D1533592

Graphic Classics:
EDGAR ALLAN POE

Graphic Classics Volume One
Third Edition
2006

Edited by Tom Pomplun

EUREKA PRODUCTIONS
8778 Oak Grove Road, Mount Horeb, Wisconsin 53572
www.graphicclassics.com

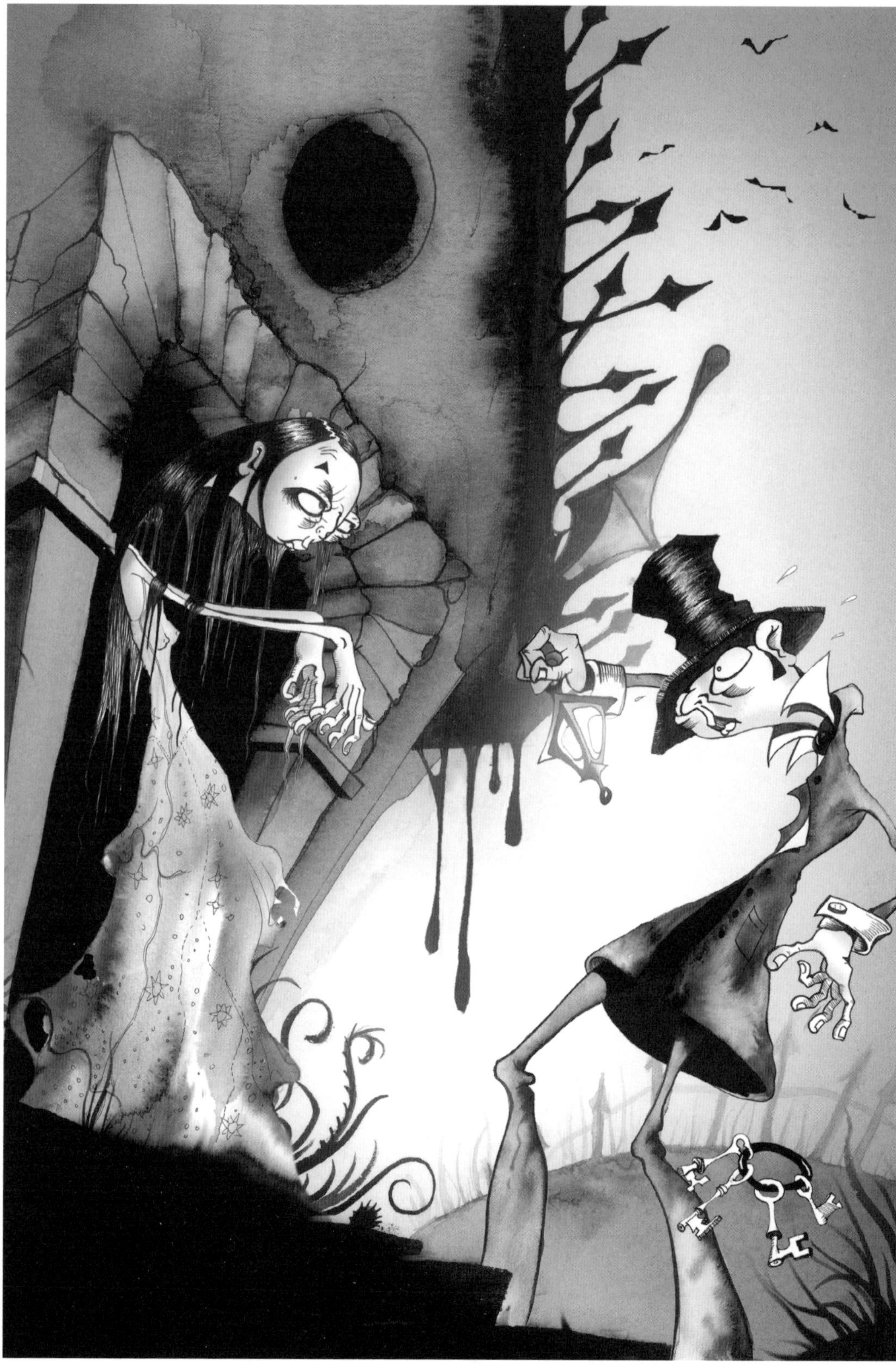

THE PREMATURE BURIAL ©2006 ANNIE OWENS

Graphic Classics:
EDGAR ALLAN POE

© 2004 MATT HOWARTH

The Tell-Tale Heart *adapted & illustrated by Rick Geary* 4

King Pest *adapted by Antonella Caputo, illustrated by Anton Emdin and Glenn Smith* 22

The Premature Burial *adapted by Tom Pomplun, illustrated by Joe Ollmann* 39

Eldorado *illustrated by Roger Langridge* 48

Spirits of the Dead *illustrated by Andy Ewen* 50

The Imp of the Perverse *adapted by Tom Pomplun, illustrated by Lance Tooks* 52

The Raven *illustrated by J.B. Bonivert, Steven Cerio, Skot Olsen, M.K. Brown, Michael Manning, Ryan Inzana, Mary Fleener, Evert Geradts, Toni Pawlowsky & Todd Lovering* . 57

The Masque of the Red Death *adapted & illustrated by Stanley W. Shaw* 67

Never Bet the Devil Your Head *adapted & illustrated by Milton Knight* 81

Hop-Frog *illustrated by Lisa K. Weber* 94

The Cask of Amontillado *adapted & illustrated by Pedro Lopez* 106

The Fall of the House of Usher *adapted & illustrated by Matt Howarth* 117

About the Artists & Writers 141

Cover by Marcel de Jong and Ramon Contini / Back cover illustration by Lisa K. Weber
Additional illustrations by Skot Olsen, Annie Owens and Matt Howarth

Graphic Classics: Edgar Allan Poe is published by Eureka Productions. ISBN:13 #978-0-9746648-7-3 / ISBN:10 #0-9746648-7-1. Price US $11.95, CAN $14.50. Available from Eureka Productions, 8778 Oak Grove Road, Mount Horeb, WI 53572. Tom Pomplun, designer and publisher, tom@graphicclassics.com. Eileen Fitzgerald, editorial assistant. Compilation and all original works ©2006 Eureka Productions. All rights revert to creators after publication. Graphic Classics is a trademark of Eureka Productions. For ordering information and previews of upcoming volumes visit the Graphic Classics website at http://www.graphicclassics.com. Printed in Canada.

THE Tell-Tale HEART

By EDGAR ALLAN POE
Adapted and Illustrated by RICK GEARY

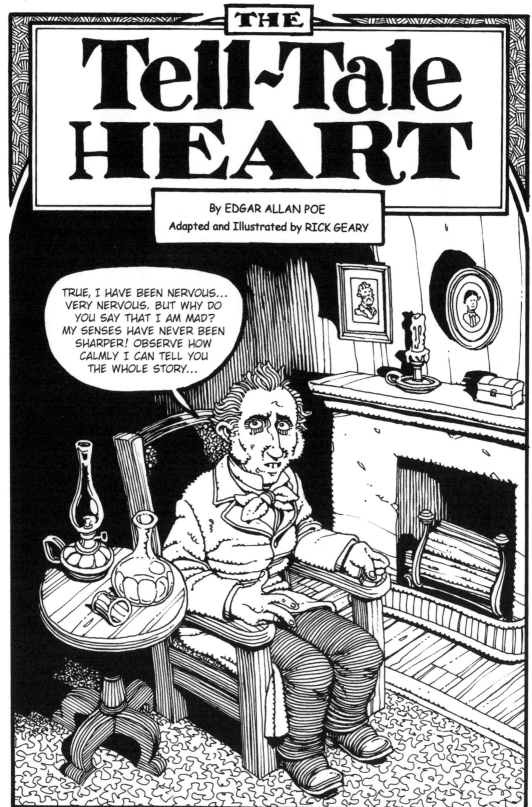

TRUE, I HAVE BEEN NERVOUS... VERY NERVOUS. BUT WHY DO YOU SAY THAT I AM MAD? MY SENSES HAVE NEVER BEEN SHARPER! OBSERVE HOW CALMLY I CAN TELL YOU THE WHOLE STORY...

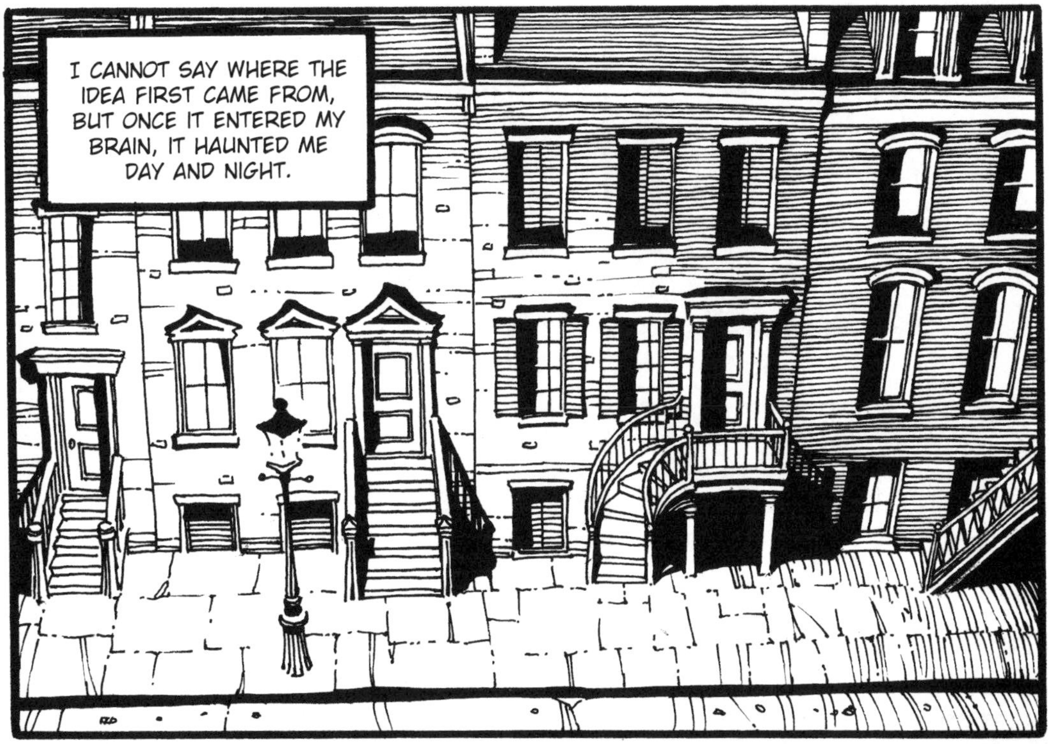
I CANNOT SAY WHERE THE IDEA FIRST CAME FROM, BUT ONCE IT ENTERED MY BRAIN, IT HAUNTED ME DAY AND NIGHT.

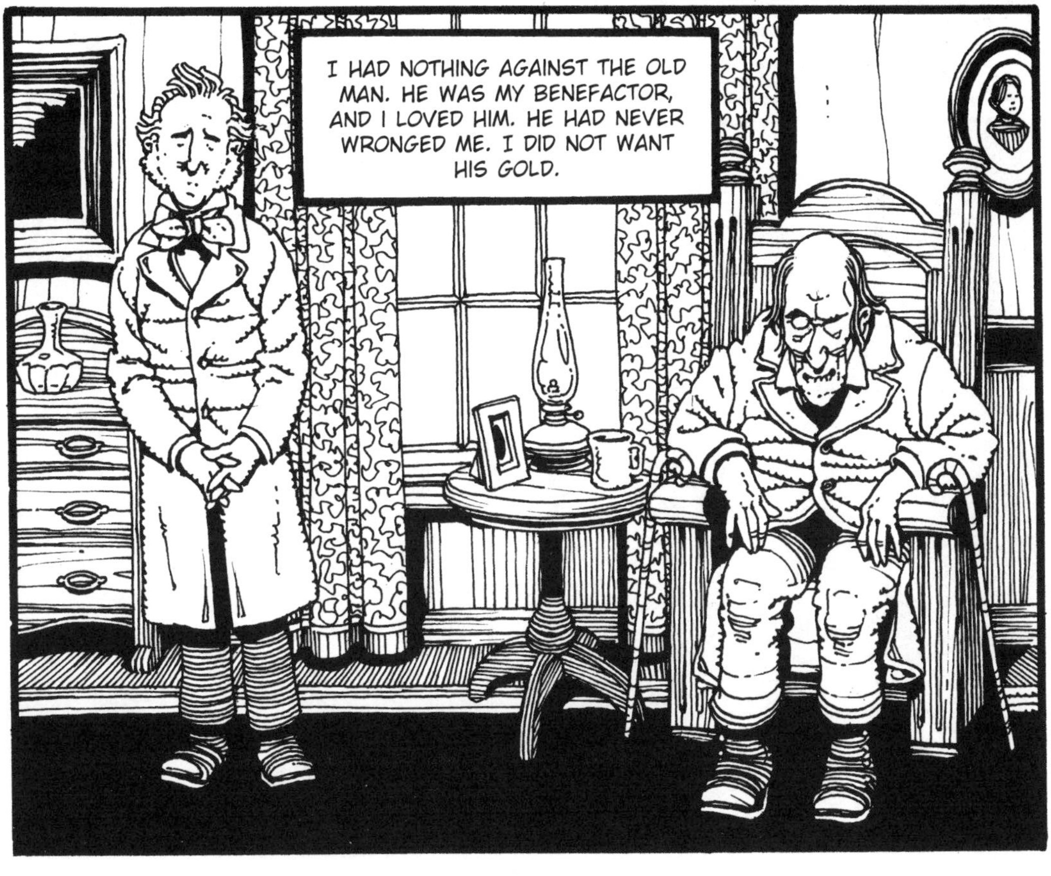
I HAD NOTHING AGAINST THE OLD MAN. HE WAS MY BENEFACTOR, AND I LOVED HIM. HE HAD NEVER WRONGED ME. I DID NOT WANT HIS GOLD.

I THINK IT WAS HIS EYE...
YES, IT WAS THIS!

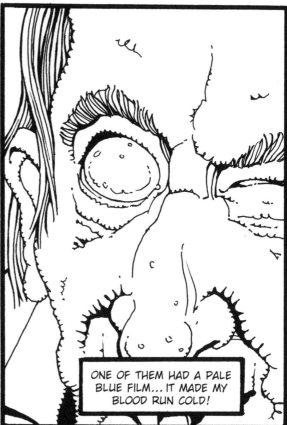

ONE OF THEM HAD A PALE
BLUE FILM... IT MADE MY
BLOOD RUN COLD!

GRADUALLY I MADE UP MY MIND TO
TAKE THE OLD MAN'S LIFE... AND RID
MYSELF OF THAT EYE FOREVER!

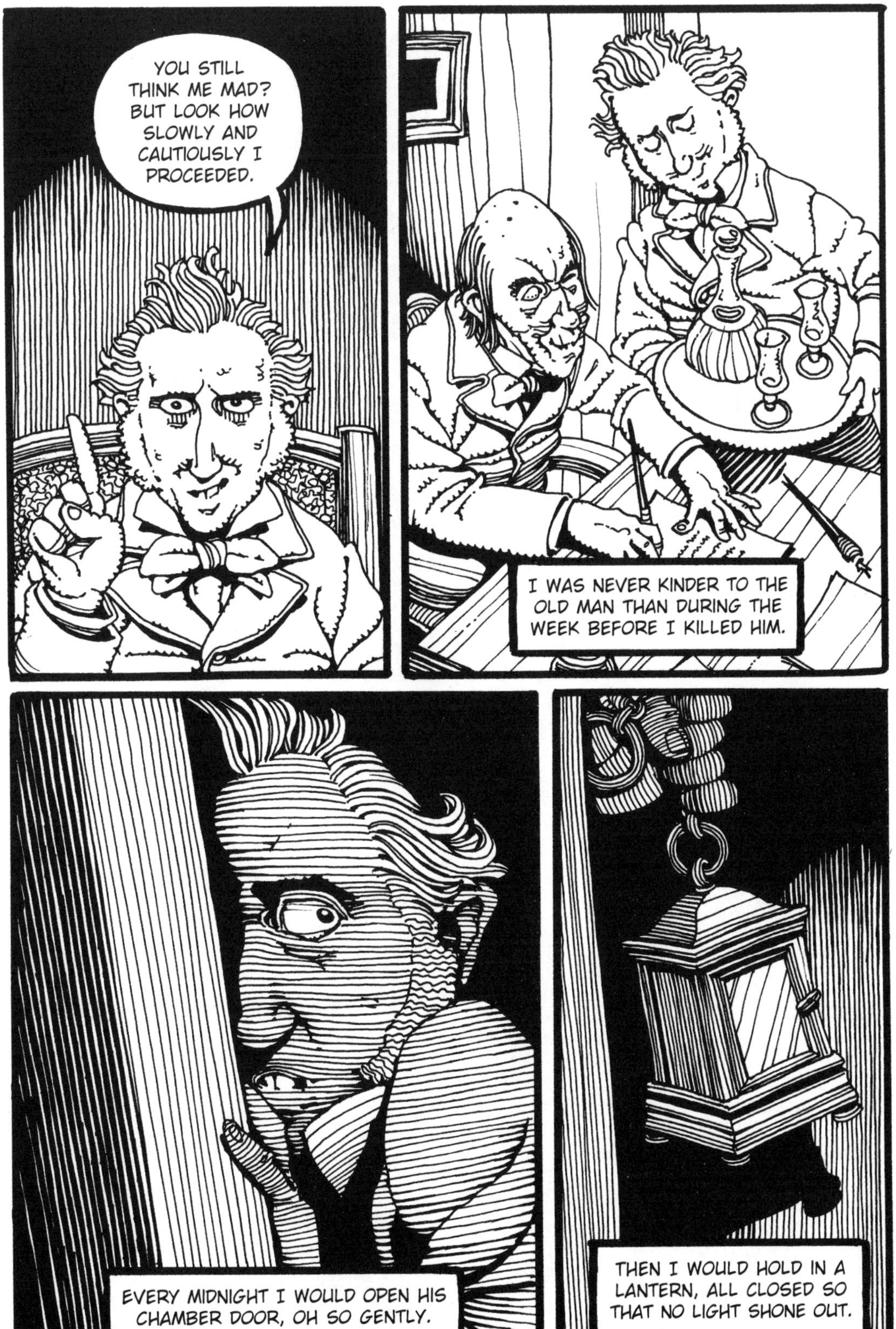
YOU STILL THINK ME MAD? BUT LOOK HOW SLOWLY AND CAUTIOUSLY I PROCEEDED.
I WAS NEVER KINDER TO THE OLD MAN THAN DURING THE WEEK BEFORE I KILLED HIM.
EVERY MIDNIGHT I WOULD OPEN HIS CHAMBER DOOR, OH SO GENTLY.
THEN I WOULD HOLD IN A LANTERN, ALL CLOSED SO THAT NO LIGHT SHONE OUT.

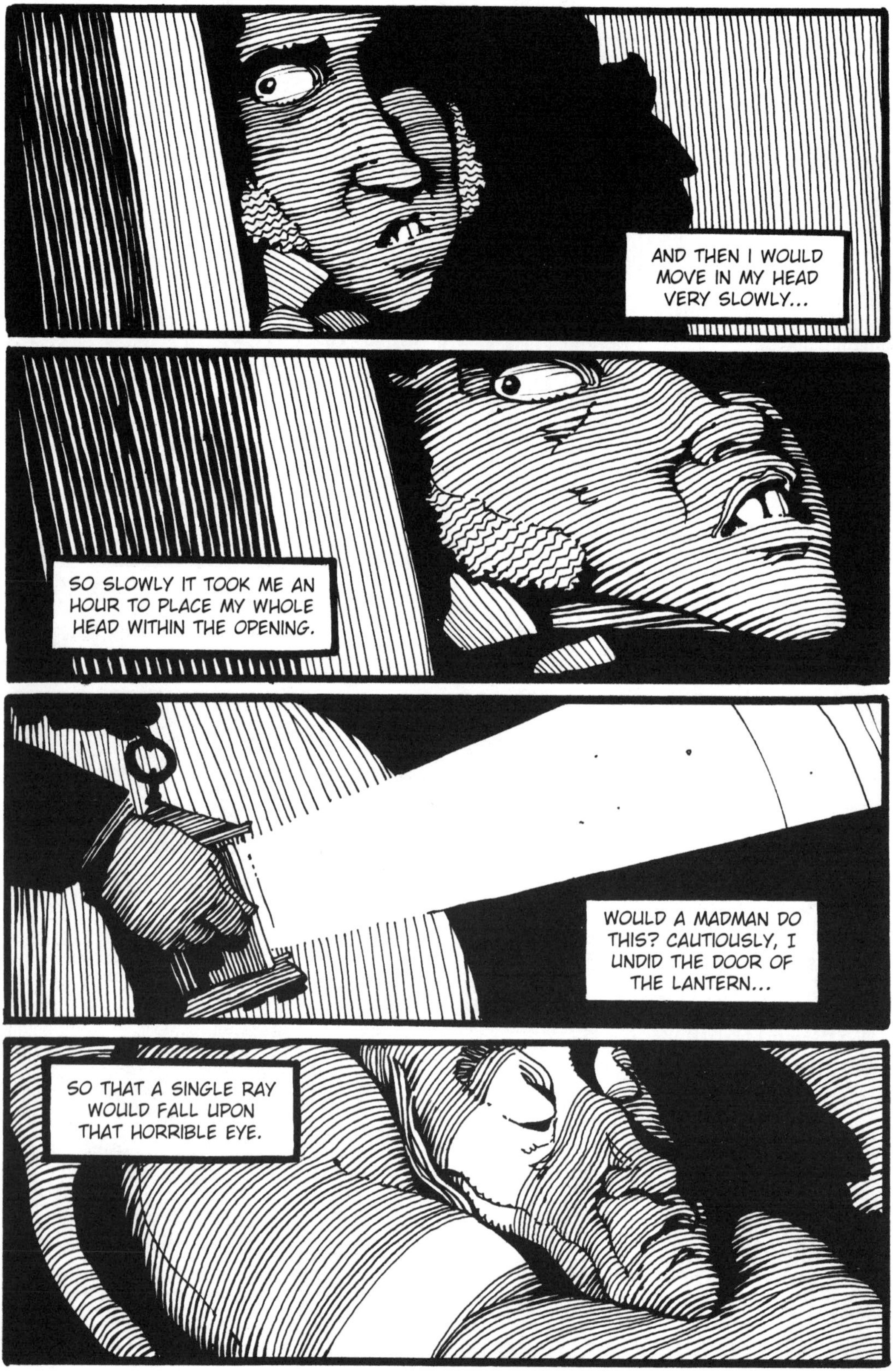
AND THEN I WOULD MOVE IN MY HEAD VERY SLOWLY...
SO SLOWLY IT TOOK ME AN HOUR TO PLACE MY WHOLE HEAD WITHIN THE OPENING.
WOULD A MADMAN DO THIS? CAUTIOUSLY, I UNDID THE DOOR OF THE LANTERN...
SO THAT A SINGLE RAY WOULD FALL UPON THAT HORRIBLE EYE.

FOR SEVEN NIGHTS, I FOUND THE EYE CLOSED AND COULD NOT DO THE DEED.

FOR I DID NOT HATE THE OLD MAN... ONLY HIS EVIL EYE.

ON THE EIGHTH NIGHT, I WAS MORE THAN USUALLY CAREFUL IN OPENING THE DOOR.

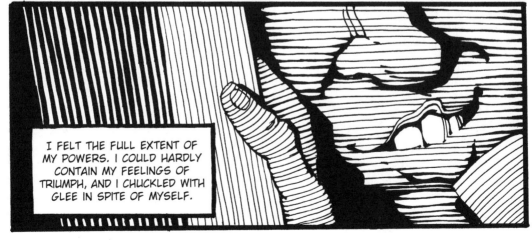

I FELT THE FULL EXTENT OF MY POWERS. I COULD HARDLY CONTAIN MY FEELINGS OF TRIUMPH, AND I CHUCKLED WITH GLEE IN SPITE OF MYSELF.

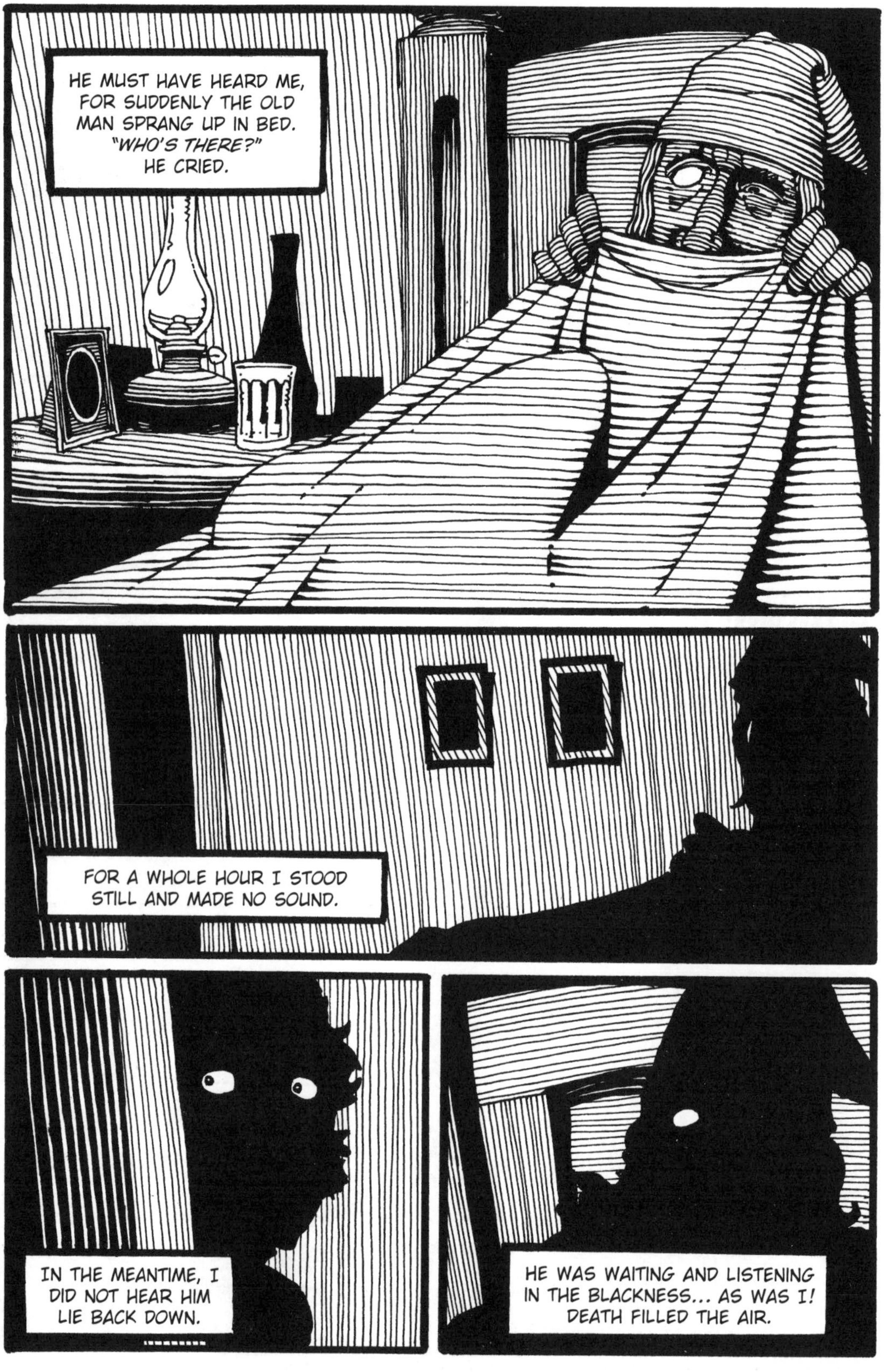
HE MUST HAVE HEARD ME, FOR SUDDENLY THE OLD MAN SPRANG UP IN BED. "WHO'S THERE?" HE CRIED.
FOR A WHOLE HOUR I STOOD STILL AND MADE NO SOUND.
IN THE MEANTIME, I DID NOT HEAR HIM LIE BACK DOWN.
HE WAS WAITING AND LISTENING IN THE BLACKNESS... AS WAS I! DEATH FILLED THE AIR.

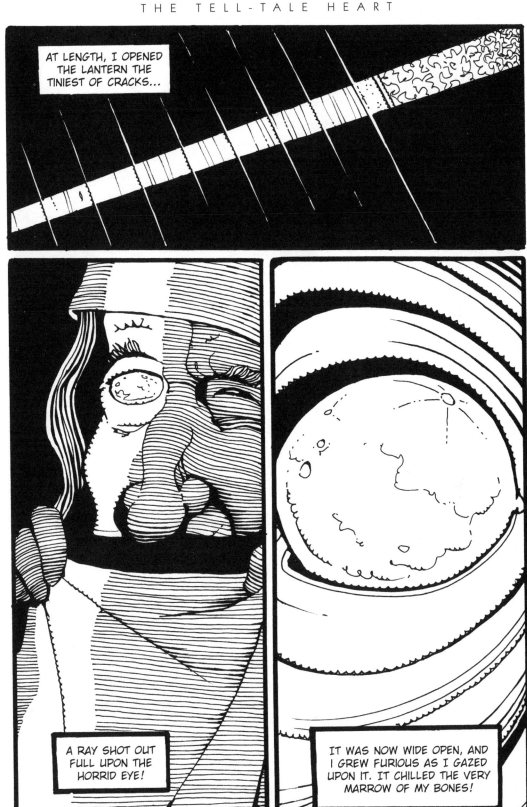

AT LENGTH, I OPENED THE LANTERN THE TINIEST OF CRACKS...

A RAY SHOT OUT FULL UPON THE HORRID EYE!

IT WAS NOW WIDE OPEN, AND I GREW FURIOUS AS I GAZED UPON IT. IT CHILLED THE VERY MARROW OF MY BONES!

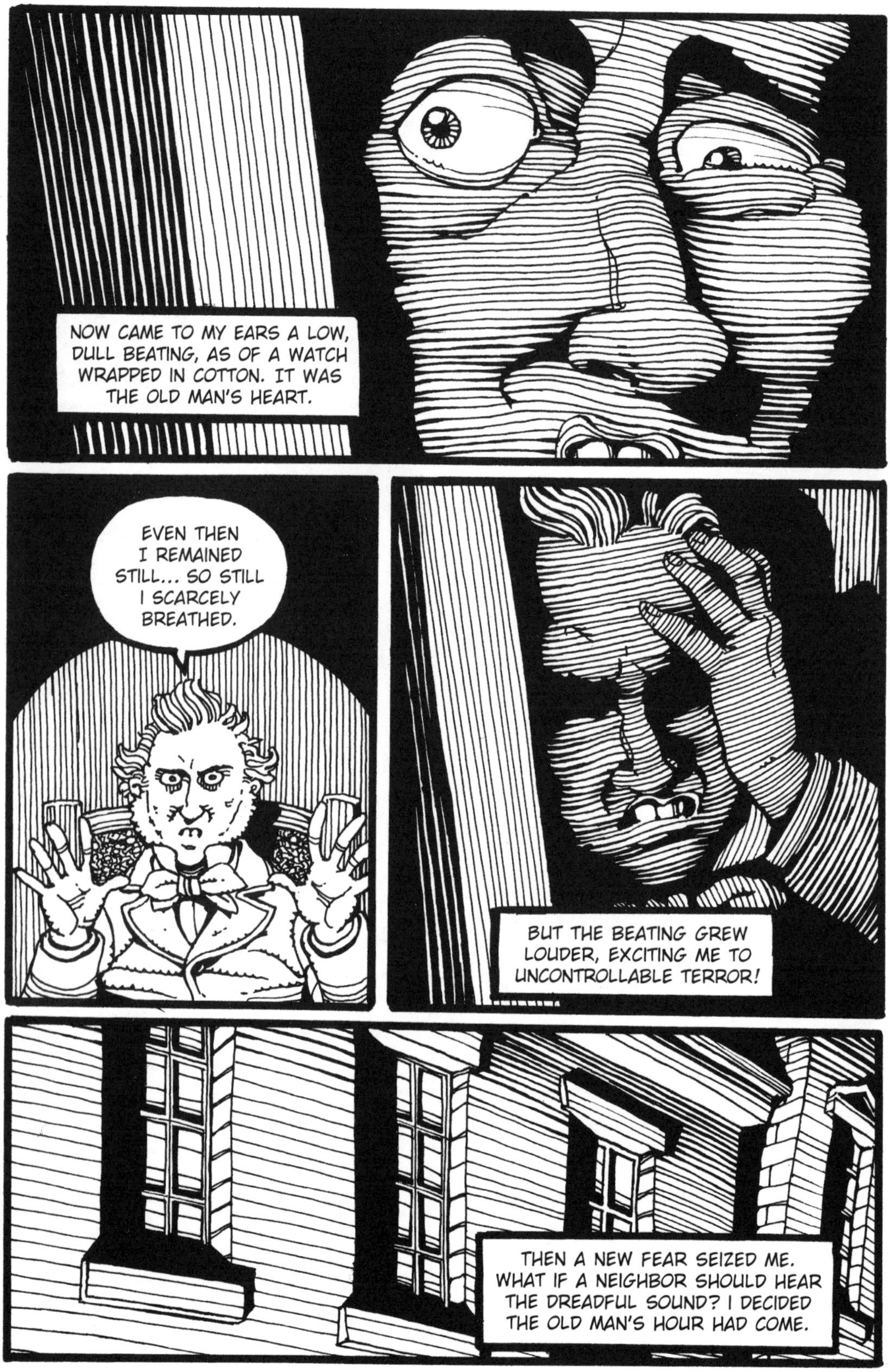
NOW CAME TO MY EARS A LOW, DULL BEATING, AS OF A WATCH WRAPPED IN COTTON. IT WAS THE OLD MAN'S HEART.
EVEN THEN I REMAINED STILL... SO STILL I SCARCELY BREATHED.
BUT THE BEATING GREW LOUDER, EXCITING ME TO UNCONTROLLABLE TERROR!
THEN A NEW FEAR SEIZED ME. WHAT IF A NEIGHBOR SHOULD HEAR THE DREADFUL SOUND? I DECIDED THE OLD MAN'S HOUR HAD COME.

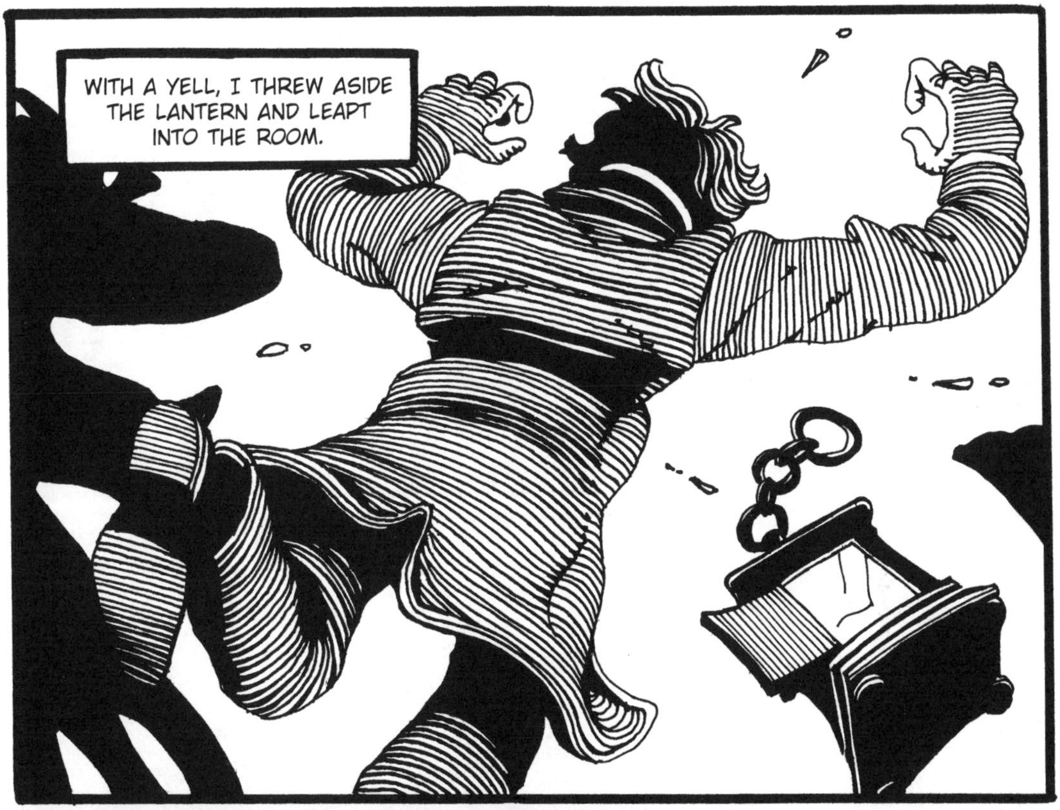
WITH A YELL, I THREW ASIDE THE LANTERN AND LEAPT INTO THE ROOM.

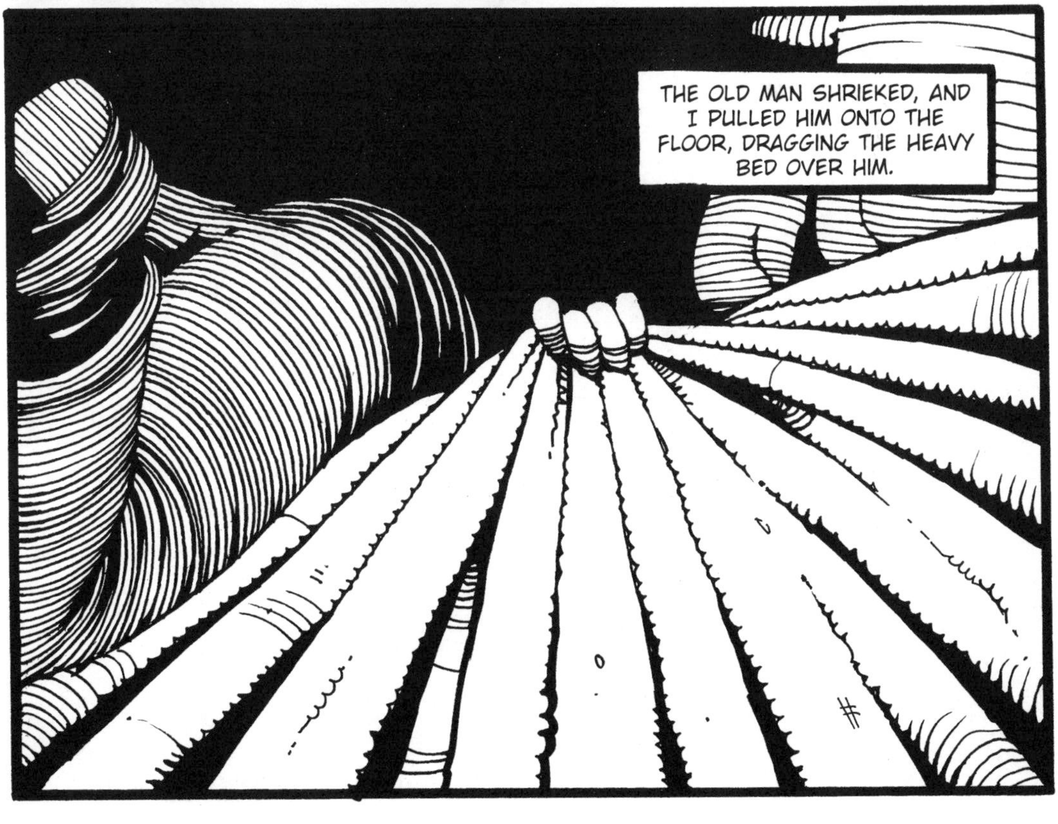
THE OLD MAN SHRIEKED, AND I PULLED HIM ONTO THE FLOOR, DRAGGING THE HEAVY BED OVER HIM.

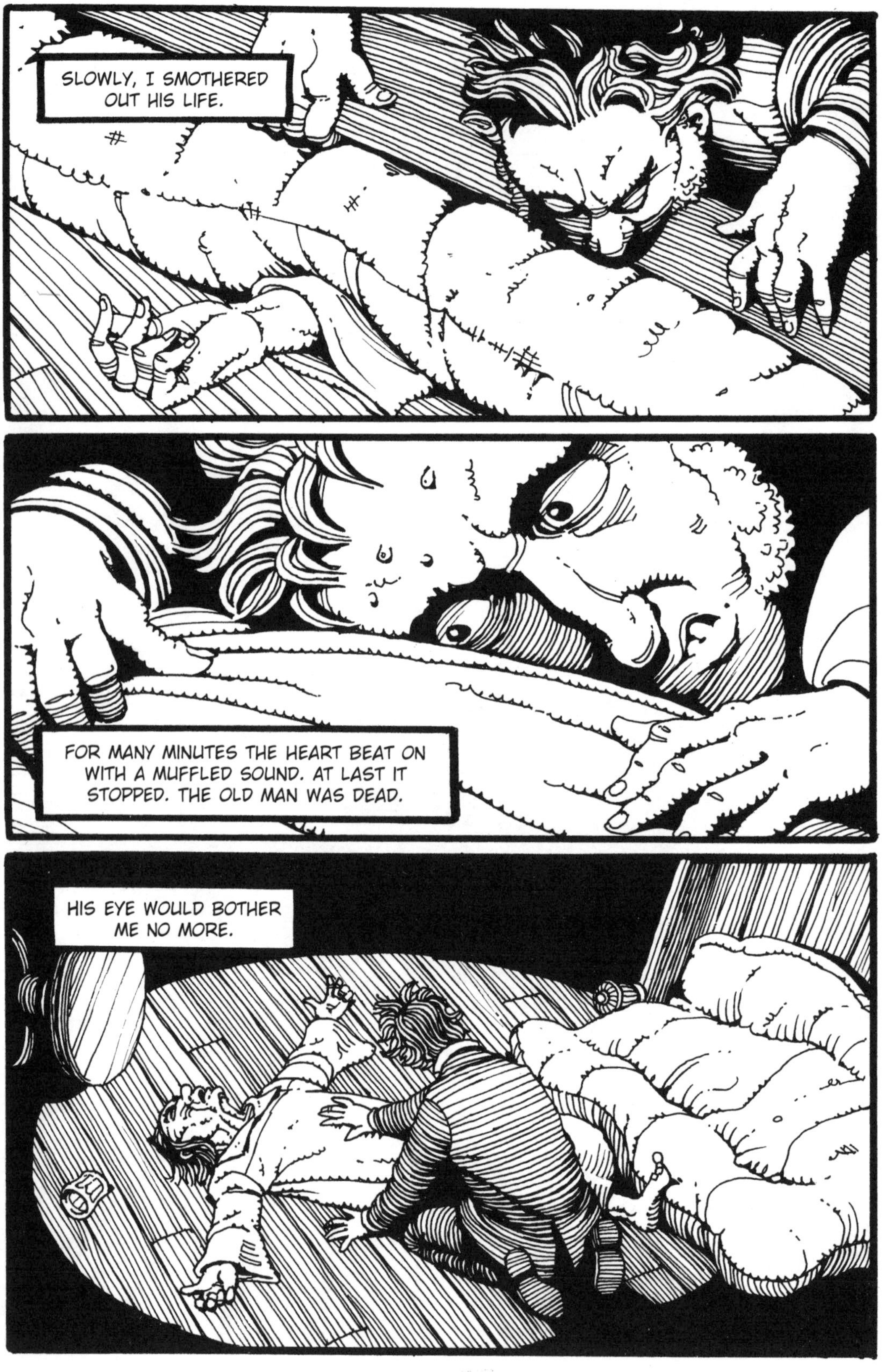
SLOWLY, I SMOTHERED OUT HIS LIFE.
FOR MANY MINUTES THE HEART BEAT ON WITH A MUFFLED SOUND. AT LAST IT STOPPED. THE OLD MAN WAS DEAD.
HIS EYE WOULD BOTHER ME NO MORE.

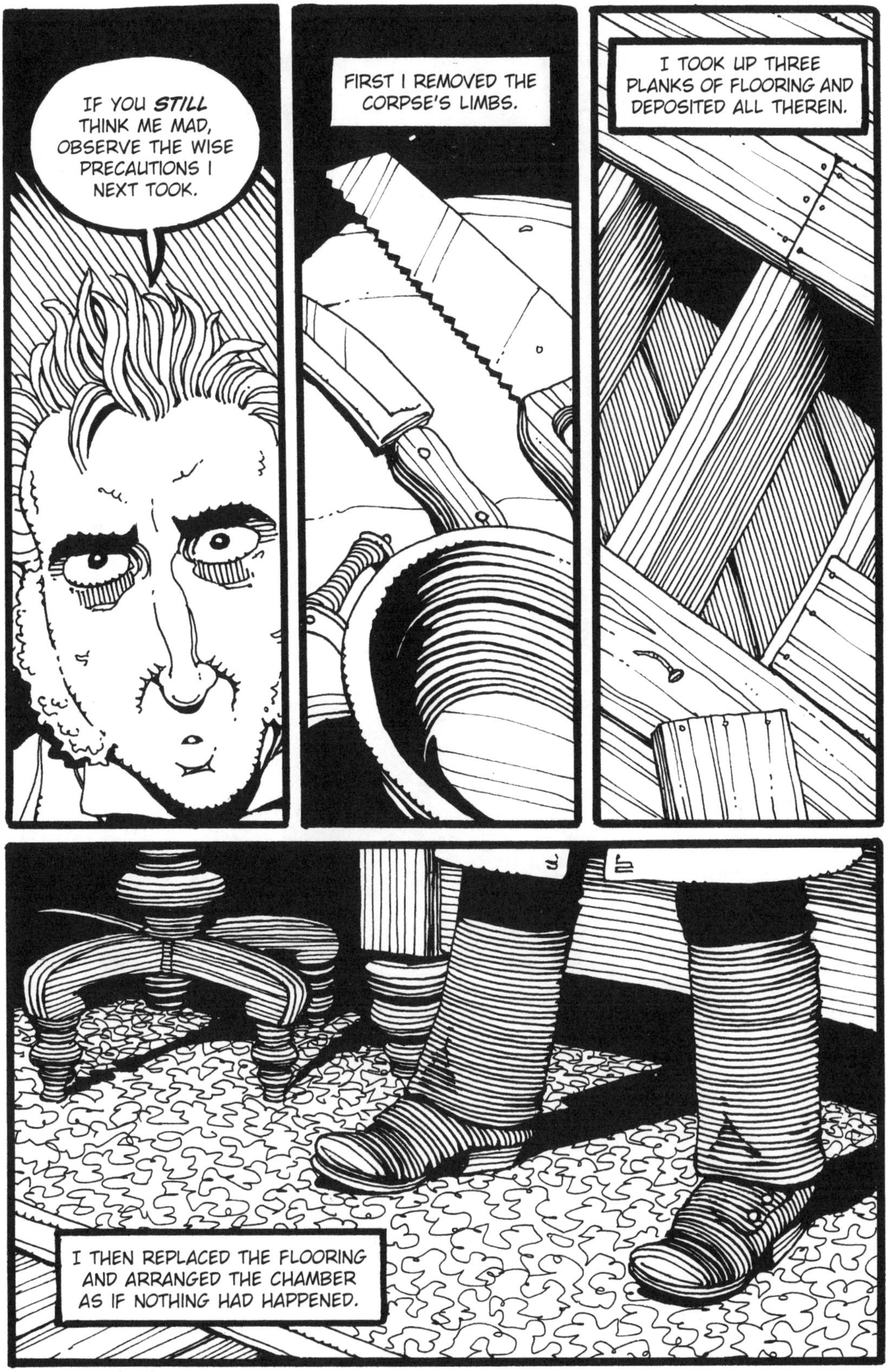
IF YOU STILL THINK ME MAD, OBSERVE THE WISE PRECAUTIONS I NEXT TOOK.
FIRST I REMOVED THE CORPSE'S LIMBS.
I TOOK UP THREE PLANKS OF FLOORING AND DEPOSITED ALL THEREIN.
I THEN REPLACED THE FLOORING AND ARRANGED THE CHAMBER AS IF NOTHING HAD HAPPENED.

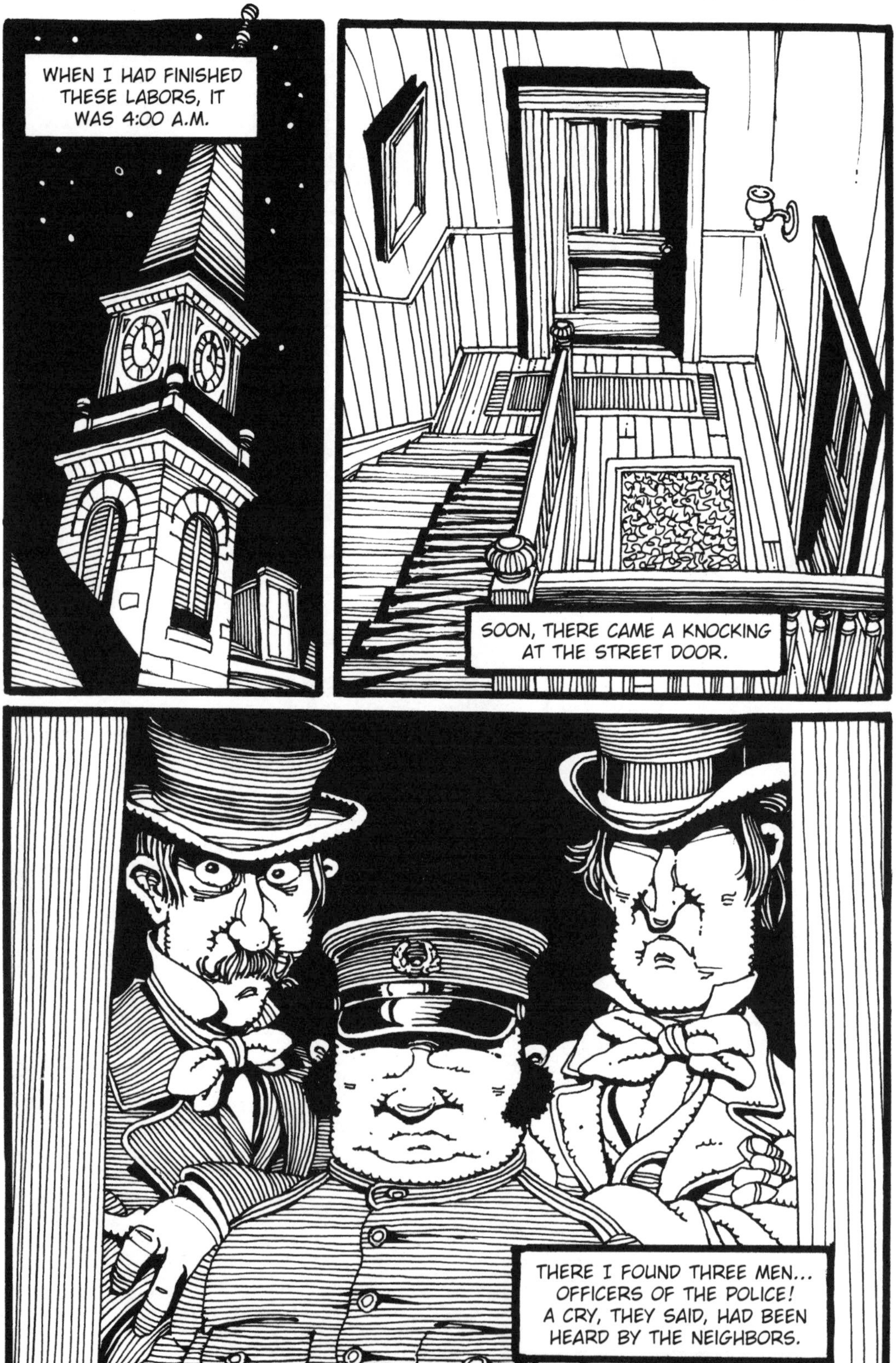
WHEN I HAD FINISHED THESE LABORS, IT WAS 4:00 A.M.
SOON, THERE CAME A KNOCKING AT THE STREET DOOR.
THERE I FOUND THREE MEN... OFFICERS OF THE POLICE! A CRY, THEY SAID, HAD BEEN HEARD BY THE NEIGHBORS.

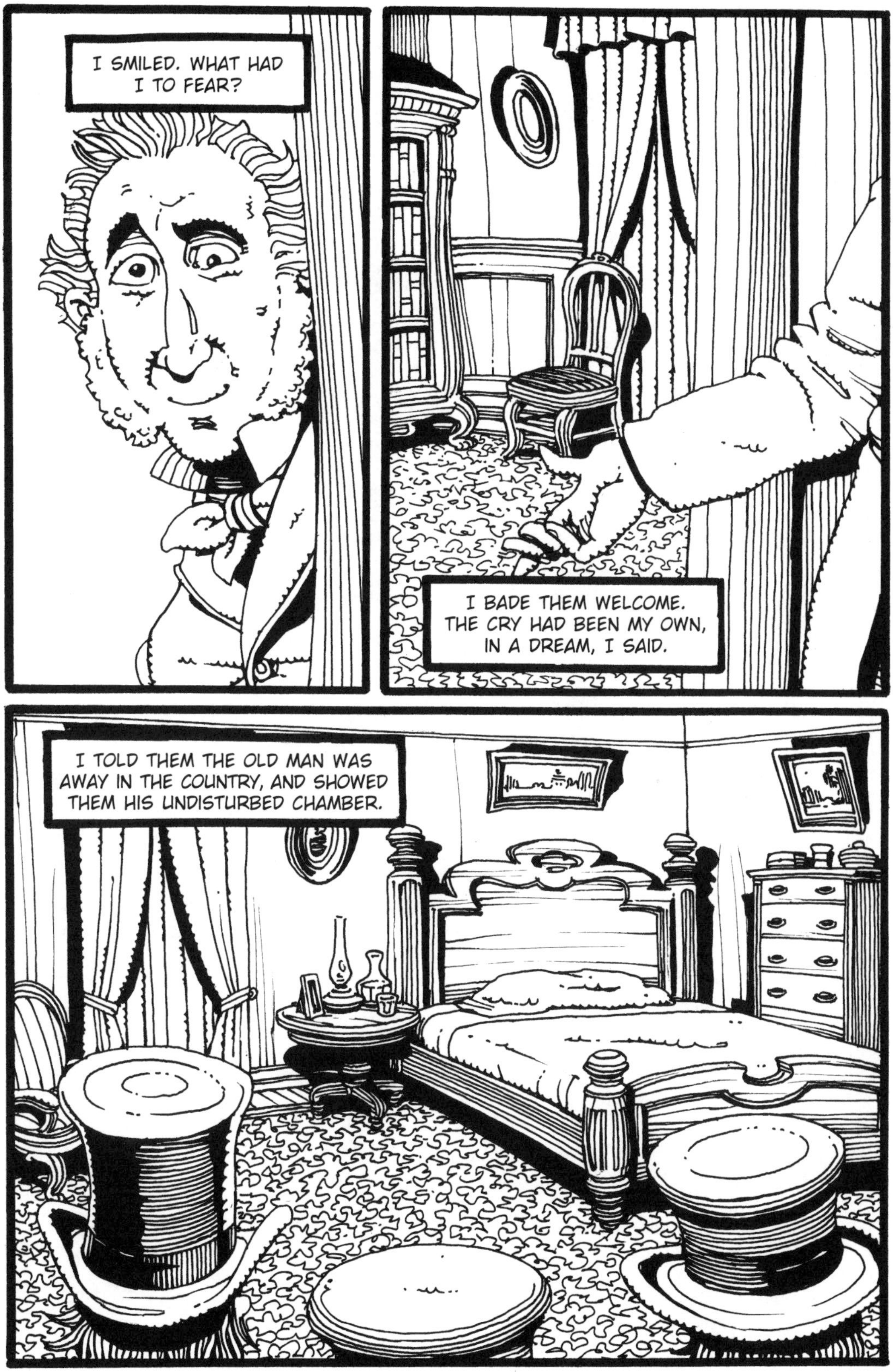
I SMILED. WHAT HAD I TO FEAR?
I BADE THEM WELCOME. THE CRY HAD BEEN MY OWN, IN A DREAM, I SAID.
I TOLD THEM THE OLD MAN WAS AWAY IN THE COUNTRY, AND SHOWED THEM HIS UNDISTURBED CHAMBER.

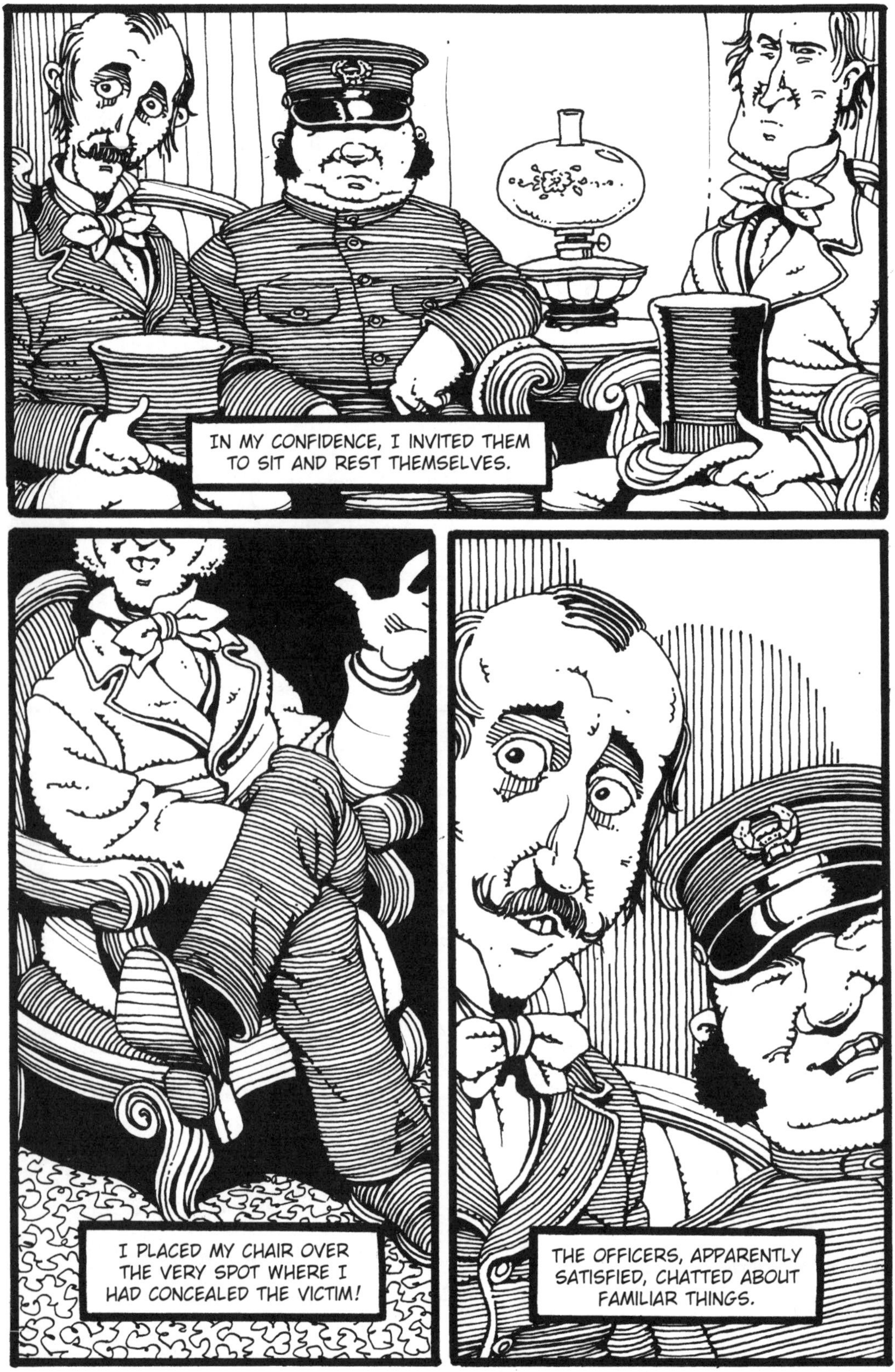
IN MY CONFIDENCE, I INVITED THEM TO SIT AND REST THEMSELVES.
I PLACED MY CHAIR OVER THE VERY SPOT WHERE I HAD CONCEALED THE VICTIM!
THE OFFICERS, APPARENTLY SATISFIED, CHATTED ABOUT FAMILIAR THINGS.

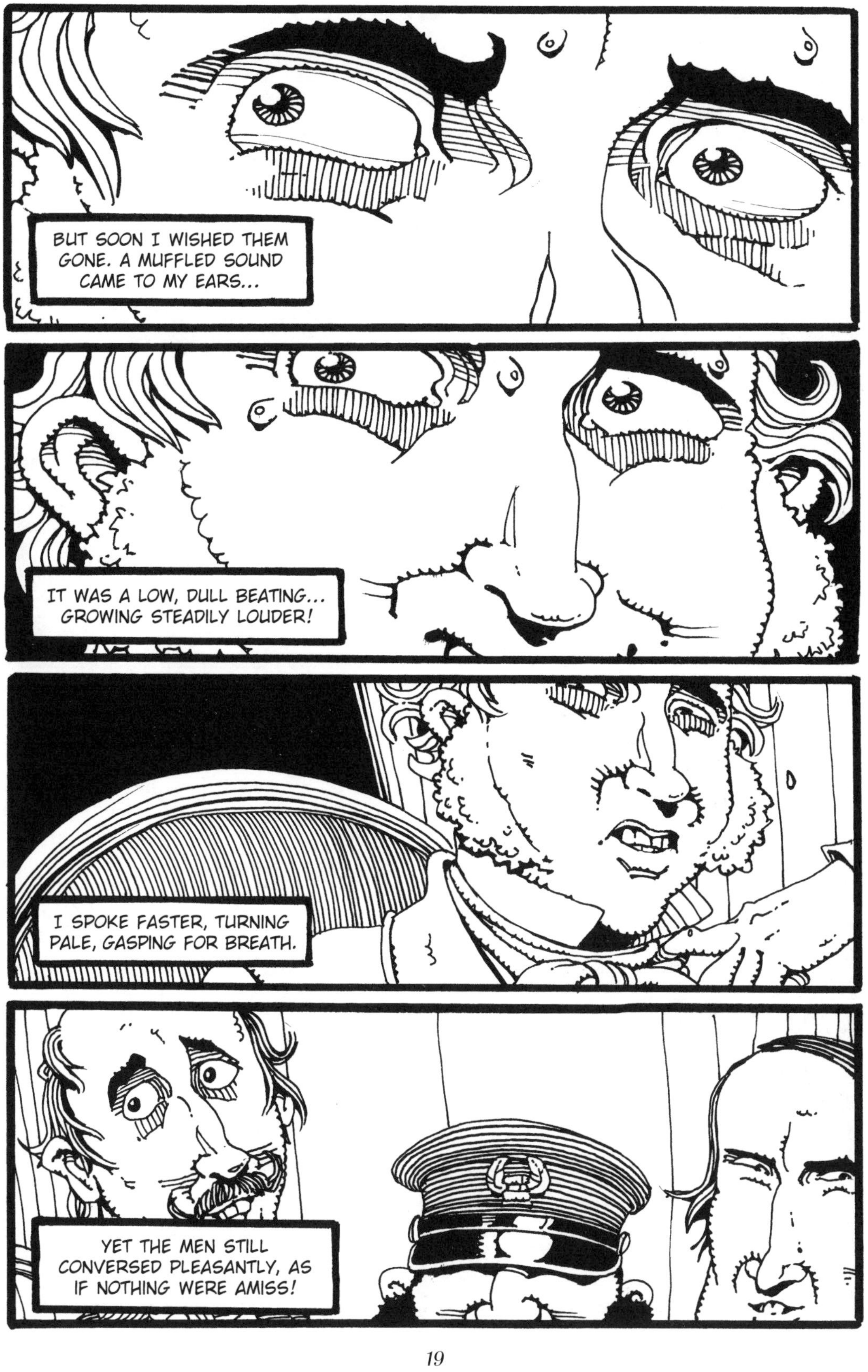
BUT SOON I WISHED THEM GONE. A MUFFLED SOUND CAME TO MY EARS...
IT WAS A LOW, DULL BEATING... GROWING STEADILY LOUDER!
I SPOKE FASTER, TURNING PALE, GASPING FOR BREATH.
YET THE MEN STILL CONVERSED PLEASANTLY, AS IF NOTHING WERE AMISS!

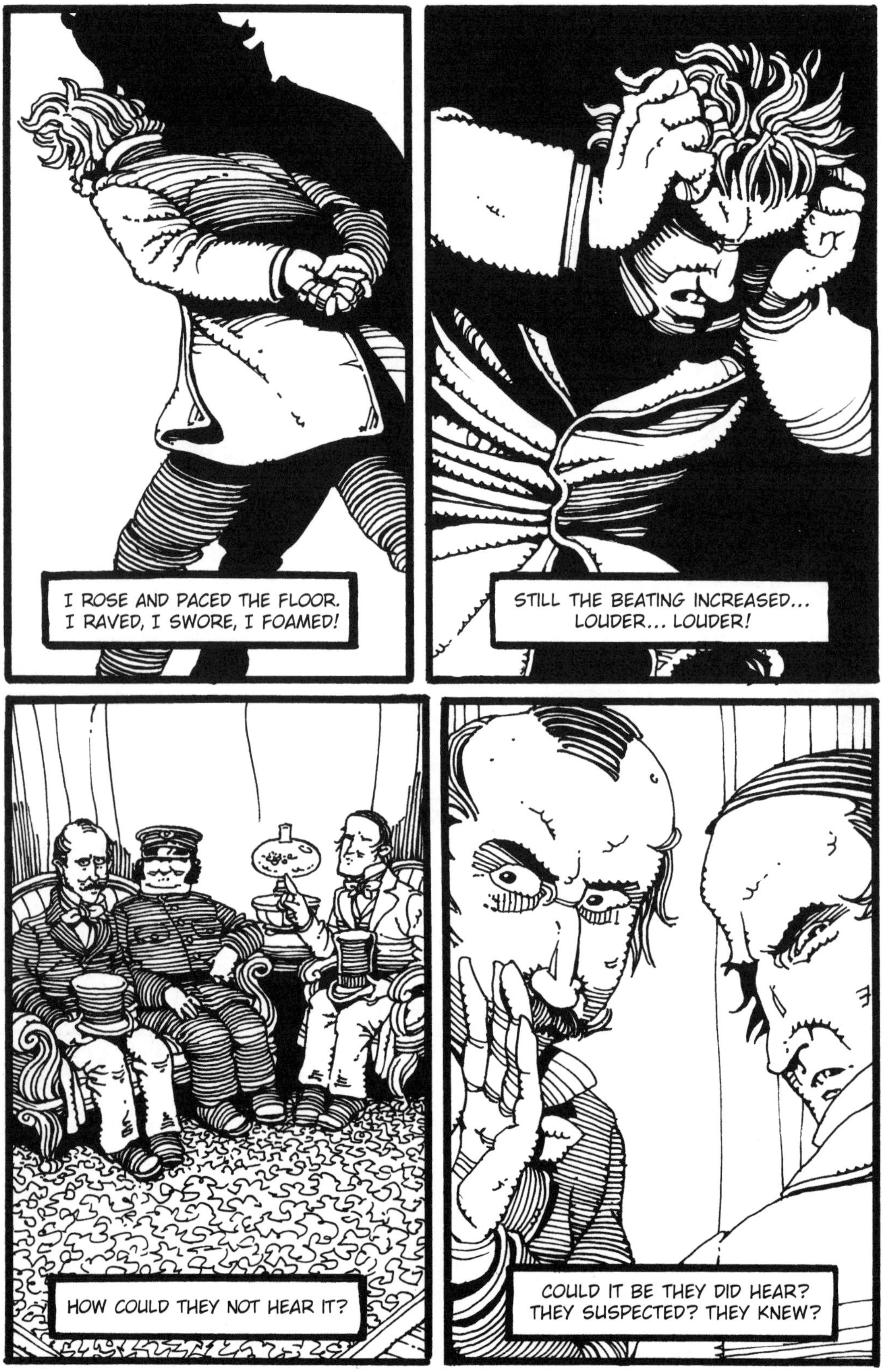
I ROSE AND PACED THE FLOOR. I RAVED, I SWORE, I FOAMED!
STILL THE BEATING INCREASED... LOUDER... LOUDER!
HOW COULD THEY NOT HEAR IT?
COULD IT BE THEY DID HEAR? THEY SUSPECTED? THEY KNEW?

THEY WERE MOCKING MY HORROR! I COULD BEAR THEIR SMILES NO LONGER!

LOUDER... LOUDER! IT WAS INTOLERABLE! I FELT I MUST SCREAM OR DIE!

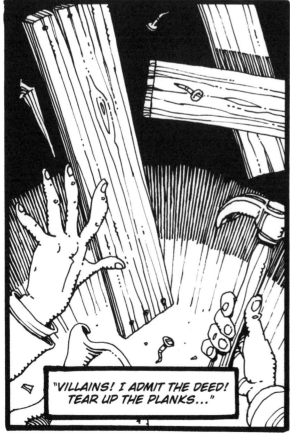

"VILLAINS! I ADMIT THE DEED! TEAR UP THE PLANKS..."

"HERE, HERE IT IS! IT IS THE BEATING OF HIS HIDEOUS HEART!"

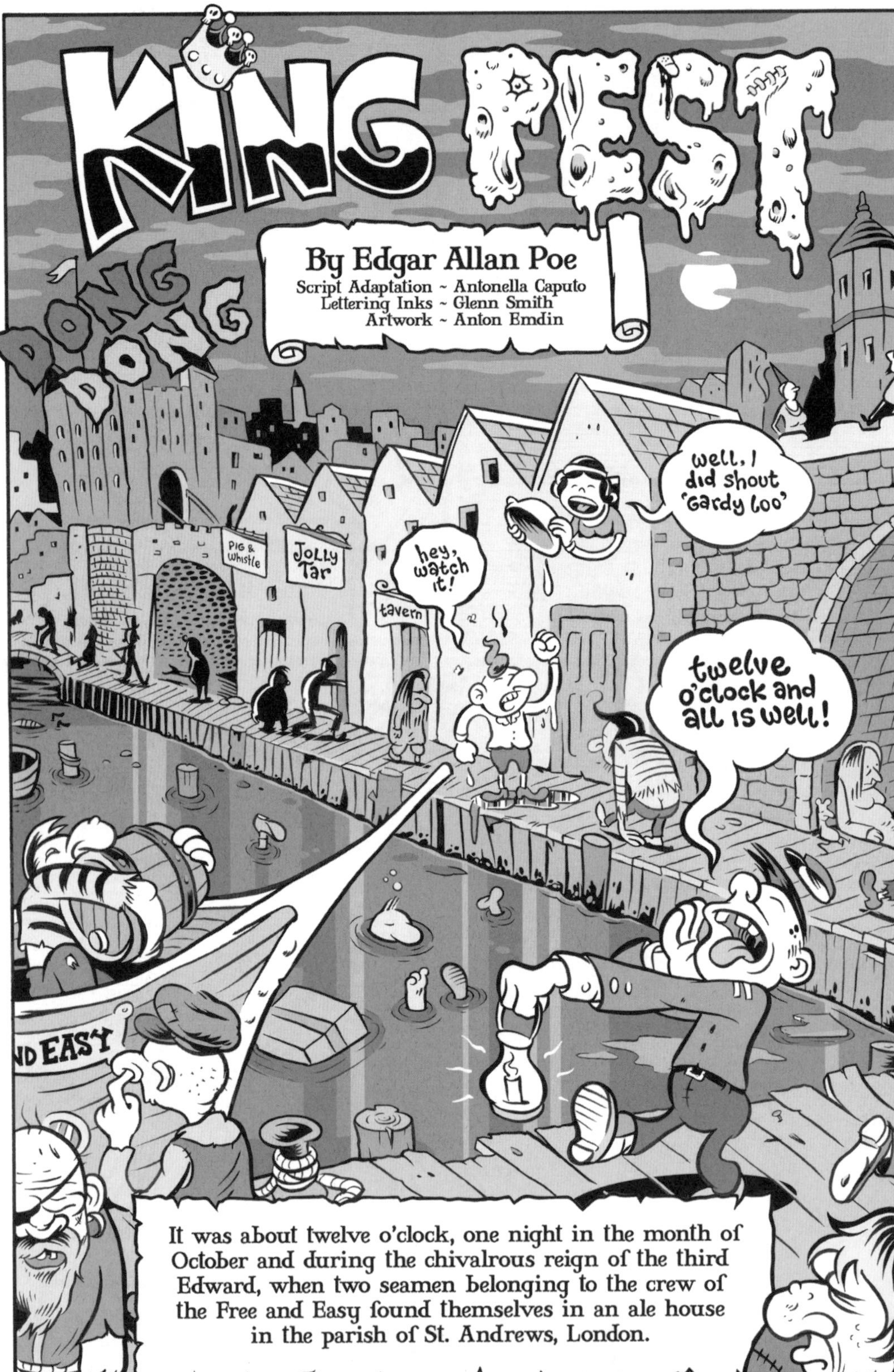
KING PEST
By Edgar Allan Poe
Script Adaptation ~ Antonella Caputo
Lettering Inks ~ Glenn Smith
Artwork ~ Anton Emdin
DONG DONG
PIG & Whistle
JOLLY Tar
tavern
hey, watch it!
well, I did shout 'Gardy Loo'
twelve o'clock and all is well!
ND EASY
It was about twelve o'clock, one night in the month of October and during the chivalrous reign of the third Edward, when two seamen belonging to the crew of the Free and Easy found themselves in an ale house in the parish of St. Andrews, London.

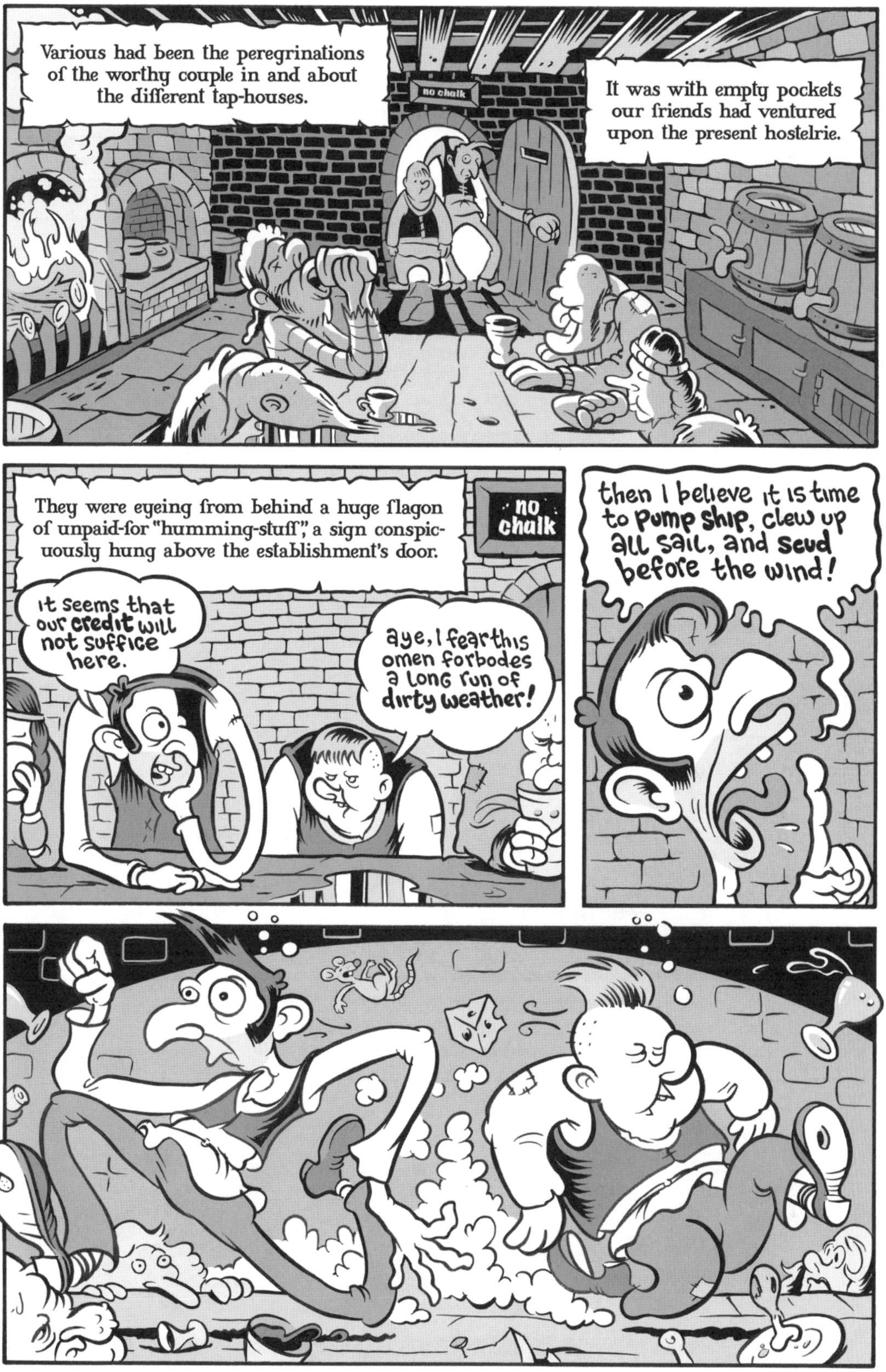
Various had been the peregrinations of the worthy couple in and about the different tap-houses.
no chalk
It was with empty pockets our friends had ventured upon the present hostelrie.
They were eyeing from behind a huge flagon of unpaid-for "humming-stuff," a sign conspicuously hung above the establishment's door.
no chalk
it seems that our credit will not suffice here.
aye, I fear this omen forbodes a long run of dirty weather!
then I believe it is time to pump ship, clew up all sail, and scud before the wind!

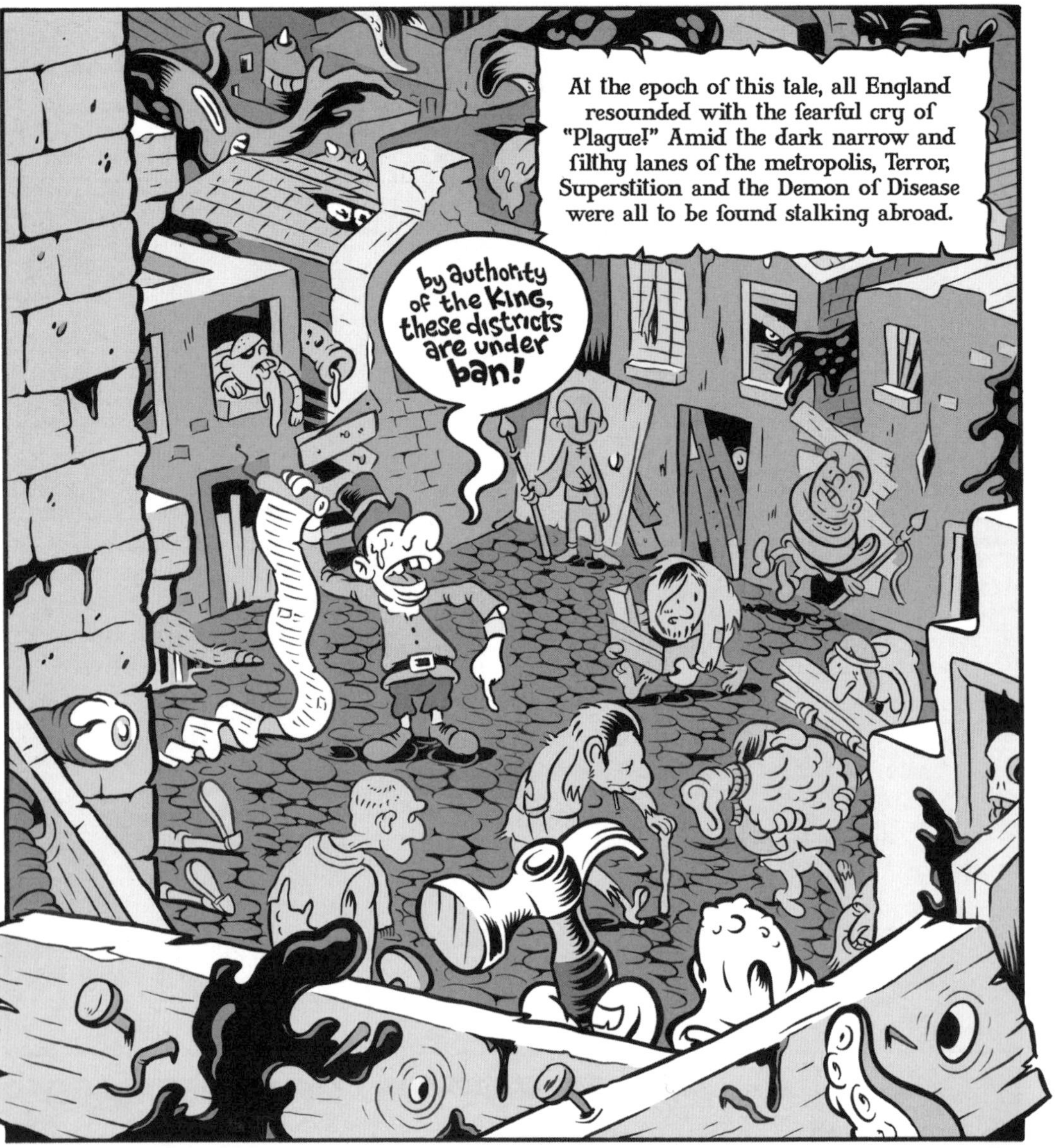
At the epoch of this tale, all England resounded with the fearful cry of "Plague!" Amid the dark narrow and filthy lanes of the metropolis, Terror, Superstition and the Demon of Disease were all to be found stalking abroad.
by authority of the KING, these districts are under ban!

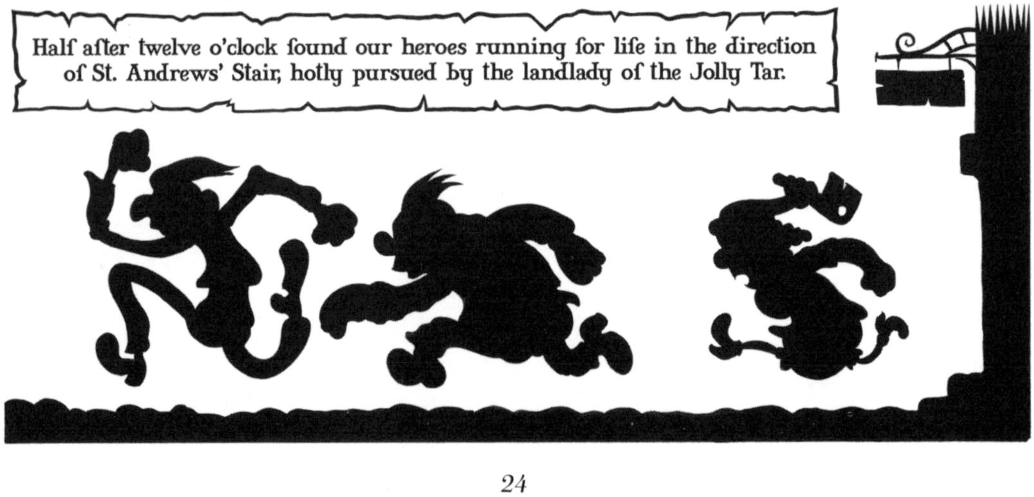
Half after twelve o'clock found our heroes running for life in the direction of St. Andrews' Stair, hotly pursued by the landlady of the Jolly Tar.

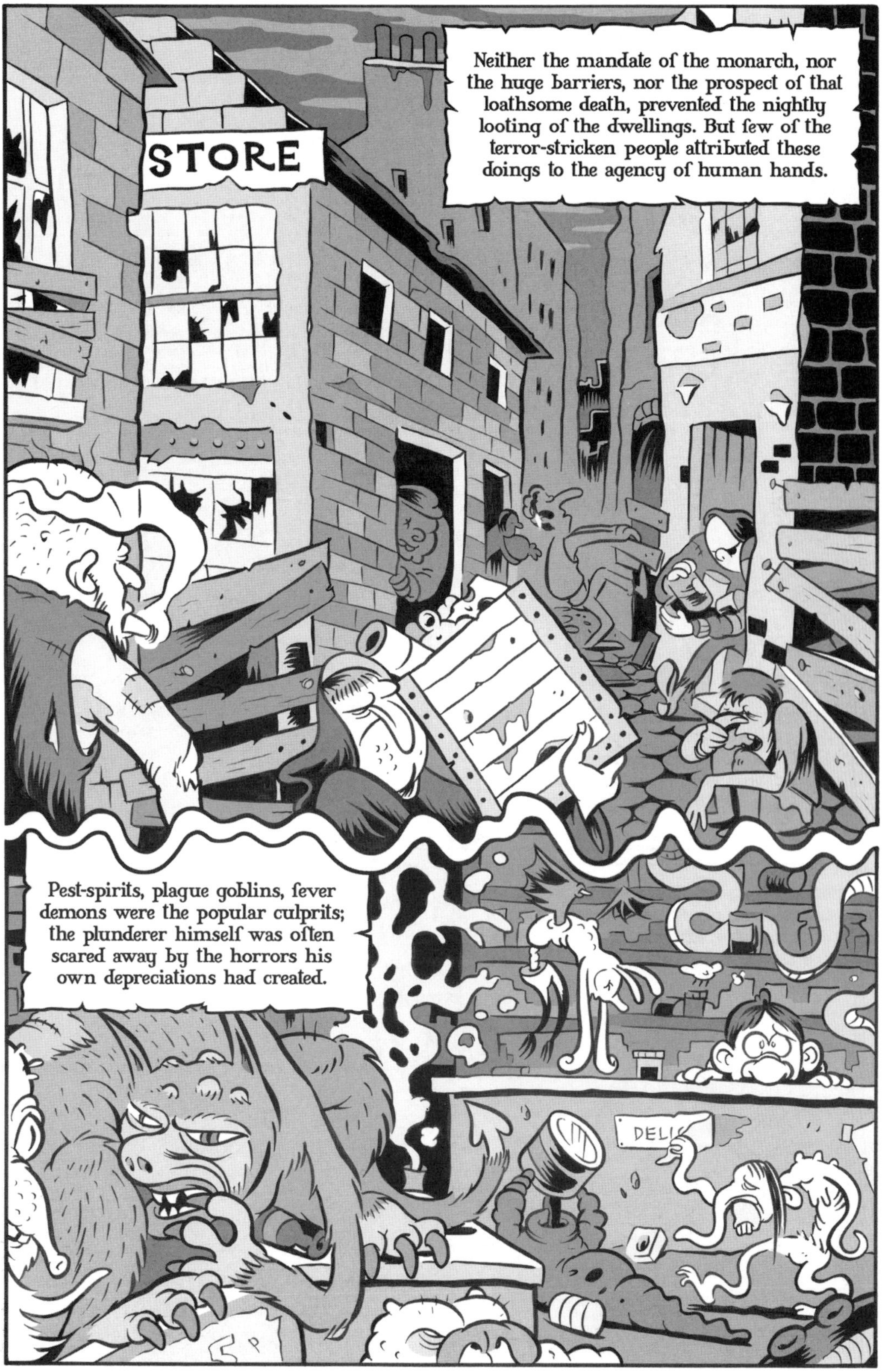
Neither the mandate of the monarch, nor the huge barriers, nor the prospect of that loathsome death, prevented the nightly looting of the dwellings. But few of the terror-stricken people attributed these doings to the agency of human hands.
STORE
Pest-spirits, plague goblins, fever demons were the popular culprits; the plunderer himself was often scared away by the horrors his own depreciations had created.
DELI

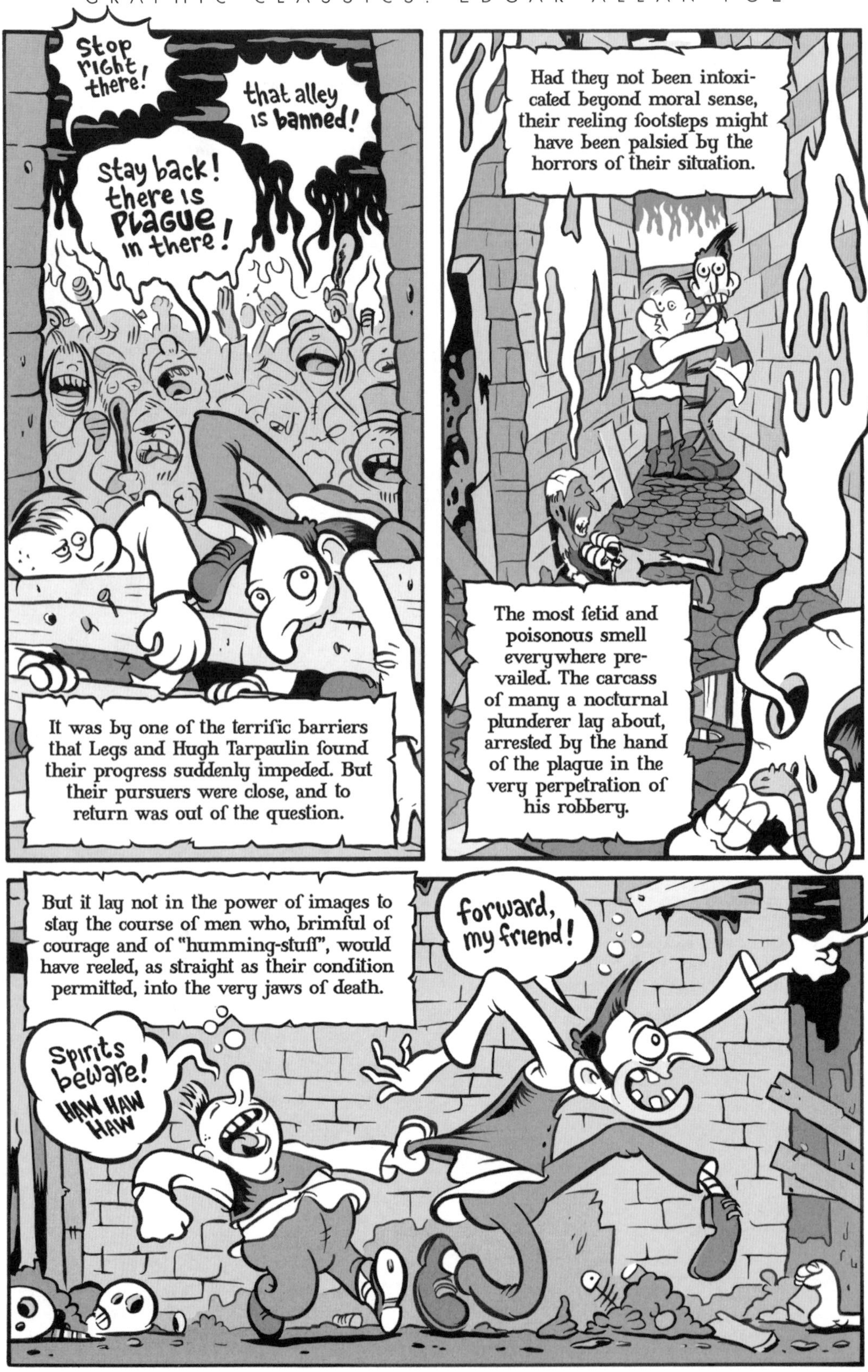

Stop right there!
that alley is banned!
stay back! there is PLAGUE in there!
It was by one of the terrific barriers that Legs and Hugh Tarpaulin found their progress suddenly impeded. But their pursuers were close, and to return was out of the question.
Had they not been intoxicated beyond moral sense, their reeling footsteps might have been palsied by the horrors of their situation.
The most fetid and poisonous smell everywhere prevailed. The carcass of many a nocturnal plunderer lay about, arrested by the hand of the plague in the very perpetration of his robbery.
But it lay not in the power of images to stay the course of men who, brimful of courage and of "humming-stuff", would have reeled, as straight as their condition permitted, into the very jaws of death.
forward, my friend!
Spirits beware! HAW HAW HAW

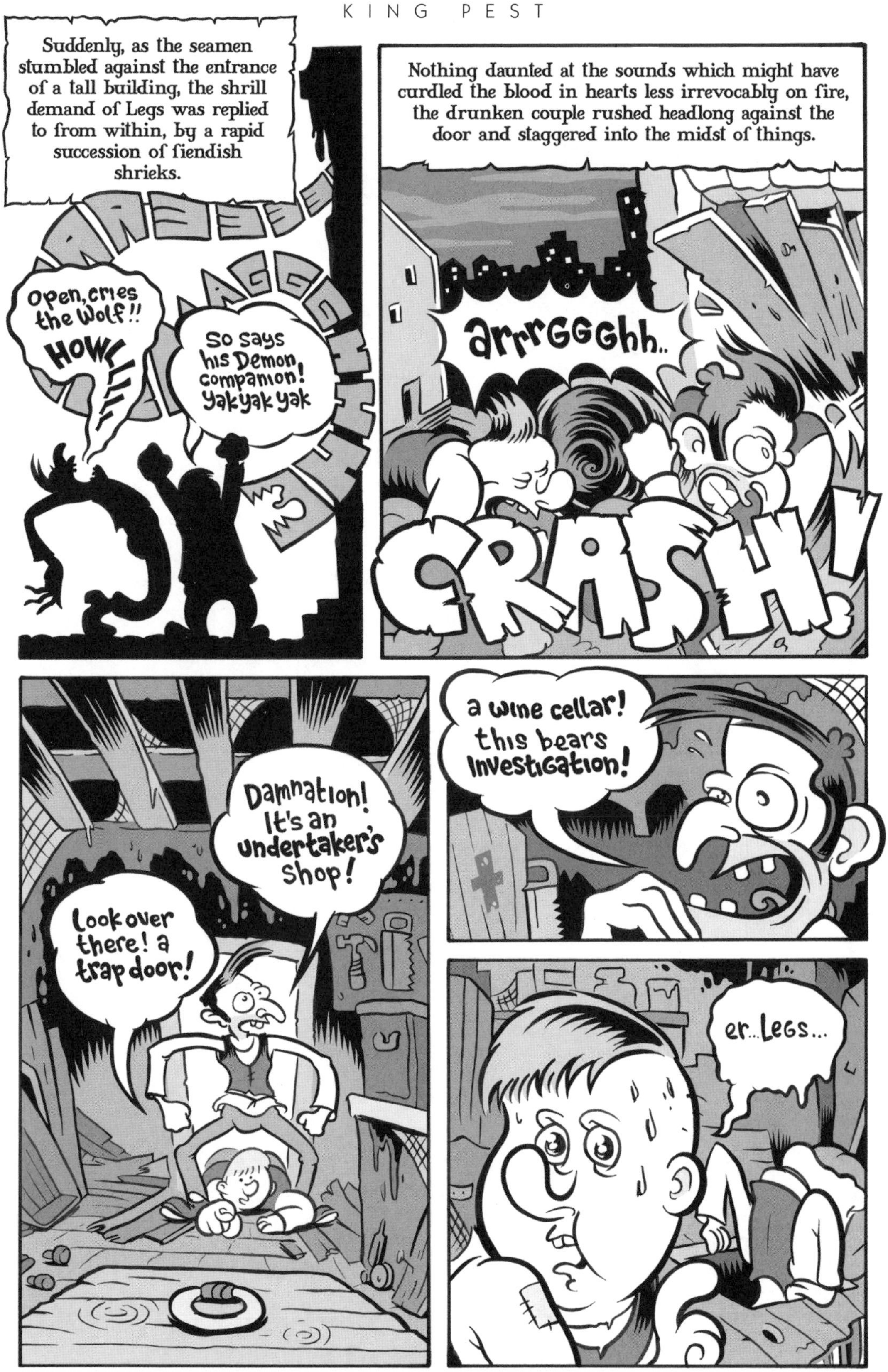
Suddenly, as the seamen stumbled against the entrance of a tall building, the shrill demand of Legs was replied to from within, by a rapid succession of fiendish shrieks.
Open, cries the Wolf!! HOWL!
So says his Demon companion! Yakyakyak
Nothing daunted at the sounds which might have curdled the blood in hearts less irrevocably on fire, the drunken couple rushed headlong against the door and staggered into the midst of things.
arrrGGGhh..
CRASH!
Damnation! It's an undertaker's shop!
Look over there! a trap door!
a wine cellar! this bears investigation!
er...Legs...

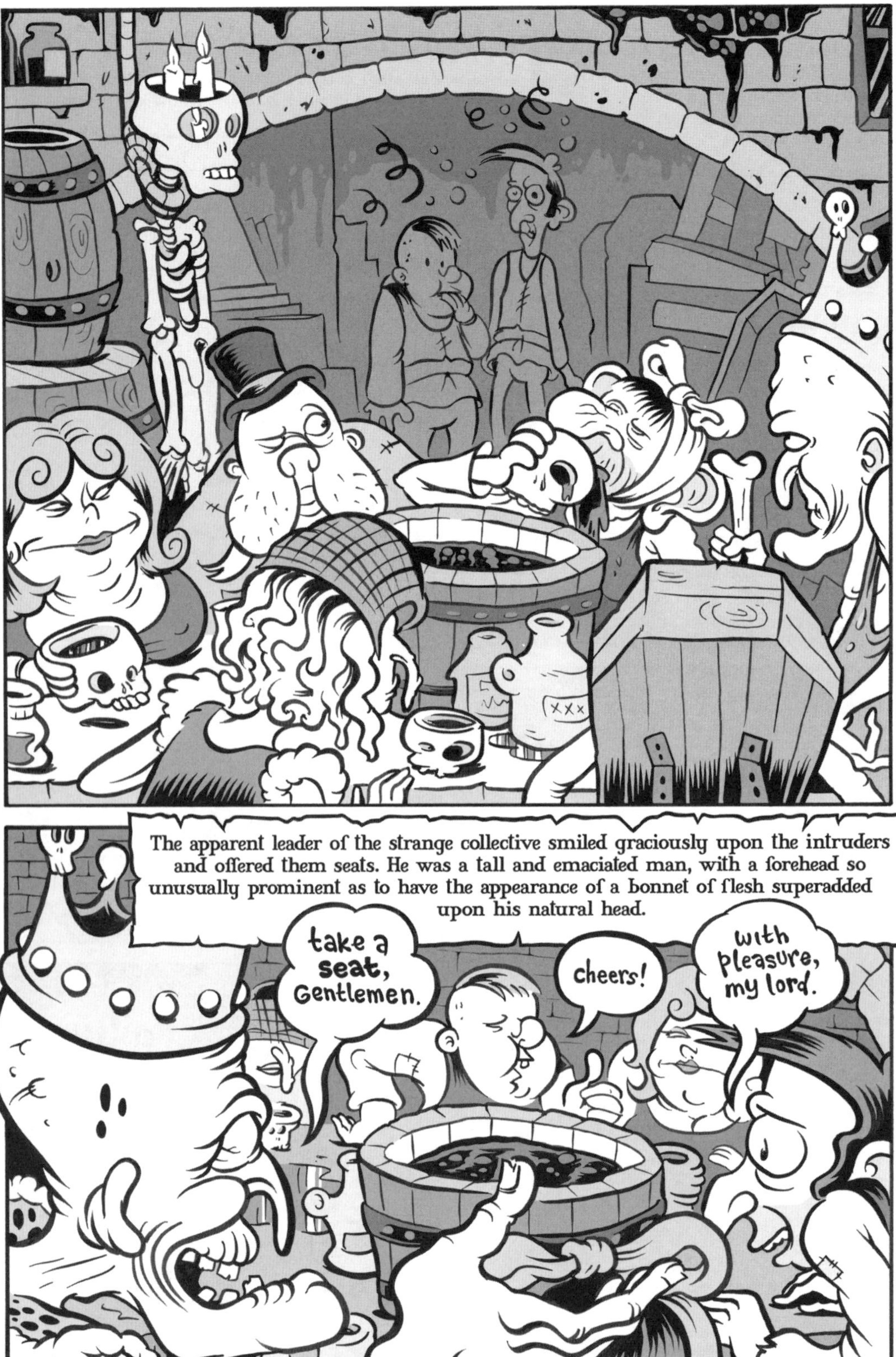
The apparent leader of the strange collective smiled graciously upon the intruders and offered them seats. He was a tall and emaciated man, with a forehead so unusually prominent as to have the appearance of a bonnet of flesh superadded upon his natural head.
take a seat, Gentlemen.
cheers!
with pleasure, my lord.

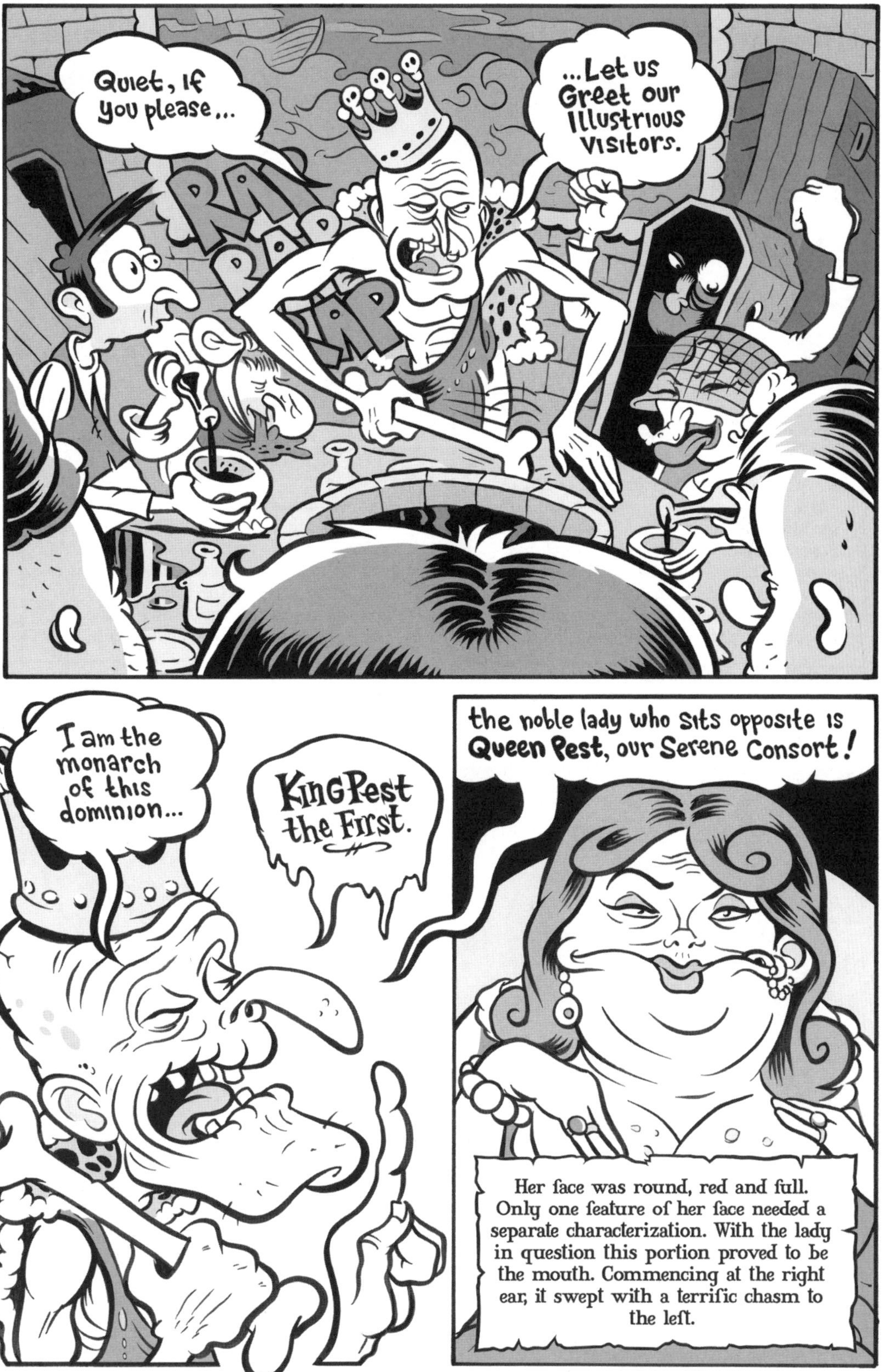
Quiet, if you please,...
...Let us Greet our Illustrious visitors.
I am the monarch of this dominion...
King Pest the First.
the noble lady who sits opposite is **Queen Pest**, our Serene Consort!
Her face was round, red and full. Only one feature of her face needed a separate characterization. With the lady in question this portion proved to be the mouth. Commencing at the right ear, it swept with a terrific chasm to the left.

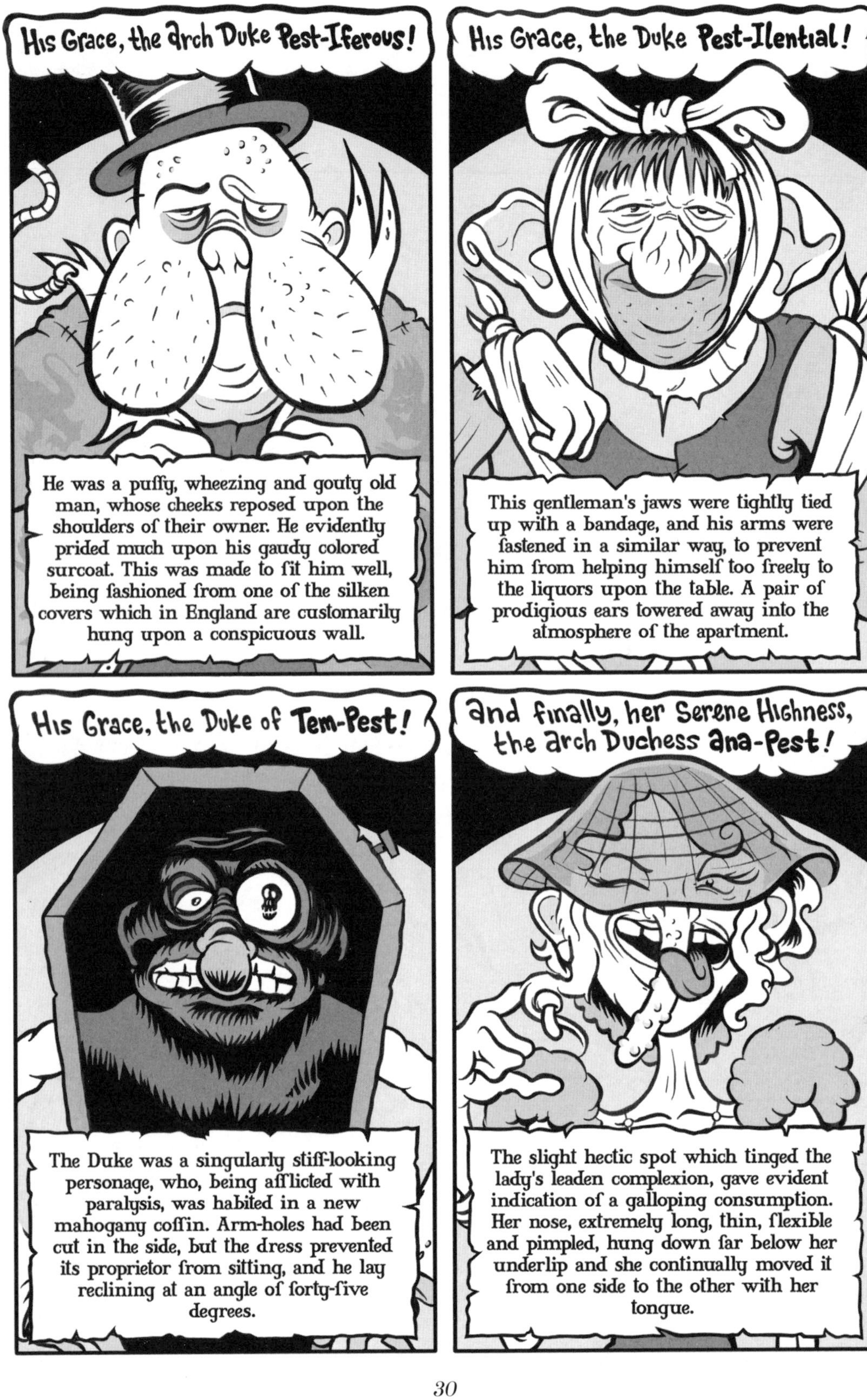
His Grace, the Arch Duke Pest-Iferous!
He was a puffy, wheezing and gouty old man, whose cheeks reposed upon the shoulders of their owner. He evidently prided much upon his gaudy colored surcoat. This was made to fit him well, being fashioned from one of the silken covers which in England are customarily hung upon a conspicuous wall.
His Grace, the Duke Pest-Ilential!
This gentleman's jaws were tightly tied up with a bandage, and his arms were fastened in a similar way, to prevent him from helping himself too freely to the liquors upon the table. A pair of prodigious ears towered away into the atmosphere of the apartment.
His Grace, the Duke of Tem-Pest!
The Duke was a singularly stiff-looking personage, who, being afflicted with paralysis, was habited in a new mahogany coffin. Arm-holes had been cut in the side, but the dress prevented its proprietor from sitting, and he lay reclining at an angle of forty-five degrees.
And finally, her Serene Highness, the Arch Duchess Ana-Pest!
The slight hectic spot which tinged the lady's leaden complexion, gave evident indication of a galloping consumption. Her nose, extremely long, thin, flexible and pimpled, hung down far below her underlip and she continually moved it from one side to the other with her tongue.

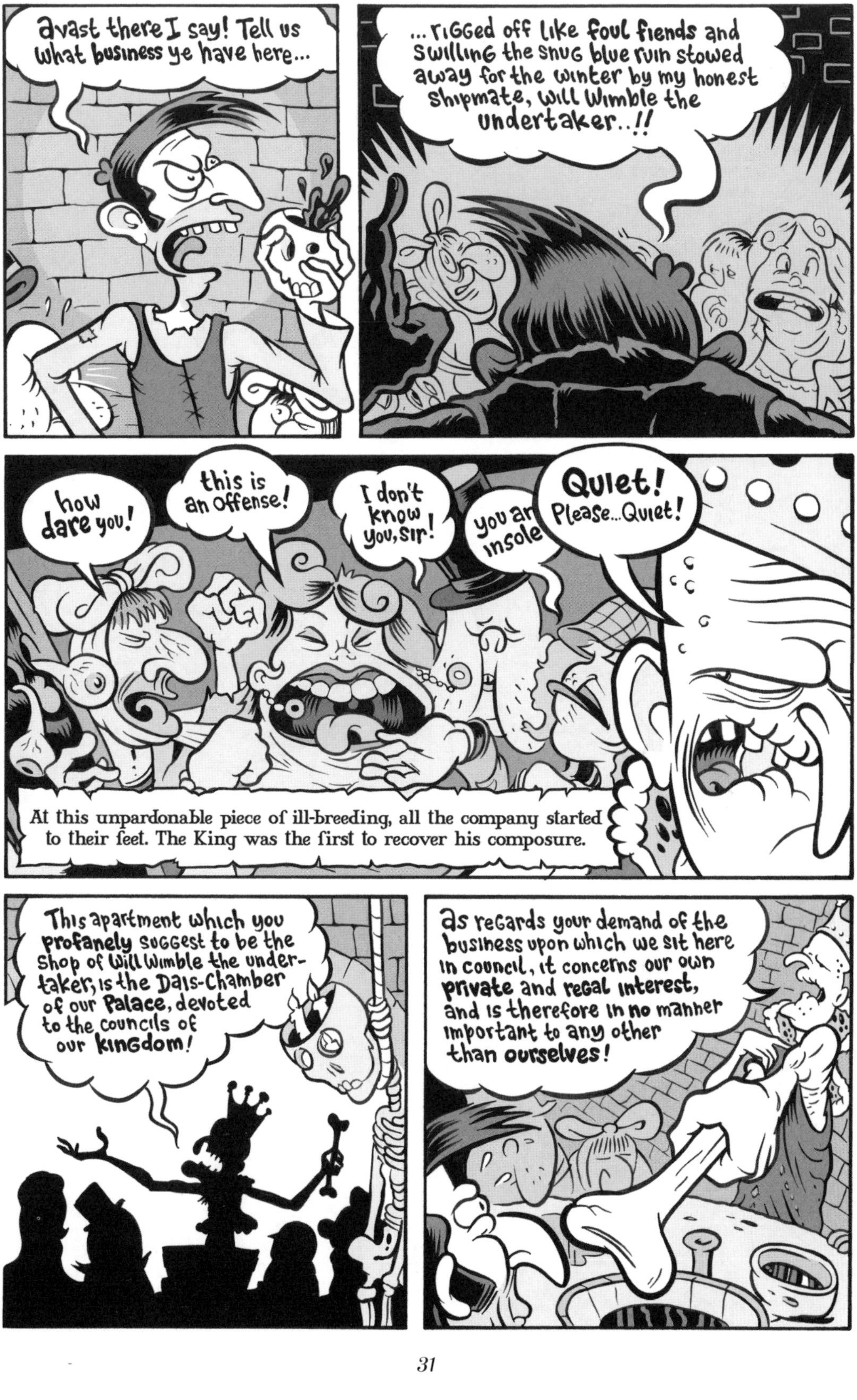
avast there I say! Tell us what business ye have here...
...rigged off like foul fiends and swilling the snug blue ruin stowed away for the winter by my honest shipmate, Will Wimble the undertaker..!!
how dare you!
this is an offense!
I don't know you, sir!
you ar insole
Quiet! Please...Quiet!
At this unpardonable piece of ill-breeding, all the company started to their feet. The King was the first to recover his composure.
This apartment which you profanely suggest to be the shop of Will Wimble the undertaker, is the Dais-Chamber of our Palace, devoted to the councils of our kingdom!
as regards your demand of the business upon which we sit here in council, it concerns our own private and regal interest, and is therefore in no manner important to any other than ourselves!

But we will explain that we are here this night to examine, analyze and thoroughly determine the incomprehensible nature of those inestimable treasures of the palate: the wines, ales and liqueurs of this Goodly Metropolis...

...and by so doing to advance, not more our own designs, than the true welfare of that unearthly sovereign whose name is DEATH!

~whose name is Davey Jones...!

tee hee

Profane varlet! Profane and execrable wretch! We have condescended to make reply to thy rude enquiries..!

Oops! heehee

We nevertheless believe it our duty to **penalize** thee and thy companion each with a Gallon of **Black Strap.**

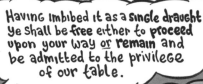

Having imbibed it as a **single draught** ye shall be **free** either to **proceed** upon your way **or remain** and be admitted to the privilege of our table.

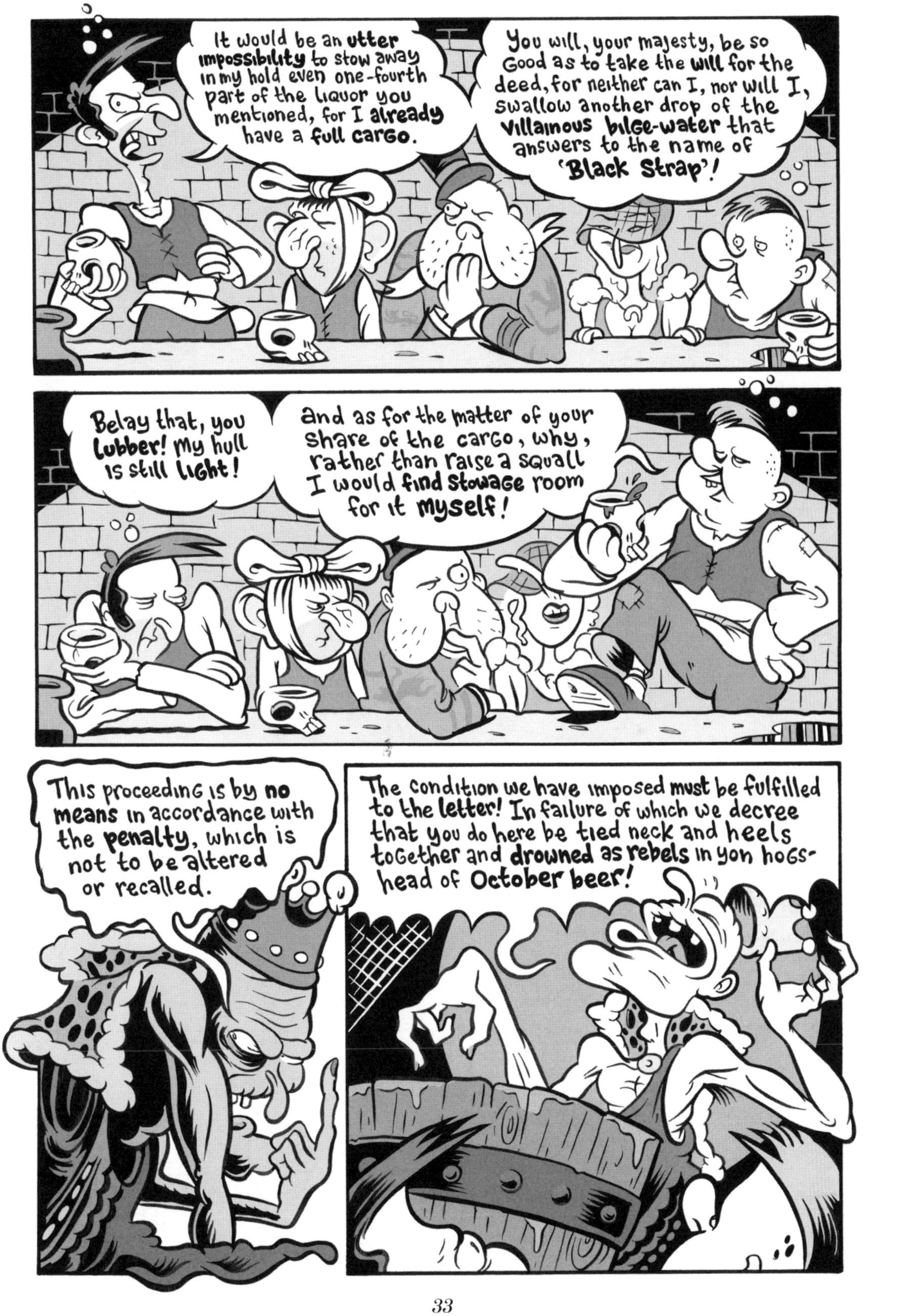
It would be an utter impossibility to stow away in my hold even one-fourth part of the liquor you mentioned, for I already have a full cargo.
You will, your majesty, be so Good as to take the will for the deed, for neither can I, nor will I, swallow another drop of the villainous bilge-water that answers to the name of 'Black Strap'!
Belay that, you lubber! My hull is still light!
And as for the matter of your share of the cargo, why, rather than raise a squall I would find stowage room for it myself!
This proceeding is by no means in accordance with the penalty, which is not to be altered or recalled.
The condition we have imposed must be fulfilled to the letter! In failure of which we decree that you do here be tied neck and heels together and drowned as rebels in yon hogs-head of October beer!

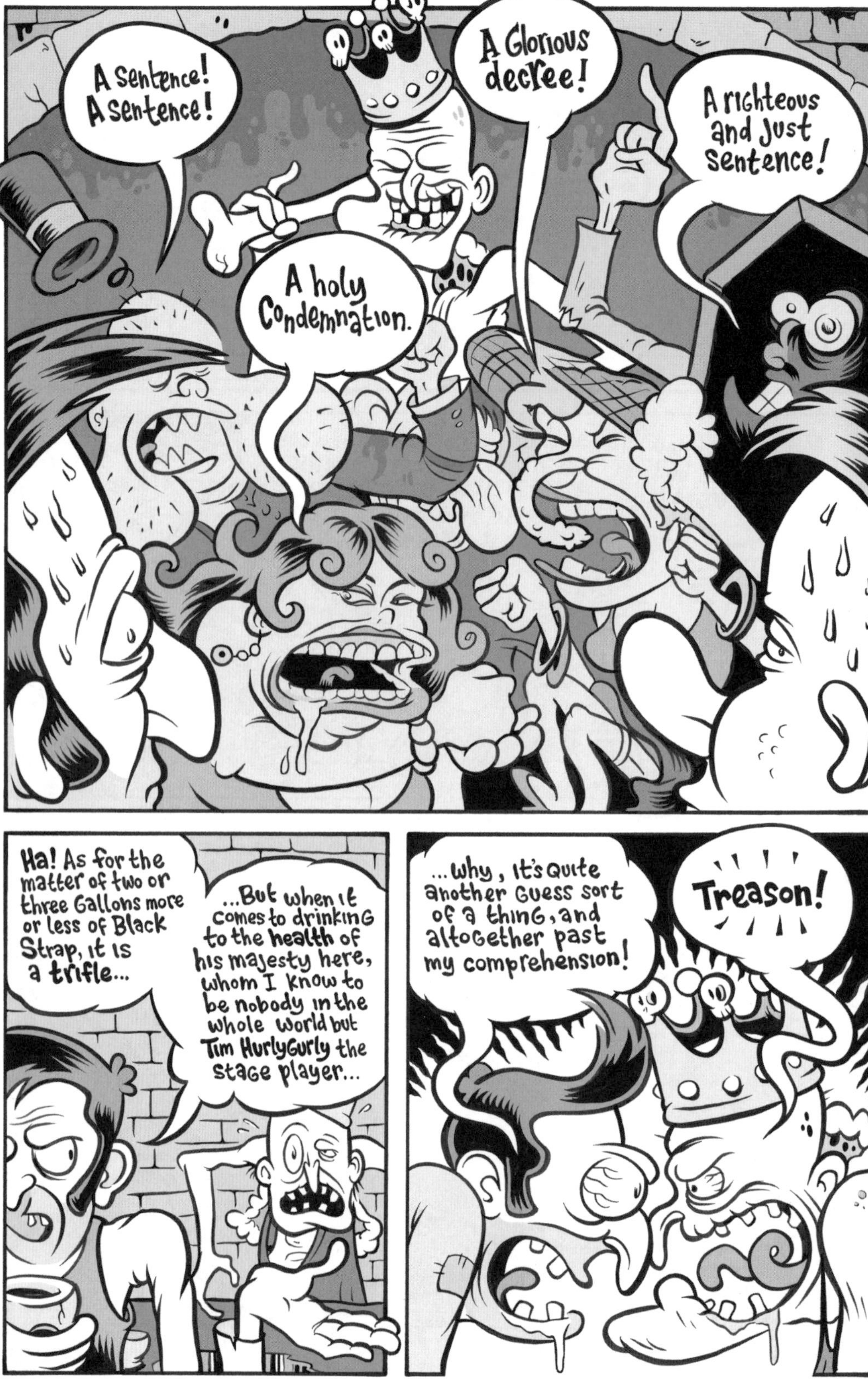
A sentence! A sentence!
A Glorious decree!
A righteous and just sentence!
A holy Condemnation.
Ha! As for the matter of two or three Gallons more or less of Black Strap, it is a trifle...
...But when it comes to drinking to the health of his majesty here, whom I know to be nobody in the whole world but Tim HurlyGurly the stage player...
...why, it's quite another guess sort of a thing, and altogether past my comprehension!
Treason!

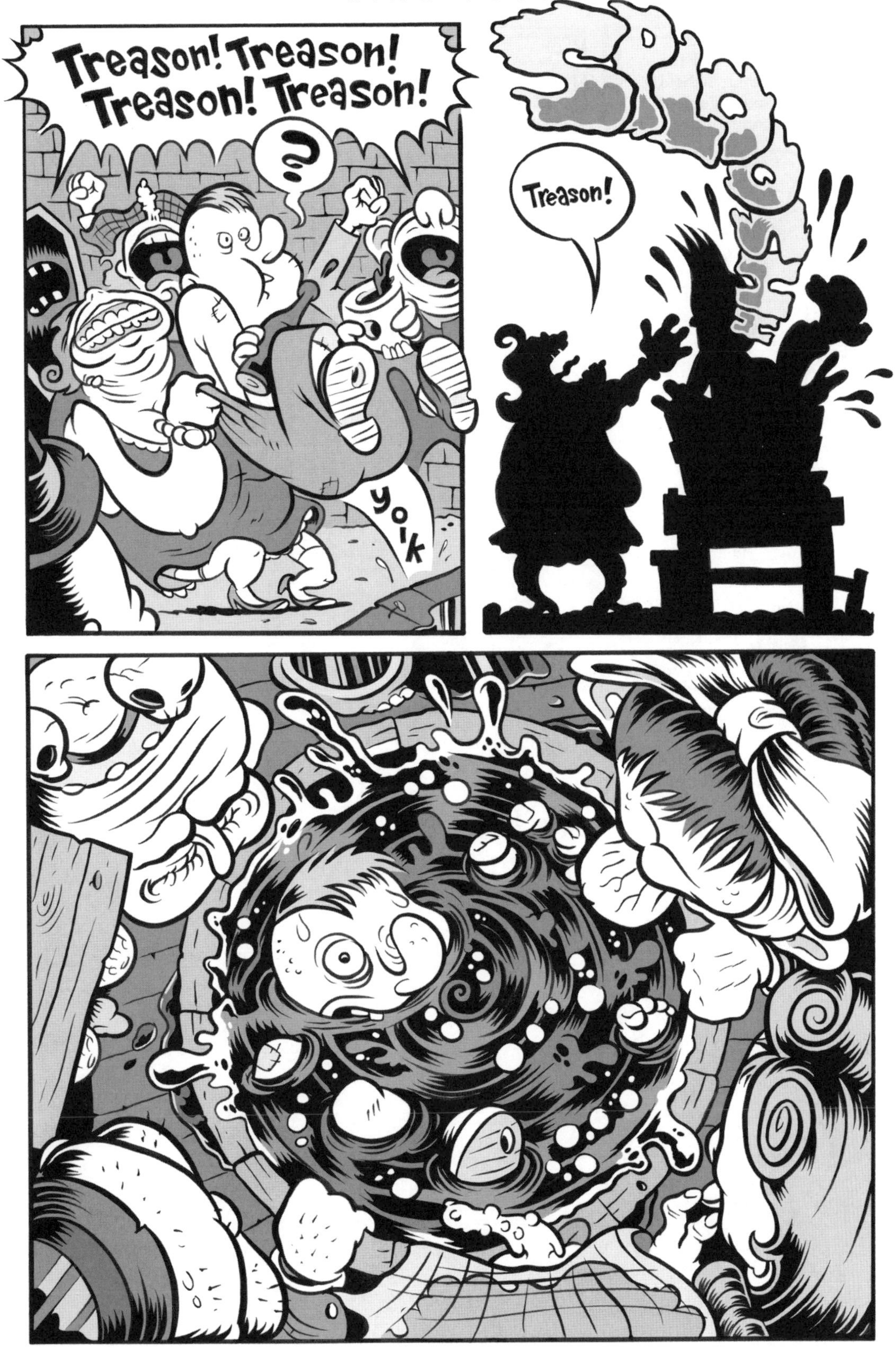
Treason! Treason!
Treason! Treason!
?
YOIK
SPLOOSH
Treason!

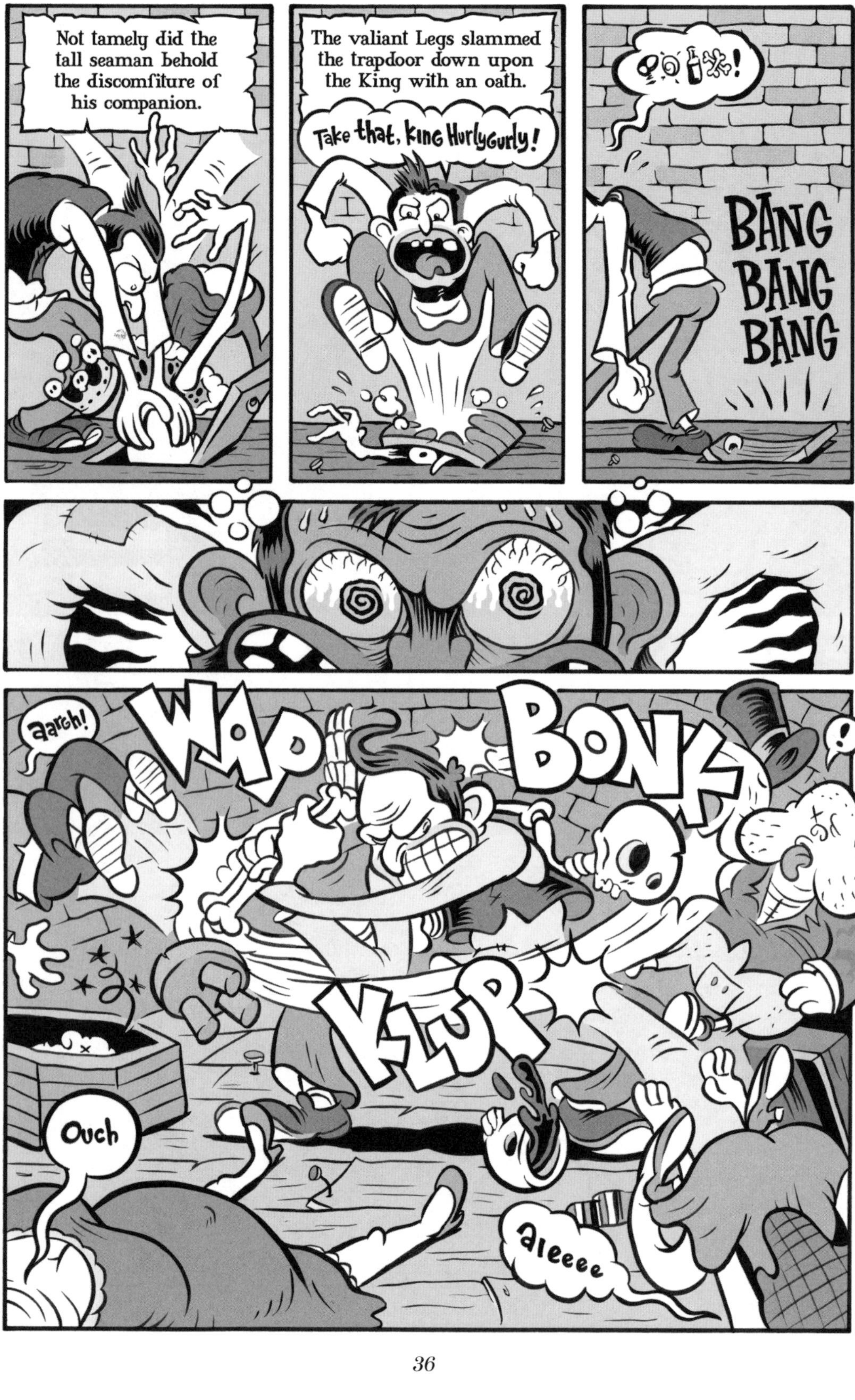
Not tamely did the tall seaman behold the discomfiture of his companion.
The valiant Legs slammed the trapdoor down upon the King with an oath.
Take that, King Hurlygurly!
BANG
BANG
BANG
WAP
BONK
!
aarch!
KLUP
Ouch
aieeee

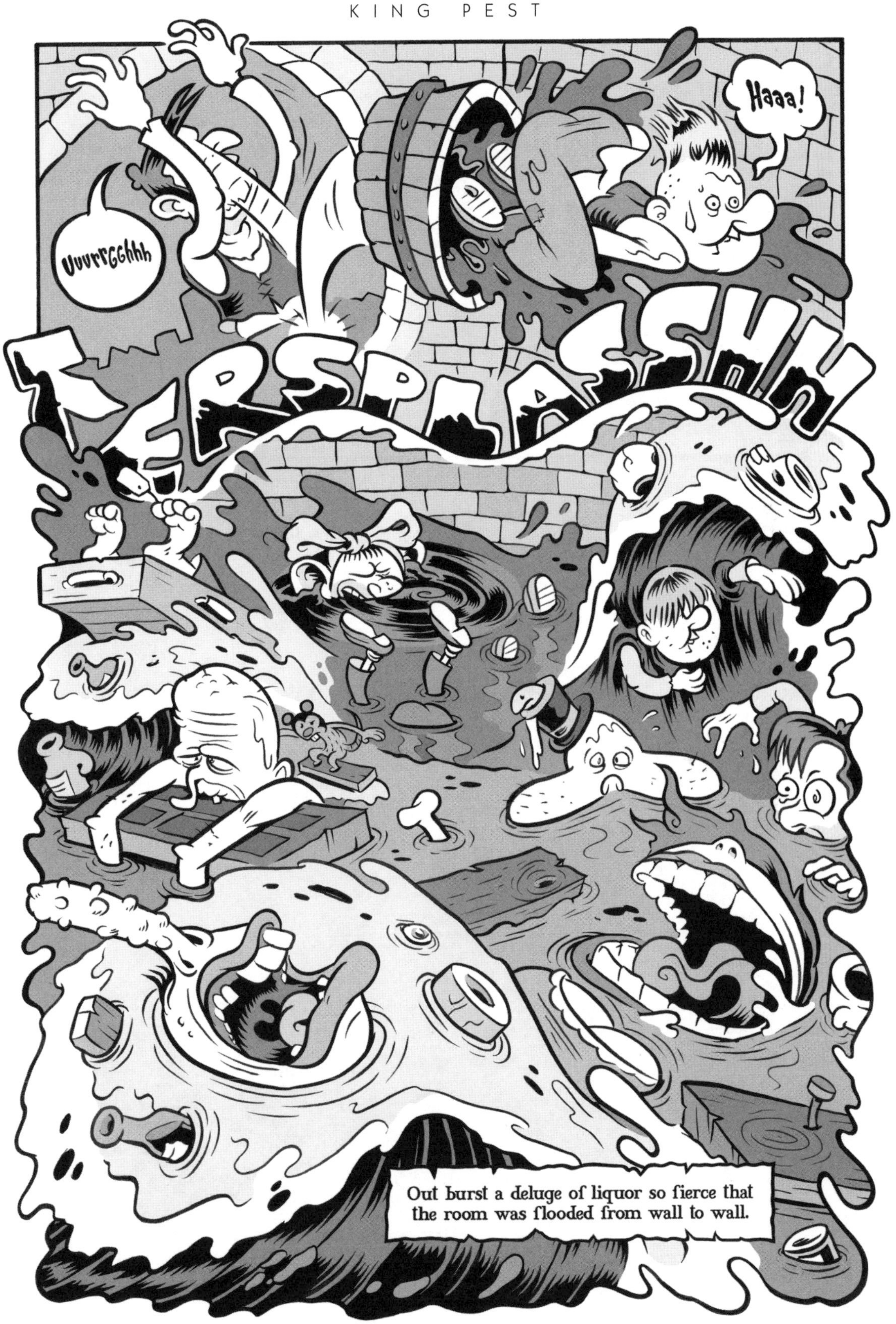
Haaa!
UuurrGGhhh
KERSPLASSHH
Out burst a deluge of liquor so fierce that the room was flooded from wall to wall.

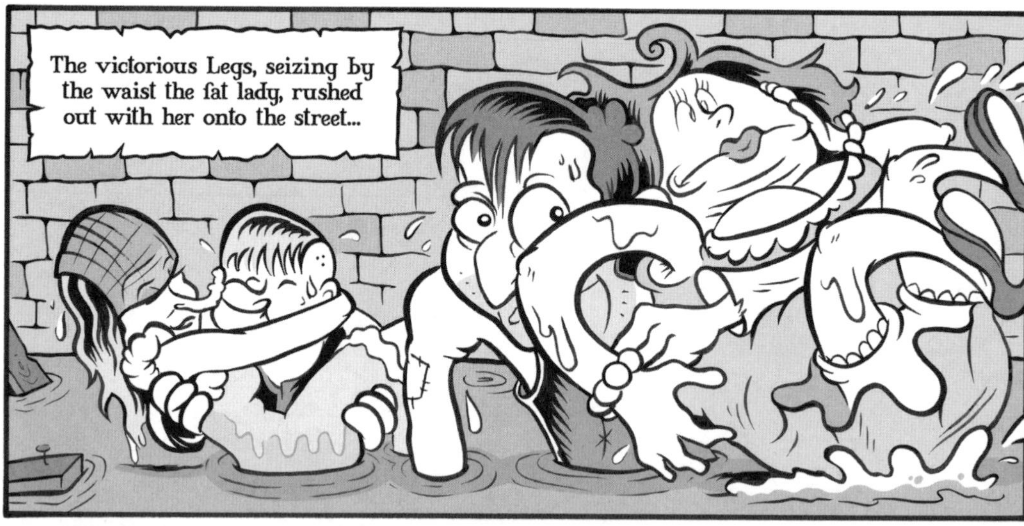
The victorious Legs, seizing by the waist the fat lady, rushed out with her onto the street...

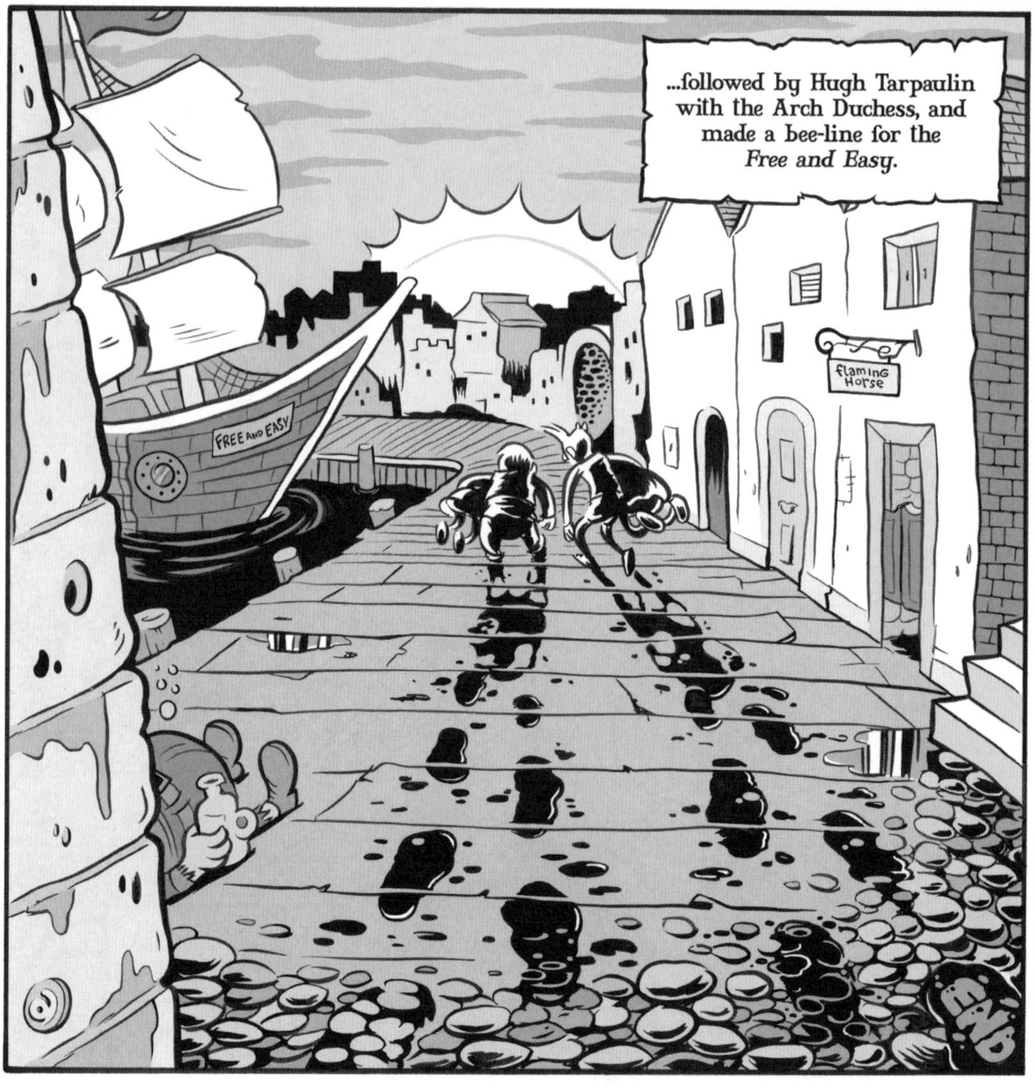
...followed by Hugh Tarpaulin with the Arch Duchess, and made a bee-line for the *Free and Easy*.
flaming Horse
FREE AND EASY
END

ILLUSTRATIONS ©2006 ANTON EMDIN

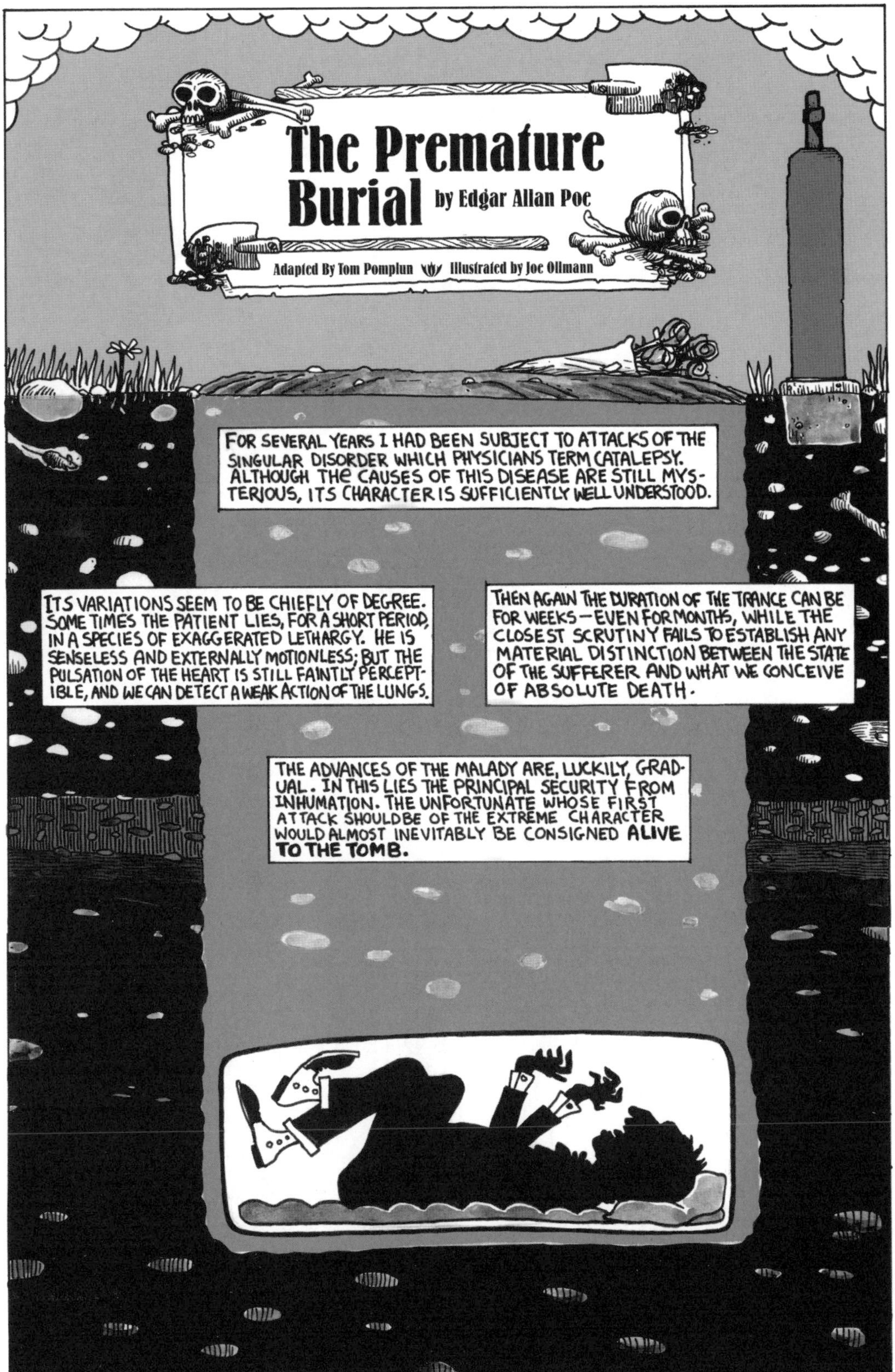
The Premature Burial
by Edgar Allan Poe
Adapted By Tom Pomplun
Illustrated by Joe Ollmann
FOR SEVERAL YEARS I HAD BEEN SUBJECT TO ATTACKS OF THE SINGULAR DISORDER WHICH PHYSICIANS TERM CATALEPSY. ALTHOUGH THE CAUSES OF THIS DISEASE ARE STILL MYSTERIOUS, ITS CHARACTER IS SUFFICIENTLY WELL UNDERSTOOD.
ITS VARIATIONS SEEM TO BE CHIEFLY OF DEGREE. SOME TIMES THE PATIENT LIES, FOR A SHORT PERIOD, IN A SPECIES OF EXAGGERATED LETHARGY. HE IS SENSELESS AND EXTERNALLY MOTIONLESS; BUT THE PULSATION OF THE HEART IS STILL FAINTLY PERCEPTIBLE, AND WE CAN DETECT A WEAK ACTION OF THE LUNGS.
THEN AGAIN THE DURATION OF THE TRANCE CAN BE FOR WEEKS—EVEN FOR MONTHS, WHILE THE CLOSEST SCRUTINY FAILS TO ESTABLISH ANY MATERIAL DISTINCTION BETWEEN THE STATE OF THE SUFFERER AND WHAT WE CONCEIVE OF ABSOLUTE DEATH.
THE ADVANCES OF THE MALADY ARE, LUCKILY, GRADUAL. IN THIS LIES THE PRINCIPAL SECURITY FROM INHUMATION. THE UNFORTUNATE WHOSE FIRST ATTACK SHOULDBE OF THE EXTREME CHARACTER WOULD ALMOST INEVITABLY BE CONSIGNED ALIVE TO THE TOMB.

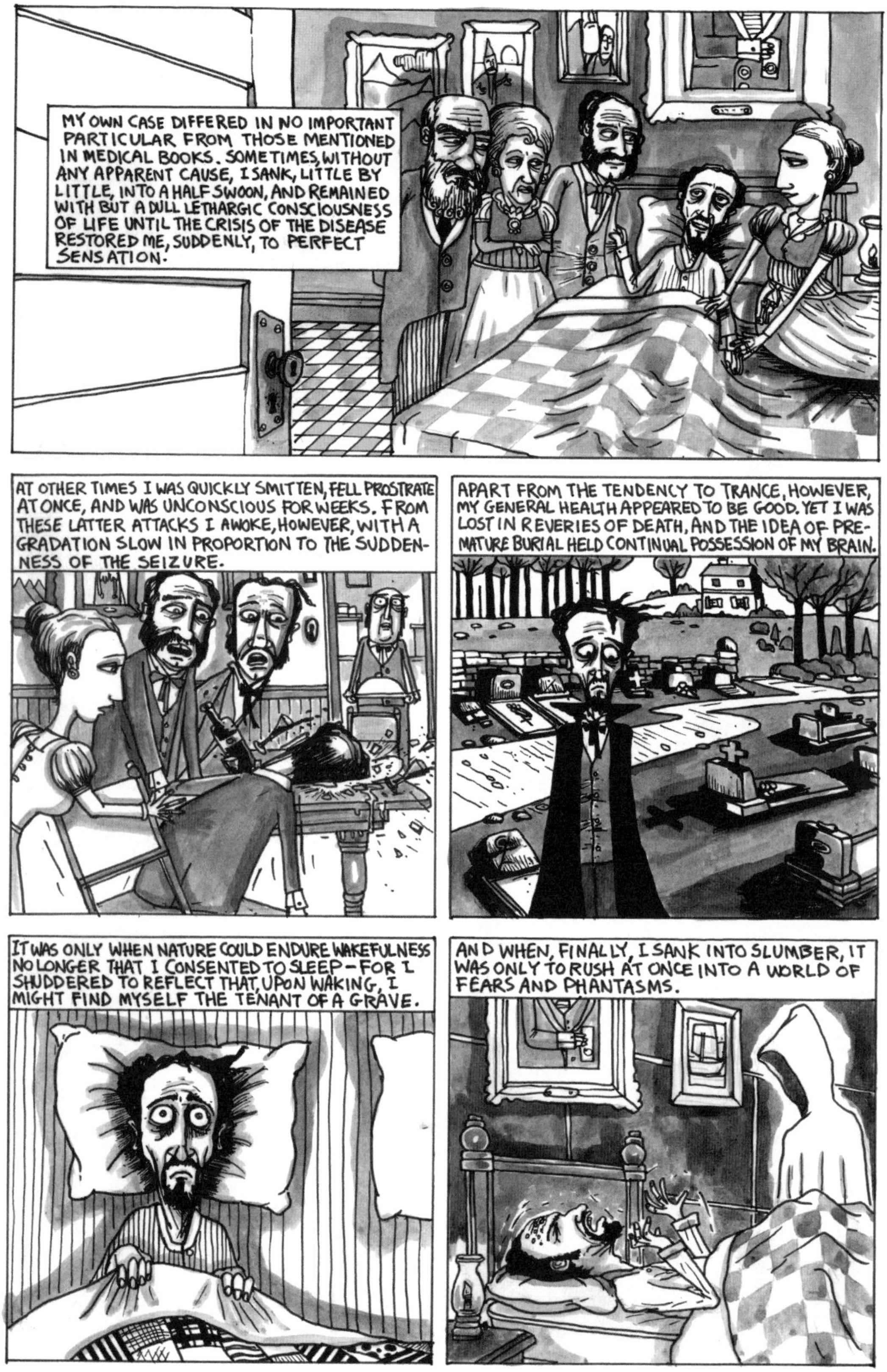
MY OWN CASE DIFFERED IN NO IMPORTANT PARTICULAR FROM THOSE MENTIONED IN MEDICAL BOOKS. SOMETIMES, WITHOUT ANY APPARENT CAUSE, I SANK, LITTLE BY LITTLE, INTO A HALF SWOON, AND REMAINED WITH BUT A DULL LETHARGIC CONSCIOUSNESS OF LIFE UNTIL THE CRISIS OF THE DISEASE RESTORED ME, SUDDENLY, TO PERFECT SENSATION.
AT OTHER TIMES I WAS QUICKLY SMITTEN, FELL PROSTRATE AT ONCE, AND WAS UNCONSCIOUS FOR WEEKS. FROM THESE LATTER ATTACKS I AWOKE, HOWEVER, WITH A GRADATION SLOW IN PROPORTION TO THE SUDDENNESS OF THE SEIZURE.
APART FROM THE TENDENCY TO TRANCE, HOWEVER, MY GENERAL HEALTH APPEARED TO BE GOOD. YET I WAS LOST IN REVERIES OF DEATH, AND THE IDEA OF PREMATURE BURIAL HELD CONTINUAL POSSESSION OF MY BRAIN.
IT WAS ONLY WHEN NATURE COULD ENDURE WAKEFULNESS NO LONGER THAT I CONSENTED TO SLEEP—FOR I SHUDDERED TO REFLECT THAT, UPON WAKING, I MIGHT FIND MYSELF THE TENANT OF A GRAVE.
AND WHEN, FINALLY, I SANK INTO SLUMBER, IT WAS ONLY TO RUSH AT ONCE INTO A WORLD OF FEARS AND PHANTASMS.

ONLY RECENTLY I WAS IMMERSED IN A CATALEPTIC TRANCE OF MORE THAN USUAL PROFUNDITY. SUDDENLY A COLD VOICE WHISPERED INTO MY EAR.
ARISE!
AND WHO ART THOU?
I HAVE NO NAME IN THE REGIONS I INHABIT. I WAS MORTAL, BUT AM NOW FIEND.
COME WITH ME INTO THE OUTER NIGHT, AND LET ME UNFOLD TO THEE THE GRAVES!
BEHOLD!

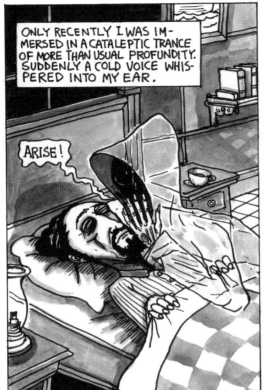

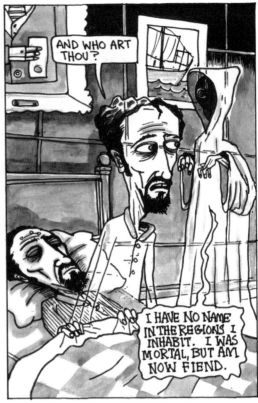

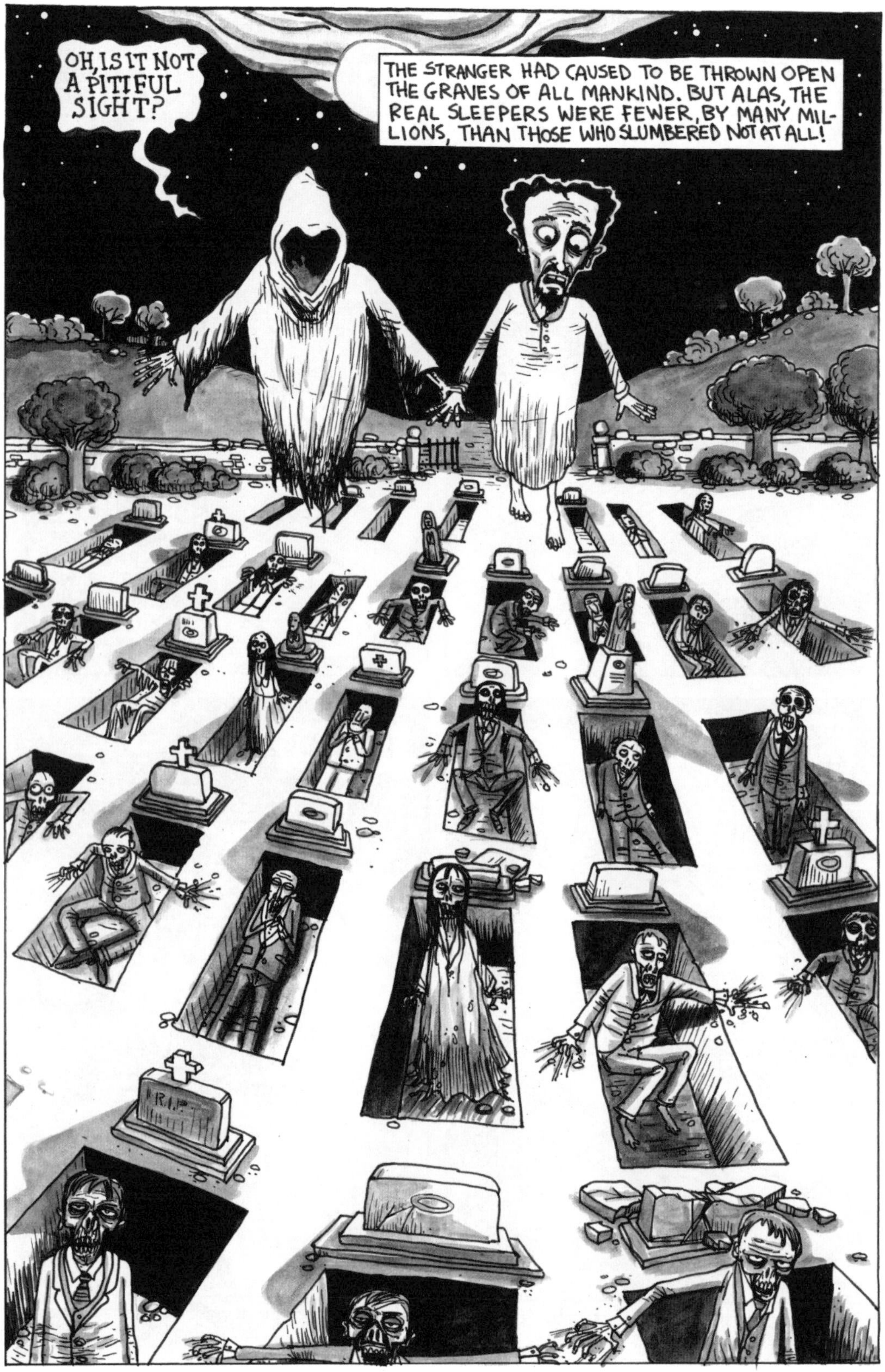
OH, IS IT NOT A PITIFUL SIGHT?
THE STRANGER HAD CAUSED TO BE THROWN OPEN THE GRAVES OF ALL MANKIND. BUT ALAS, THE REAL SLEEPERS WERE FEWER, BY MANY MILLIONS, THAN THOSE WHO SLUMBERED NOT AT ALL!
R.I.P.

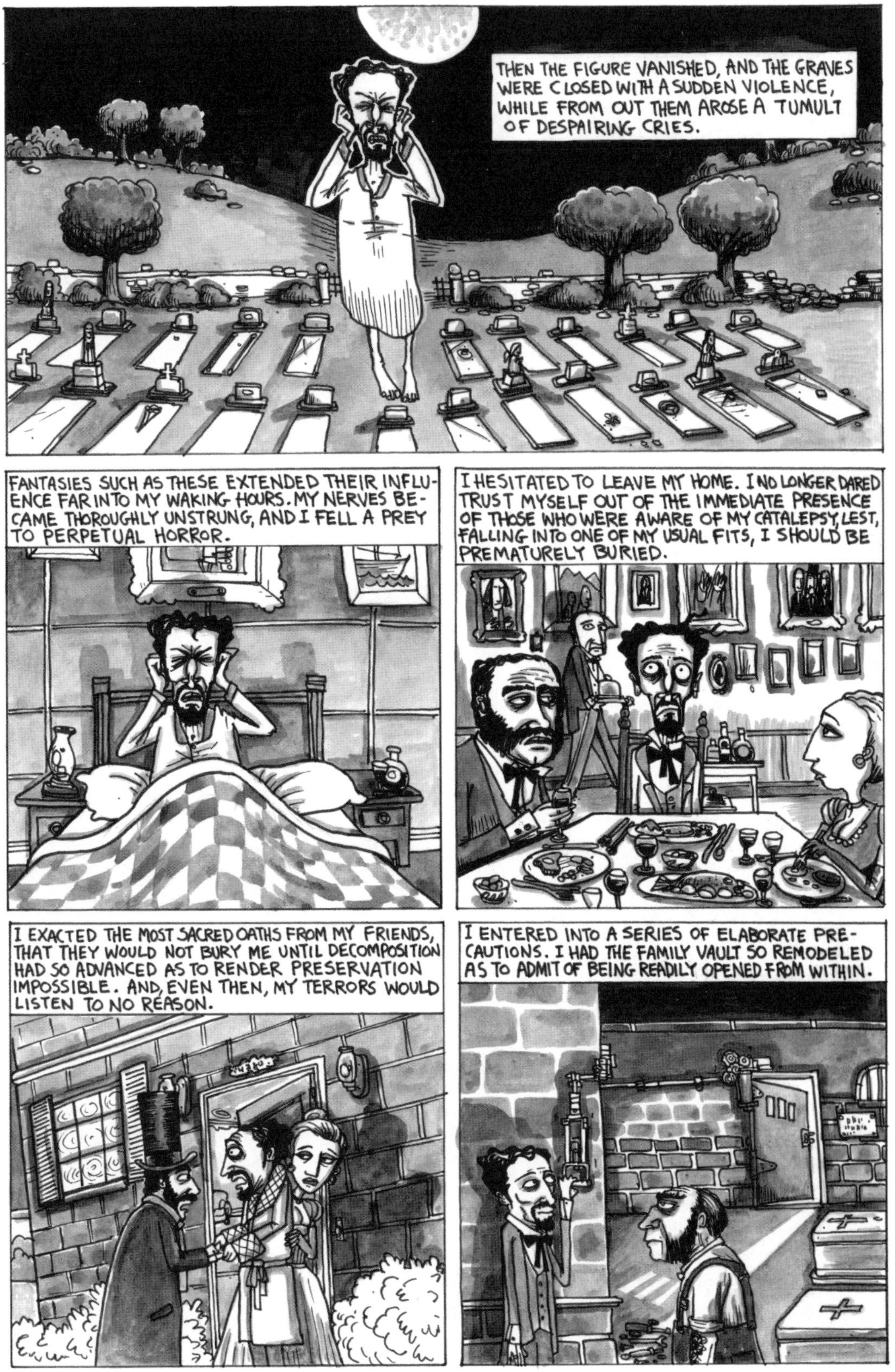
THEN THE FIGURE VANISHED, AND THE GRAVES WERE CLOSED WITH A SUDDEN VIOLENCE, WHILE FROM OUT THEM AROSE A TUMULT OF DESPAIRING CRIES.
FANTASIES SUCH AS THESE EXTENDED THEIR INFLUENCE FAR INTO MY WAKING HOURS. MY NERVES BECAME THOROUGHLY UNSTRUNG, AND I FELL A PREY TO PERPETUAL HORROR.
I HESITATED TO LEAVE MY HOME. I NO LONGER DARED TRUST MYSELF OUT OF THE IMMEDIATE PRESENCE OF THOSE WHO WERE AWARE OF MY CATALEPSY, LEST, FALLING INTO ONE OF MY USUAL FITS, I SHOULD BE PREMATURELY BURIED.
I EXACTED THE MOST SACRED OATHS FROM MY FRIENDS, THAT THEY WOULD NOT BURY ME UNTIL DECOMPOSITION HAD SO ADVANCED AS TO RENDER PRESERVATION IMPOSSIBLE. AND, EVEN THEN, MY TERRORS WOULD LISTEN TO NO REASON.
I ENTERED INTO A SERIES OF ELABORATE PRECAUTIONS. I HAD THE FAMILY VAULT SO REMODELED AS TO ADMIT OF BEING READILY OPENED FROM WITHIN.

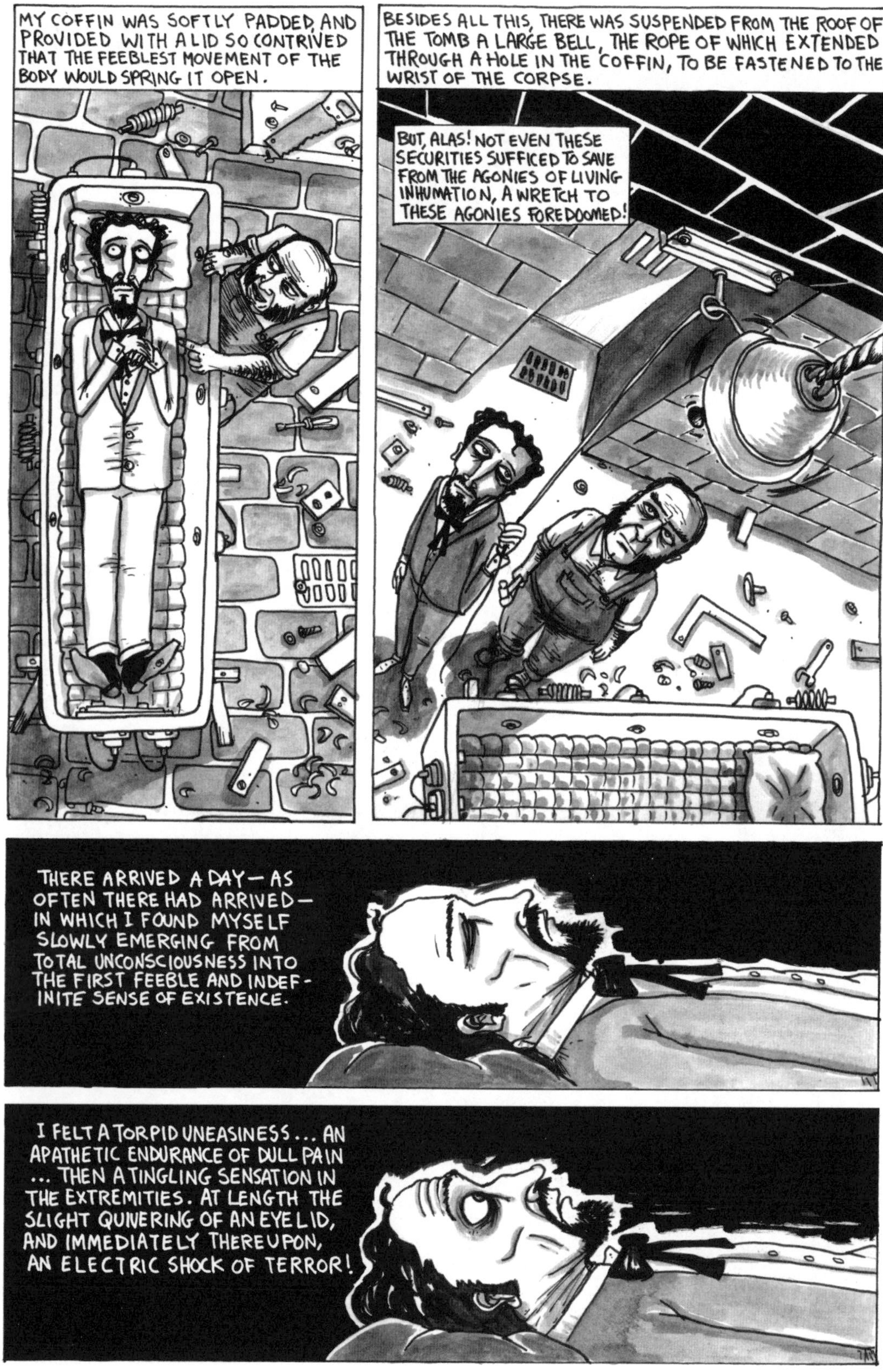
MY COFFIN WAS SOFTLY PADDED, AND PROVIDED WITH A LID SO CONTRIVED THAT THE FEEBLEST MOVEMENT OF THE BODY WOULD SPRING IT OPEN.
BESIDES ALL THIS, THERE WAS SUSPENDED FROM THE ROOF OF THE TOMB A LARGE BELL, THE ROPE OF WHICH EXTENDED THROUGH A HOLE IN THE COFFIN, TO BE FASTENED TO THE WRIST OF THE CORPSE.
BUT, ALAS! NOT EVEN THESE SECURITIES SUFFICED TO SAVE FROM THE AGONIES OF LIVING INHUMATION, A WRETCH TO THESE AGONIES FOREDOOMED!
THERE ARRIVED A DAY—AS OFTEN THERE HAD ARRIVED—IN WHICH I FOUND MYSELF SLOWLY EMERGING FROM TOTAL UNCONSCIOUSNESS INTO THE FIRST FEEBLE AND INDEFINITE SENSE OF EXISTENCE.
I FELT A TORPID UNEASINESS... AN APATHETIC ENDURANCE OF DULL PAIN ... THEN A TINGLING SENSATION IN THE EXTREMITIES. AT LENGTH THE SLIGHT QUIVERING OF AN EYELID, AND IMMEDIATELY THEREUPON, AN ELECTRIC SHOCK OF TERROR!

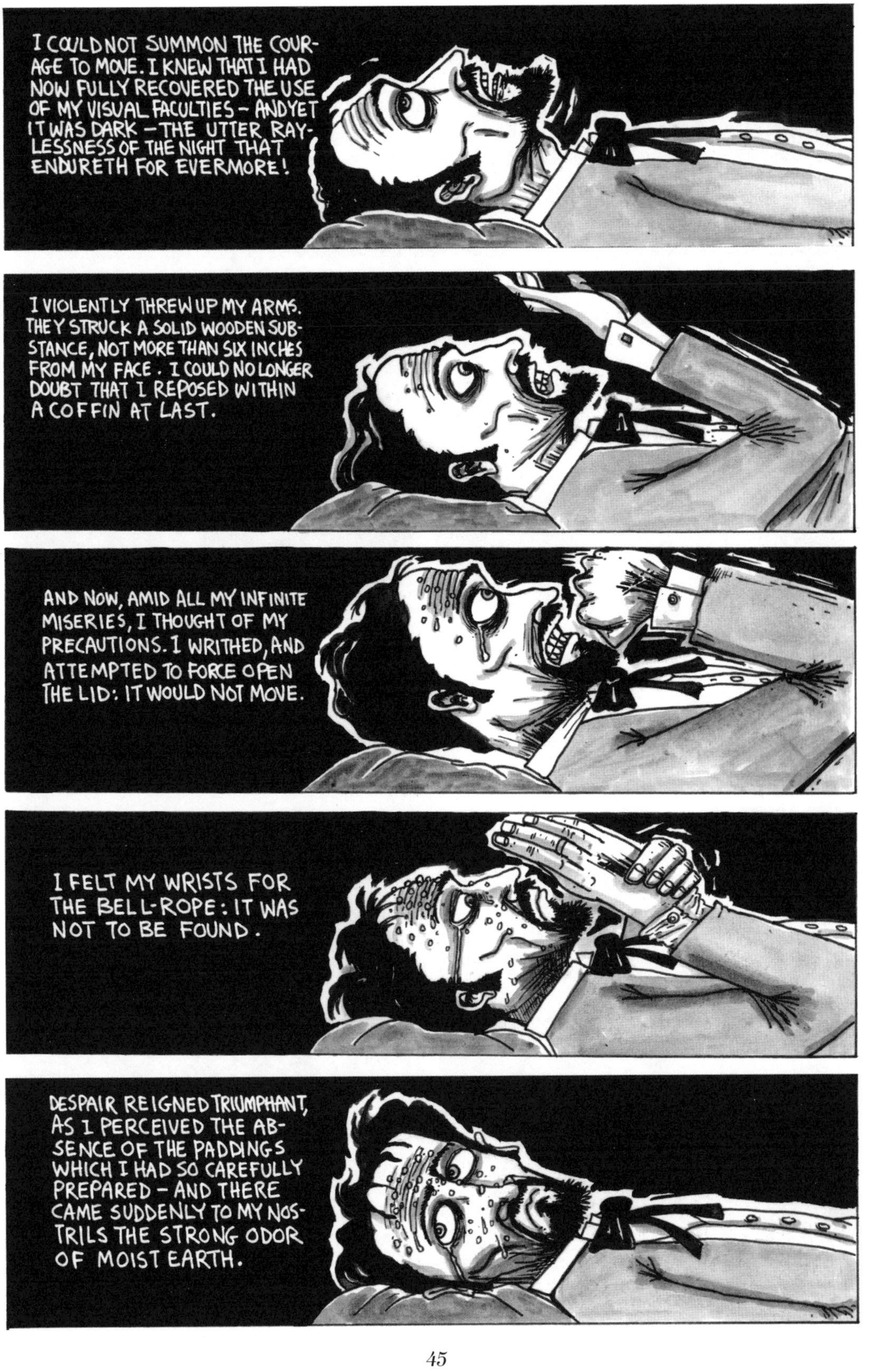
I COULD NOT SUMMON THE COURAGE TO MOVE. I KNEW THAT I HAD NOW FULLY RECOVERED THE USE OF MY VISUAL FACULTIES - AND YET IT WAS DARK - THE UTTER RAYLESSNESS OF THE NIGHT THAT ENDURETH FOR EVERMORE!
I VIOLENTLY THREW UP MY ARMS. THEY STRUCK A SOLID WOODEN SUBSTANCE, NOT MORE THAN SIX INCHES FROM MY FACE. I COULD NO LONGER DOUBT THAT I REPOSED WITHIN A COFFIN AT LAST.
AND NOW, AMID ALL MY INFINITE MISERIES, I THOUGHT OF MY PRECAUTIONS. I WRITHED, AND ATTEMPTED TO FORCE OPEN THE LID: IT WOULD NOT MOVE.
I FELT MY WRISTS FOR THE BELL-ROPE: IT WAS NOT TO BE FOUND.
DESPAIR REIGNED TRIUMPHANT, AS I PERCEIVED THE ABSENCE OF THE PADDINGS WHICH I HAD SO CAREFULLY PREPARED - AND THERE CAME SUDDENLY TO MY NOSTRILS THE STRONG ODOR OF MOIST EARTH.

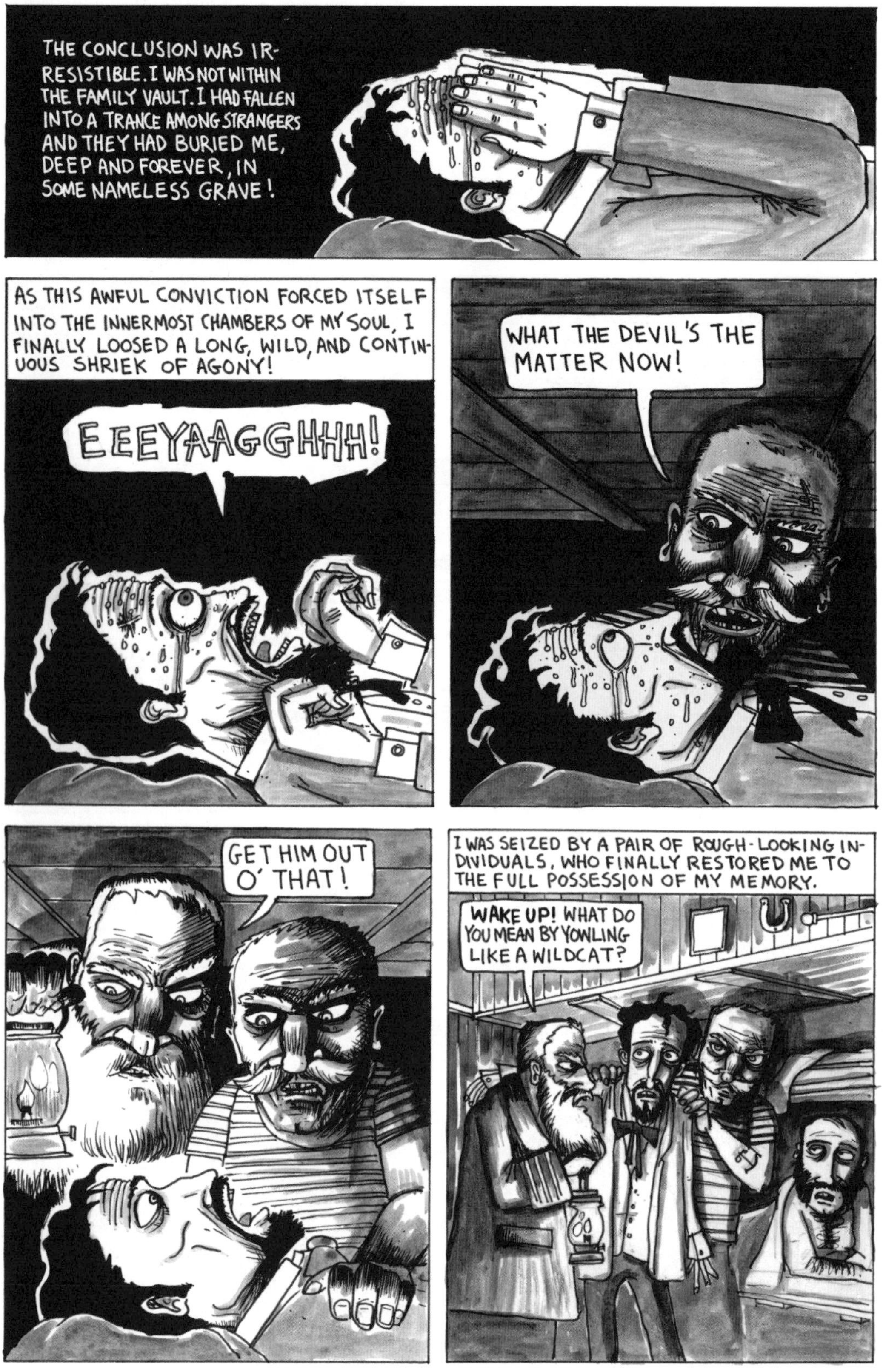
THE CONCLUSION WAS IRRESISTIBLE. I WAS NOT WITHIN THE FAMILY VAULT. I HAD FALLEN INTO A TRANCE AMONG STRANGERS AND THEY HAD BURIED ME, DEEP AND FOREVER, IN SOME NAMELESS GRAVE!
AS THIS AWFUL CONVICTION FORCED ITSELF INTO THE INNERMOST CHAMBERS OF MY SOUL, I FINALLY LOOSED A LONG, WILD, AND CONTINUOUS SHRIEK OF AGONY!
EEEYAAGGHHH!
WHAT THE DEVIL'S THE MATTER NOW!
GET HIM OUT O' THAT!
I WAS SEIZED BY A PAIR OF ROUGH-LOOKING INDIVIDUALS, WHO FINALLY RESTORED ME TO THE FULL POSSESSION OF MY MEMORY.
WAKE UP! WHAT DO YOU MEAN BY YOWLING LIKE A WILDCAT?

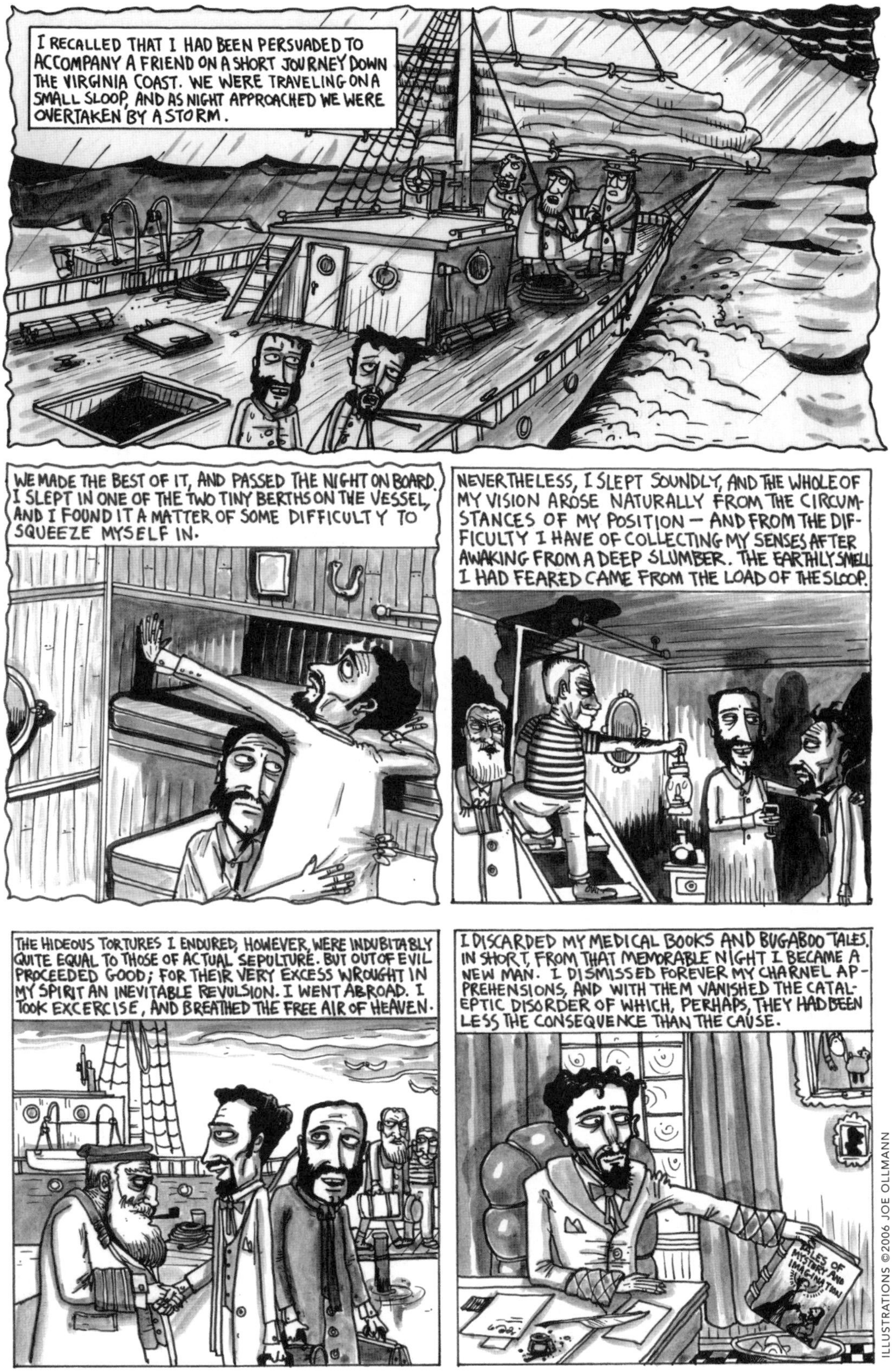
I RECALLED THAT I HAD BEEN PERSUADED TO ACCOMPANY A FRIEND ON A SHORT JOURNEY DOWN THE VIRGINIA COAST. WE WERE TRAVELING ON A SMALL SLOOP, AND AS NIGHT APPROACHED WE WERE OVERTAKEN BY A STORM.
WE MADE THE BEST OF IT, AND PASSED THE NIGHT ON BOARD. I SLEPT IN ONE OF THE TWO TINY BERTHS ON THE VESSEL, AND I FOUND IT A MATTER OF SOME DIFFICULTY TO SQUEEZE MYSELF IN.
NEVERTHELESS, I SLEPT SOUNDLY, AND THE WHOLE OF MY VISION AROSE NATURALLY FROM THE CIRCUMSTANCES OF MY POSITION — AND FROM THE DIFFICULTY I HAVE OF COLLECTING MY SENSES AFTER AWAKING FROM A DEEP SLUMBER. THE EARTHLY SMELL I HAD FEARED CAME FROM THE LOAD OF THE SLOOP.
THE HIDEOUS TORTURES I ENDURED, HOWEVER, WERE INDUBITABLY QUITE EQUAL TO THOSE OF ACTUAL SEPULTURE. BUT OUT OF EVIL PROCEEDED GOOD; FOR THEIR VERY EXCESS WROUGHT IN MY SPIRIT AN INEVITABLE REVULSION. I WENT ABROAD. I TOOK EXCERCISE, AND BREATHED THE FREE AIR OF HEAVEN.
I DISCARDED MY MEDICAL BOOKS AND BUGABOO TALES. IN SHORT, FROM THAT MEMORABLE NIGHT I BECAME A NEW MAN. I DISMISSED FOREVER MY CHARNEL APPREHENSIONS, AND WITH THEM VANISHED THE CATALEPTIC DISORDER OF WHICH, PERHAPS, THEY HAD BEEN LESS THE CONSEQUENCE THAN THE CAUSE.
TALES OF MYSTERY AND IMAGINATION

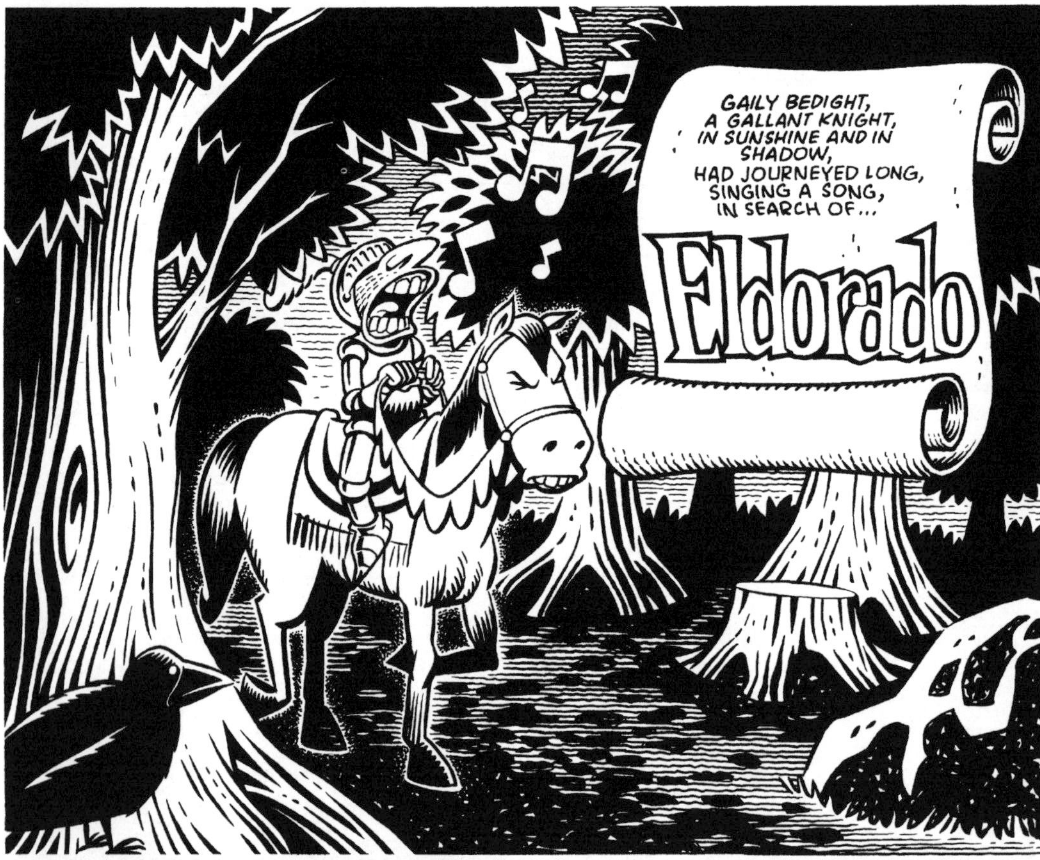
GAILY BEDIGHT,
A GALLANT KNIGHT,
IN SUNSHINE AND IN SHADOW,
HAD JOURNEYED LONG,
SINGING A SONG,
IN SEARCH OF...
Eldorado

WORDS BY **EDGAR ALLAN POE** PICTURES BY ROGER LANGRIDGE

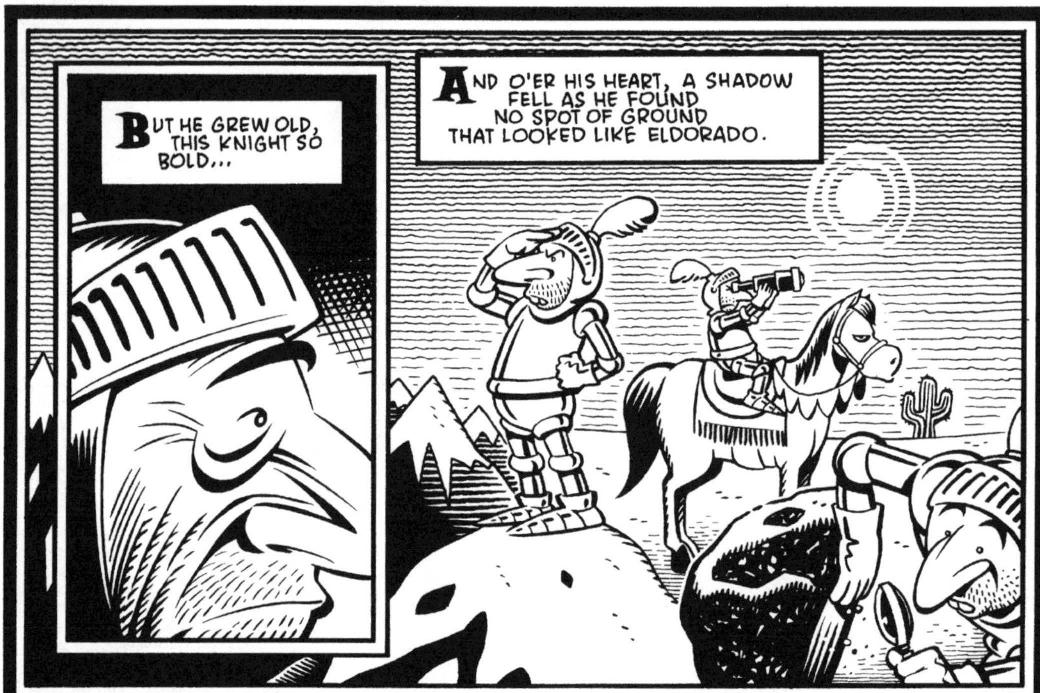
BUT HE GREW OLD,
THIS KNIGHT SO BOLD...
AND O'ER HIS HEART, A SHADOW FELL AS HE FOUND NO SPOT OF GROUND THAT LOOKED LIKE ELDORADO.

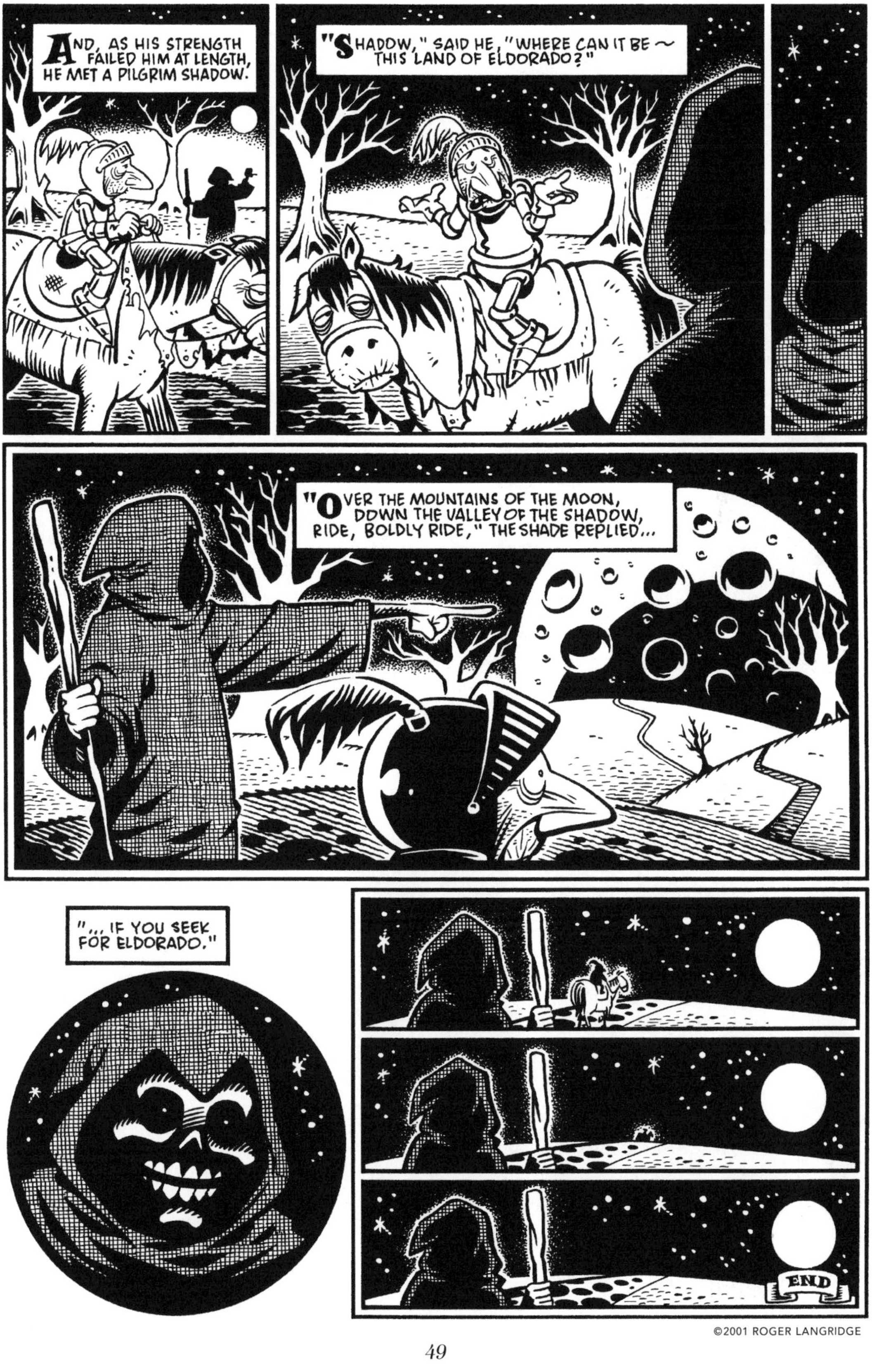
AND, AS HIS STRENGTH FAILED HIM AT LENGTH, HE MET A PILGRIM SHADOW.
"SHADOW," SAID HE, "WHERE CAN IT BE ~ THIS LAND OF ELDORADO?"
"OVER THE MOUNTAINS OF THE MOON, DOWN THE VALLEY OF THE SHADOW, RIDE, BOLDLY RIDE," THE SHADE REPLIED...
"... IF YOU SEEK FOR ELDORADO."
END

SPIRITS OF THE DEAD

by EDGAR ALLAN POE

illustrated by ANDY EWEN

Thy soul shall find itself alone
'Mid dark thoughts of the grey tomb-stone;
Not one, of all the crowd, to pry
Into thine hour of secrecy.

Be silent in that solitude,
Which is not loneliness — for then
The spirits of the dead who stood
In life before thee are again
In death around thee, and their will
Shall then overshadow thee: be still.

For the night, though clear, shall frown,
And the stars shall look not down
From their high thrones in the Heaven
With light like hope to mortals given,
But their red orbs, without beam,
To thy weariness shall seem
As a burning and a fever
Which would cling to thee for ever.

Now are thoughts thou shalt not banish,
Now are visions ne'er to vanish;
From thy spirit shall they pass
No more, like dew-drop from the grass.

The breeze, the breath of God, is still,
And the mist upon the hill
Shadowy, shadowy, yet unbroken,
Is a symbol and a token.
How it hangs upon the trees,
A mystery of mysteries!

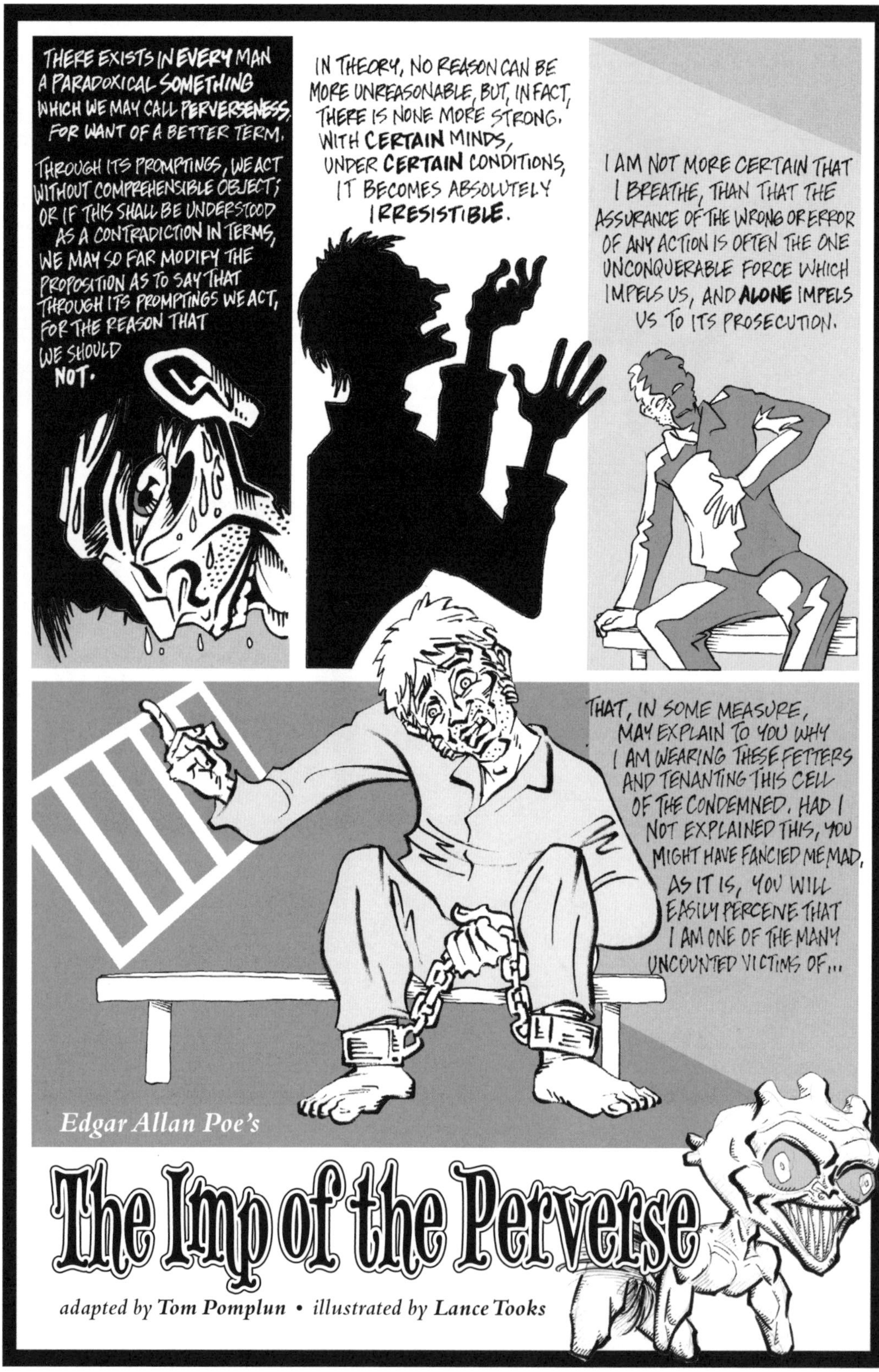
THERE EXISTS IN EVERY MAN A PARADOXICAL SOMETHING WHICH WE MAY CALL PERVERSENESS, FOR WANT OF A BETTER TERM.
THROUGH ITS PROMPTINGS, WE ACT WITHOUT COMPREHENSIBLE OBJECT; OR IF THIS SHALL BE UNDERSTOOD AS A CONTRADICTION IN TERMS, WE MAY SO FAR MODIFY THE PROPOSITION AS TO SAY THAT THROUGH ITS PROMPTINGS WE ACT, FOR THE REASON THAT WE SHOULD NOT.
IN THEORY, NO REASON CAN BE MORE UNREASONABLE, BUT, IN FACT, THERE IS NONE MORE STRONG. WITH CERTAIN MINDS, UNDER CERTAIN CONDITIONS, IT BECOMES ABSOLUTELY IRRESISTIBLE.
I AM NOT MORE CERTAIN THAT I BREATHE, THAN THAT THE ASSURANCE OF THE WRONG OR ERROR OF ANY ACTION IS OFTEN THE ONE UNCONQUERABLE FORCE WHICH IMPELS US, AND ALONE IMPELS US TO ITS PROSECUTION.
THAT, IN SOME MEASURE, MAY EXPLAIN TO YOU WHY I AM WEARING THESE FETTERS AND TENANTING THIS CELL OF THE CONDEMNED. HAD I NOT EXPLAINED THIS, YOU MIGHT HAVE FANCIED ME MAD. AS IT IS, YOU WILL EASILY PERCEIVE THAT I AM ONE OF THE MANY UNCOUNTED VICTIMS OF...
Edgar Allan Poe's
The Imp of the Perverse
adapted by Tom Pomplun • illustrated by Lance Tooks

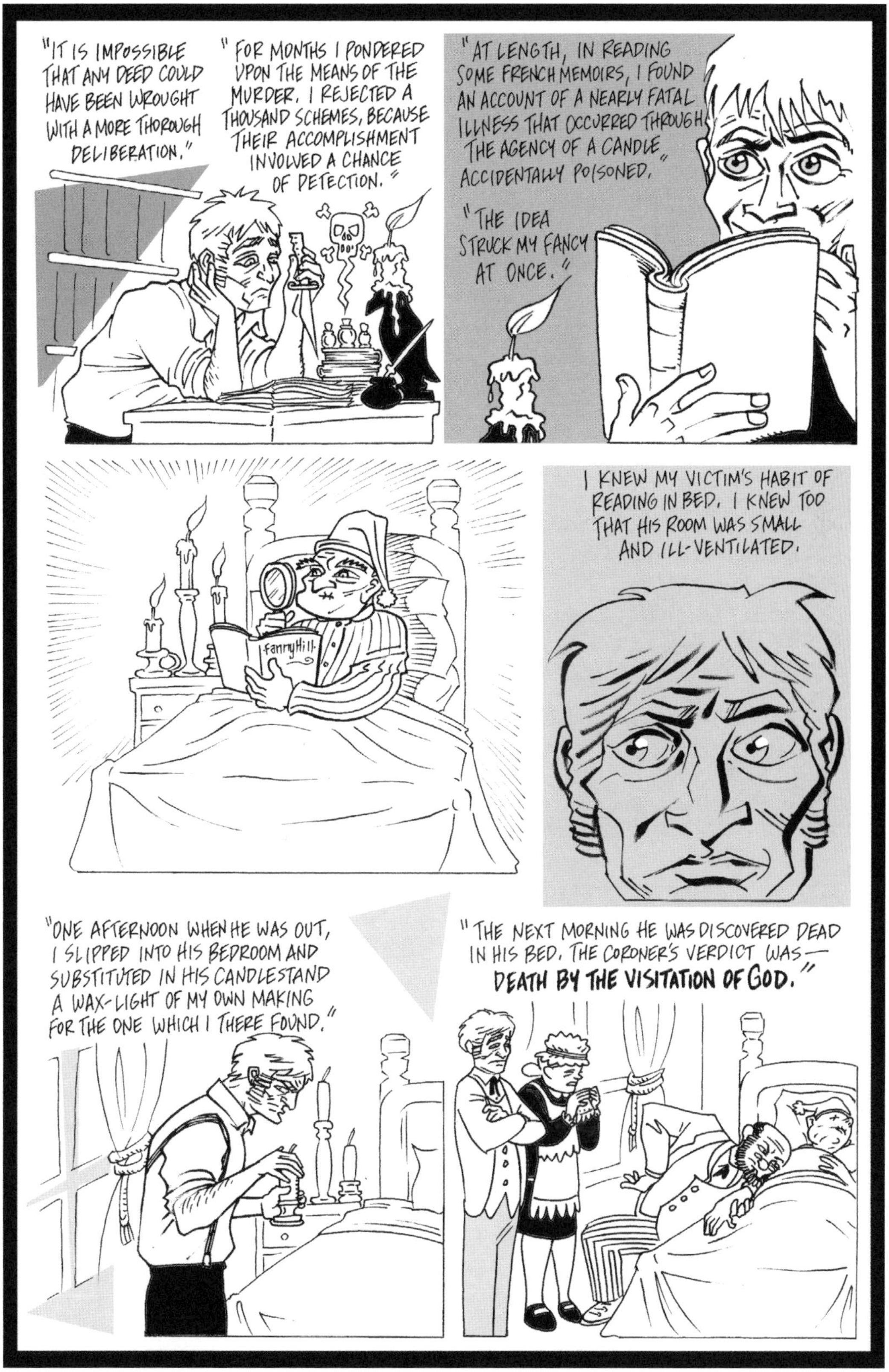
"IT IS IMPOSSIBLE THAT ANY DEED COULD HAVE BEEN WROUGHT WITH A MORE THOROUGH DELIBERATION."
"FOR MONTHS I PONDERED UPON THE MEANS OF THE MURDER. I REJECTED A THOUSAND SCHEMES, BECAUSE THEIR ACCOMPLISHMENT INVOLVED A CHANCE OF DETECTION."
"AT LENGTH, IN READING SOME FRENCH MEMOIRS, I FOUND AN ACCOUNT OF A NEARLY FATAL ILLNESS THAT OCCURRED THROUGH THE AGENCY OF A CANDLE ACCIDENTALLY POISONED.
"THE IDEA STRUCK MY FANCY AT ONCE."
Fanny Hill
I KNEW MY VICTIM'S HABIT OF READING IN BED. I KNEW TOO THAT HIS ROOM WAS SMALL AND ILL-VENTILATED.
"ONE AFTERNOON WHEN HE WAS OUT, I SLIPPED INTO HIS BEDROOM AND SUBSTITUTED IN HIS CANDLESTAND A WAX-LIGHT OF MY OWN MAKING FOR THE ONE WHICH I THERE FOUND."
"THE NEXT MORNING HE WAS DISCOVERED DEAD IN HIS BED. THE CORONER'S VERDICT WAS— DEATH BY THE VISITATION OF GOD."

I HAD DISPOSED OF THE REMAINS OF THE FATAL TAPER, AND HAD LEFT NO SHADOW OF A CLUE TO THE CRIME. HAVING INHERITED HIS ESTATE, ALL WENT WELL WITH ME FOR SEVERAL YEARS. THE IDEA OF DETECTION NEVER ONCE ENTERED MY BRAIN.

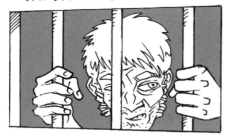

"IT IS INCONCEIVABLE HOW RICH A SENTIMENT OF SATISFACTION AROSE IN MY BOSOM AS I REFLECTED UPON MY ABSOLUTE SECURITY. IT AFFORDED ME MORE REAL DELIGHT THAN ALL THE MERE WORLDLY ADVANTAGES ACCRUING FROM MY SIN."

"BUT SLOWLY, THAT PLEASURABLE FEELING GREW, BY SCARCELY PERCEPTIBLE GRADATIONS, INTO A HAUNTING THOUGHT. I COULD SCARCELY GET RID OF IT FOR AN INSTANT."

"I WOULD PERPETUALLY CATCH MYSELF PONDERING UPON MY SECURITY, AND REPEATING, IN A LOW UNDERTONE, THE SAME PHRASE."

I AM SAFE! ... I AM SAFE!

"ONE DAY, WHILST SAUNTERING ALONG THE STREETS, I ARRESTED MYSELF IN THE ACT OF MURMURING, HALF ALOUD, THESE CUSTOMARY SYLLABLES."

I AM SA—

"IN A FIT OF PETULANCE, I REMODELLED THE USUAL PHRASE."

I AM SAFE— YES—IF I BE NOT FOOL ENOUGH TO MAKE OPEN CONFESSION!

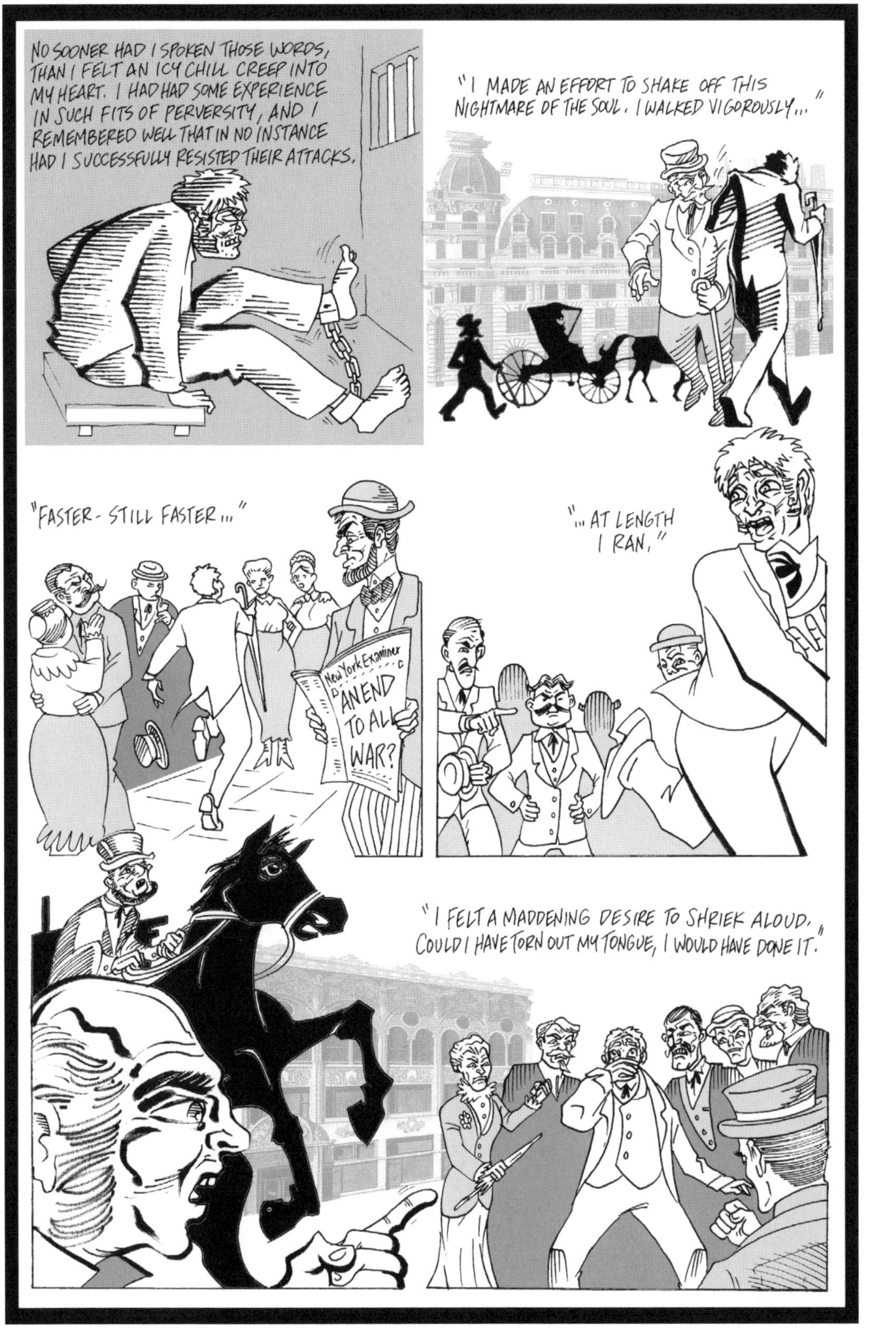
NO SOONER HAD I SPOKEN THOSE WORDS, THAN I FELT AN ICY CHILL CREEP INTO MY HEART. I HAD HAD SOME EXPERIENCE IN SUCH FITS OF PERVERSITY, AND I REMEMBERED WELL THAT IN NO INSTANCE HAD I SUCCESSFULLY RESISTED THEIR ATTACKS.
"I MADE AN EFFORT TO SHAKE OFF THIS NIGHTMARE OF THE SOUL. I WALKED VIGOROUSLY..."
"FASTER- STILL FASTER..."
New York Examiner
AN END TO ALL WAR?
"...AT LENGTH I RAN."
"I FELT A MADDENING DESIRE TO SHRIEK ALOUD. COULD I HAVE TORN OUT MY TONGUE, I WOULD HAVE DONE IT."

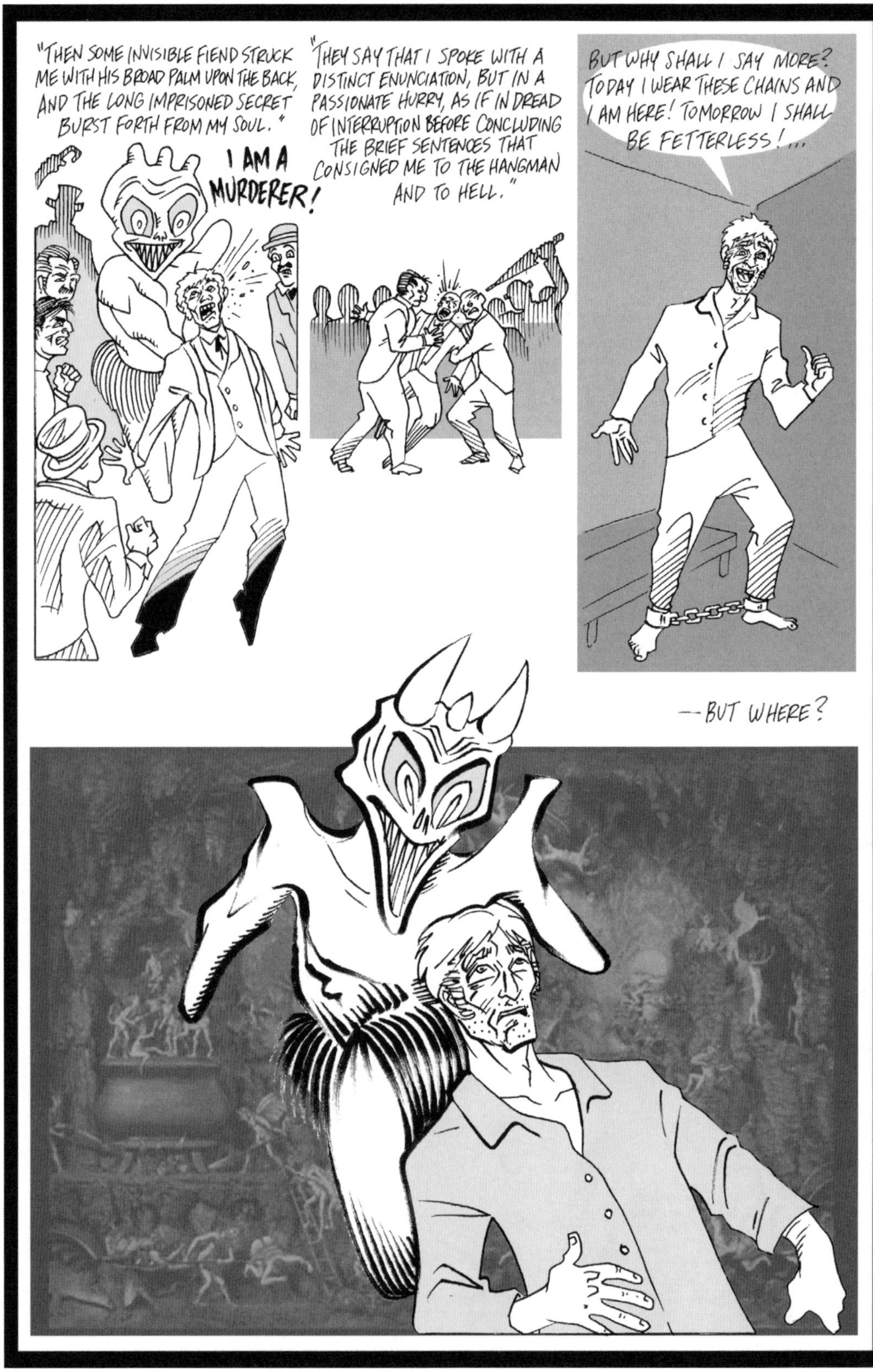
"THEN SOME INVISIBLE FIEND STRUCK ME WITH HIS BROAD PALM UPON THE BACK, AND THE LONG IMPRISONED SECRET BURST FORTH FROM MY SOUL."
I AM A MURDERER!
"THEY SAY THAT I SPOKE WITH A DISTINCT ENUNCIATION, BUT IN A PASSIONATE HURRY, AS IF IN DREAD OF INTERRUPTION BEFORE CONCLUDING THE BRIEF SENTENCES THAT CONSIGNED ME TO THE HANGMAN AND TO HELL."
BUT WHY SHALL I SAY MORE? TODAY I WEAR THESE CHAINS AND I AM HERE! TOMORROW I SHALL BE FETTERLESS!...
—BUT WHERE?

THE RAVEN

by **Edgar Allan Poe**

illustrated by

J. B. BONIVERT • STEVEN CERIO • SKOT OLSEN

M. K. BROWN • MICHAEL MANNING • RYAN INZANA• MARY FLEENER

EVERT GERADTS • TONI PAWLOWSKY • TODD LOVERING

Once upon a midnight dreary, while I pondered, weak and weary,
Over many a quaint and curious volume of forgotten lore,
While I nodded, nearly napping, suddenly there came a tapping,
As of some one gently rapping, rapping at my chamber door.
"'Tis some visitor," I muttered, "tapping at my chamber door —
Only this, and nothing more."

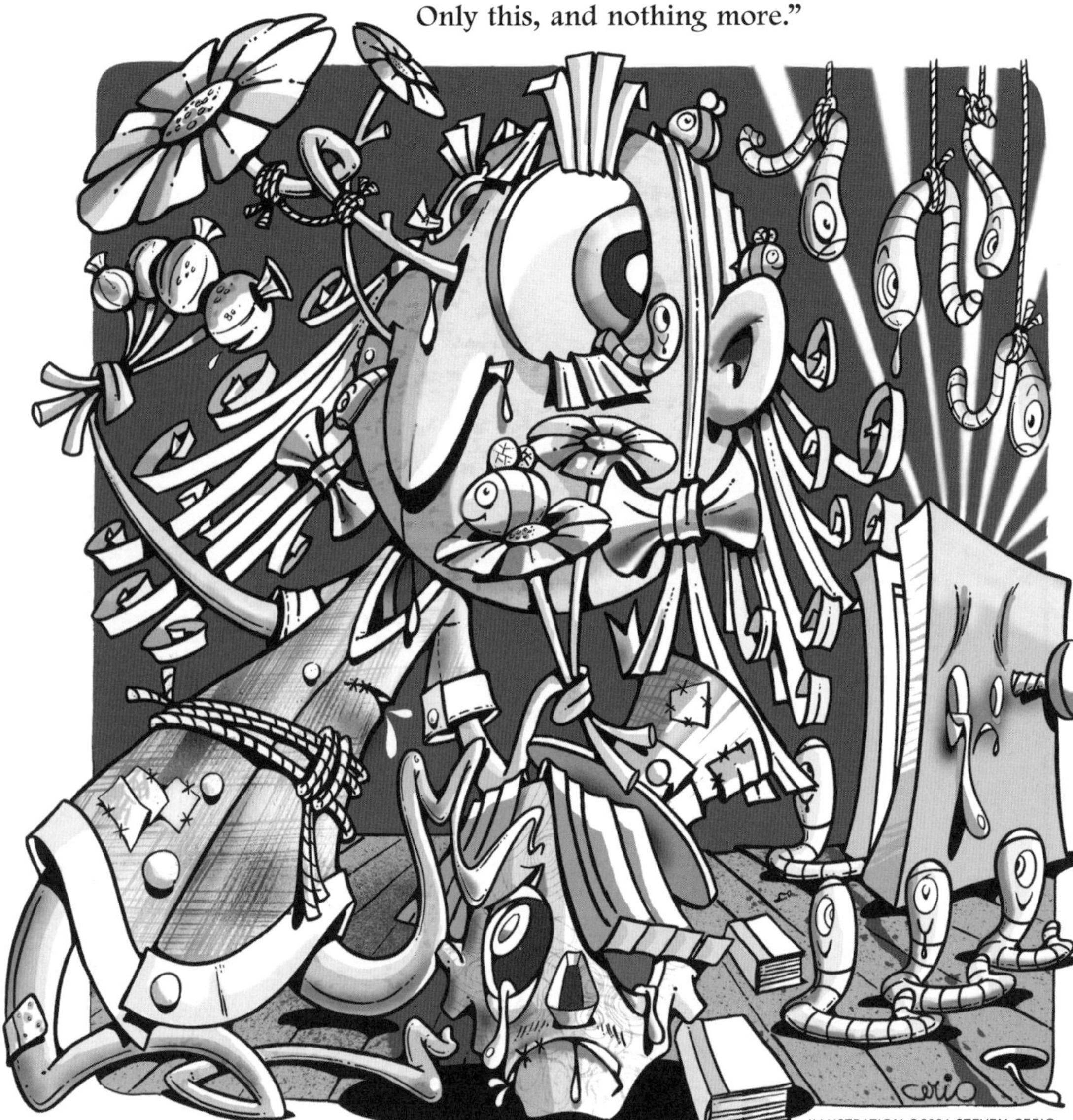
CERIO

ILLUSTRATION ©2006 STEVEN CERIO

Ah, distinctly I remember it was in the bleak December,
And each separate dying ember wrought its ghost upon the floor.
Eagerly I wished the morrow; — vainly I had sought to borrow
From my books surcease of sorrow — sorrow for the lost Lenore —
For the rare and radiant maiden whom the angels name Lenore —
Nameless here for evermore.

And the silken sad uncertain rustling of each purple curtain
Thrilled me — filled me with fantastic terrors never felt before;
So that now, to still the beating of my heart, I stood repeating
"'Tis some visitor entreating entrance at my chamber door —
Some late visitor entreating entrance at my chamber door; —
This it is, and nothing more."

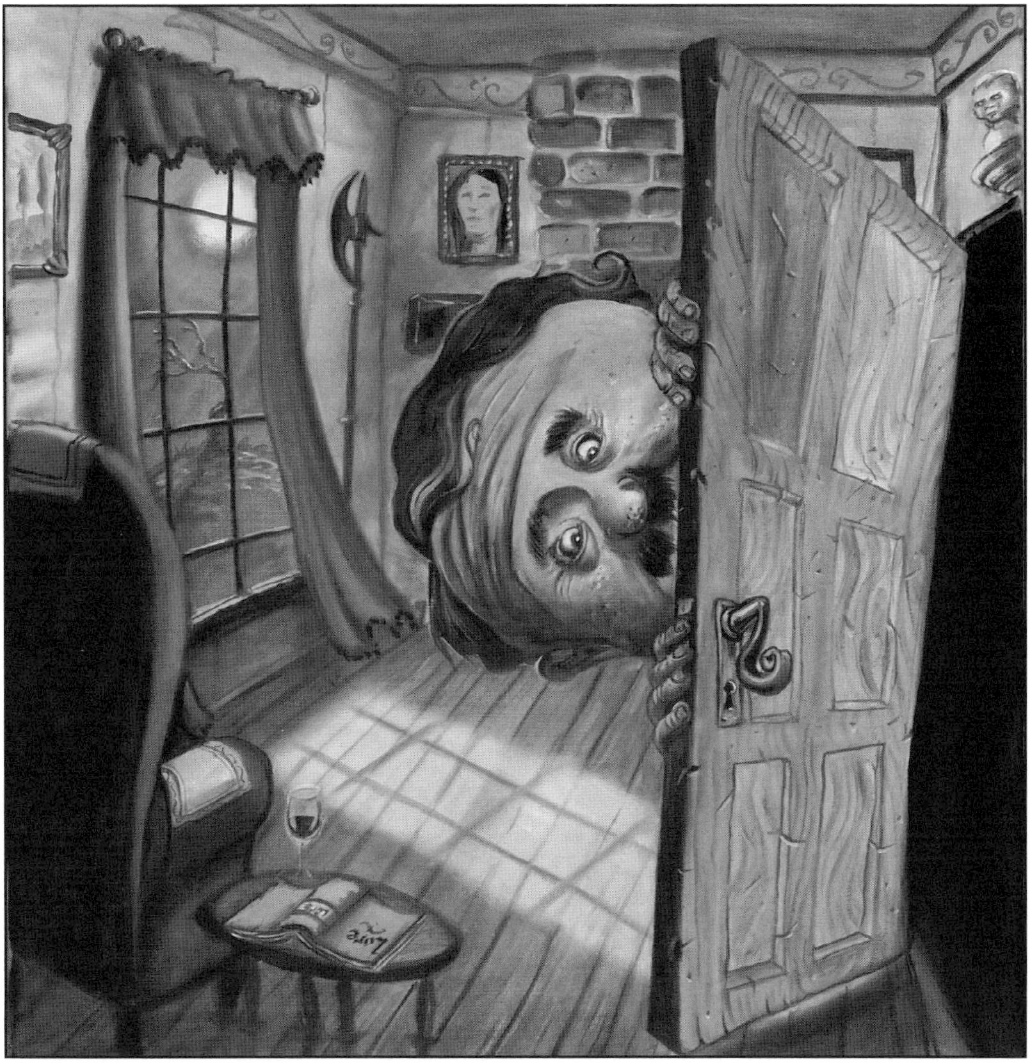

ILLUSTRATION ©2006 SKOT OLSEN

Presently my soul grew stronger; hesitating then no longer,
"Sir," said I, "or Madam, truly your forgiveness I implore;
But the fact is I was napping, and so gently you came rapping,
And so faintly you came tapping, tapping at my chamber door,
That I scarce was sure I heard you" — here I opened wide the door; —
Darkness there and nothing more.

Deep into that darkness peering, long I stood there wondering, fearing,
Doubting, dreaming dreams no mortal ever dared to dream before;
But the silence was unbroken, and the darkness gave no token,
And the only word there spoken was the whispered word, "Lenore!"
This I whispered, and an echo murmured back the word, "Lenore!" —
Merely this, and nothing more.

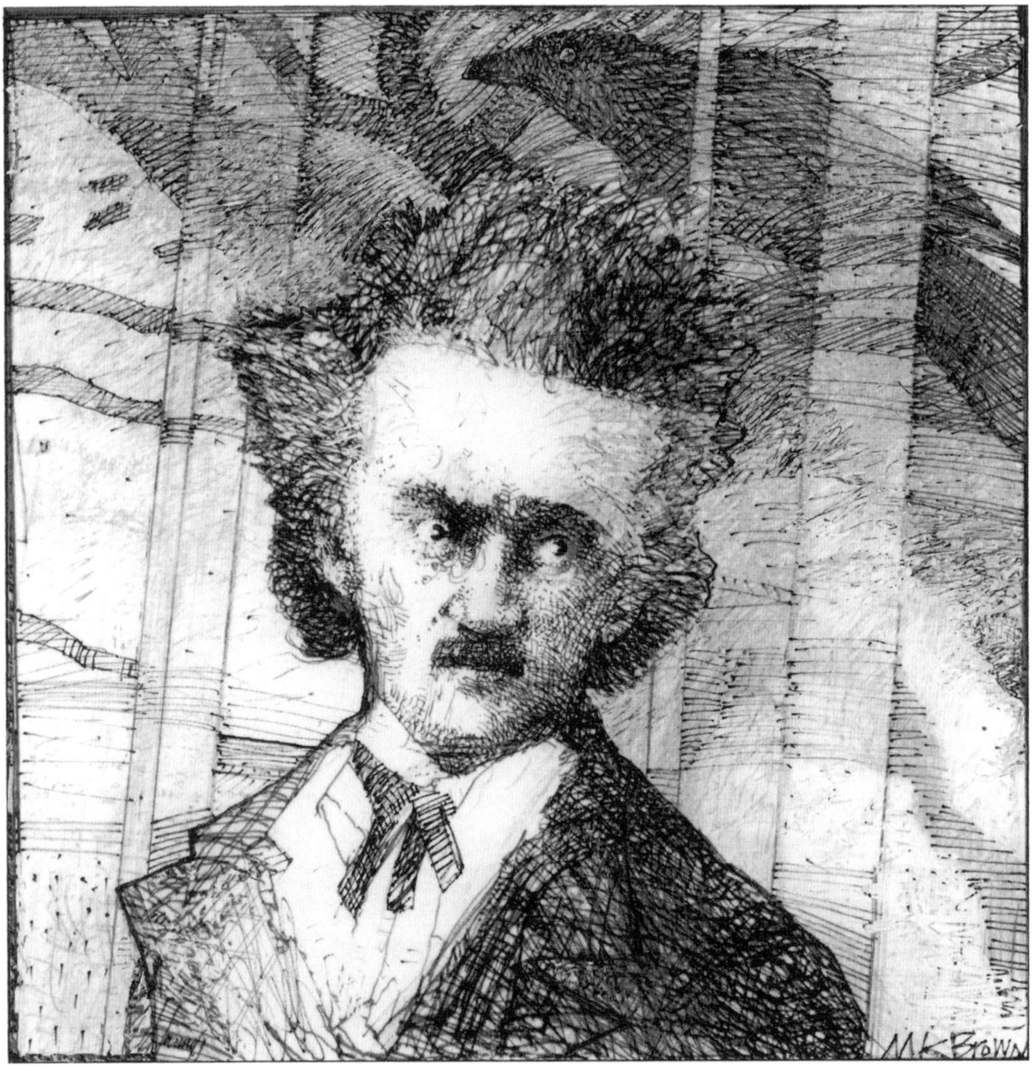
M.K. BROWN

ILLUSTRATION ©2006 M.K. BROWN

Back into the chamber turning, all my soul within me burning,
Soon I heard again a tapping somewhat louder than before.
"Surely," said I, "surely that is something at my window lattice;
Let me see, then, what thereat is, and this mystery explore —
Let my heart be still a moment and this mystery explore; —
'Tis the wind and nothing more!"

Open here I flung the shutter, when, with many a flirt and flutter,
In there stepped a stately raven of the saintly days of yore;
Not the least obeisance made he; not an instant stopped or stayed he;
But, with mien of lord or lady, perched above my chamber door —
Perched upon a bust of Pallas just above my chamber door —
Perched, and sat, and nothing more.

ILLUSTRATION ©2006 MICHAEL MANNING

Then this ebony bird beguiling my sad fancy into smiling,
By the grave and stern decorum of the countenance it wore,
"Though thy crest be shorn and shaven, thou," I said, "art sure no craven,
Ghastly grim and ancient raven wandering from the Nightly shore —
Tell me what thy lordly name is on the Night's Plutonian shore!"
Quoth the raven "Nevermore."

Much I marvelled this ungainly fowl to hear discourse so plainly,
Though its answer little meaning — little relevancy bore;
For we cannot help agreeing that no living human being
Ever yet was blessed with seeing bird above his chamber door —
Bird or beast upon the sculptured bust above his chamber door,
With such name as "Nevermore."

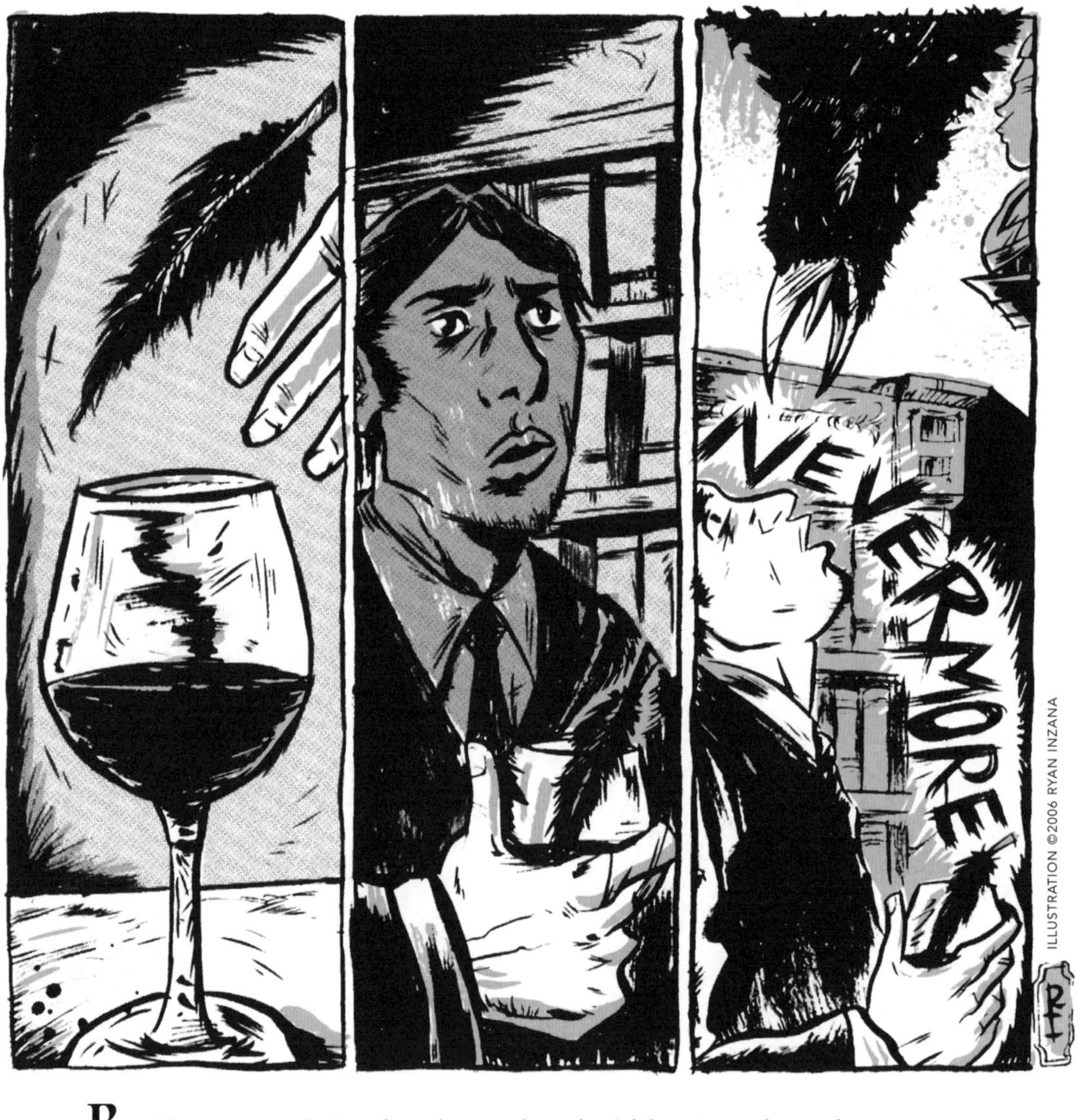
NEVERMORE
ILLUSTRATION ©2006 RYAN INZANA

But the raven, sitting lonely on the placid bust, spoke only
That one word, as if his soul in that one word he did outpour.
Nothing farther then he uttered — not a feather then he fluttered —
Till I scarcely more than muttered "Other friends have flown before —
On the morrow *he* will leave me, as my hopes have flown before."
Then the bird said "Nevermore."

Startled at the stillness broken by reply so aptly spoken,
"Doubtless," said I, "what it utters is its only stock and store
Caught from some unhappy master whom unmerciful Disaster
Followed fast and followed faster till his songs one burden bore —
Till the dirges of his Hope that melancholy burden bore
Of "Never — nevermore."

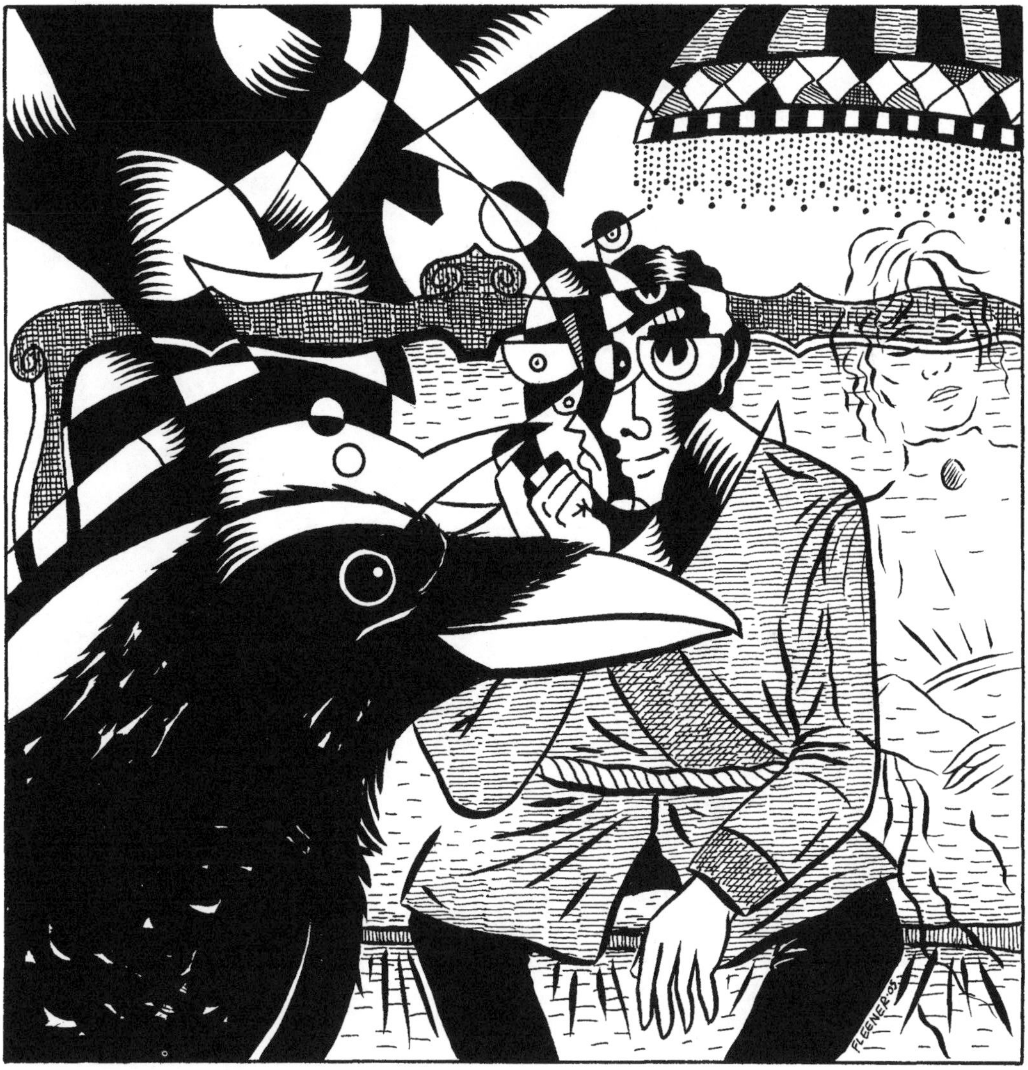
FLEENER-05

But the raven still beguiling all my sad soul into smiling,
Straight I wheeled a cushioned seat in front of bird, and bust and door;
Then, upon the velvet sinking, I betook myself to linking
Fancy unto fancy, thinking what this ominous bird of yore —
What this grim, ungainly, ghastly, gaunt and ominous bird of yore
Meant in croaking "Nevermore."

This I sat engaged in guessing, but no syllable expressing
To the fowl whose fiery eyes now burned into my bosom's core;
This and more I sat divining, with my head at ease reclining
On the cushion's velvet lining that the lamplight gloated o'er,
But whose velvet violet lining with the lamplight gloating o'er,
She shall press, ah, nevermore!

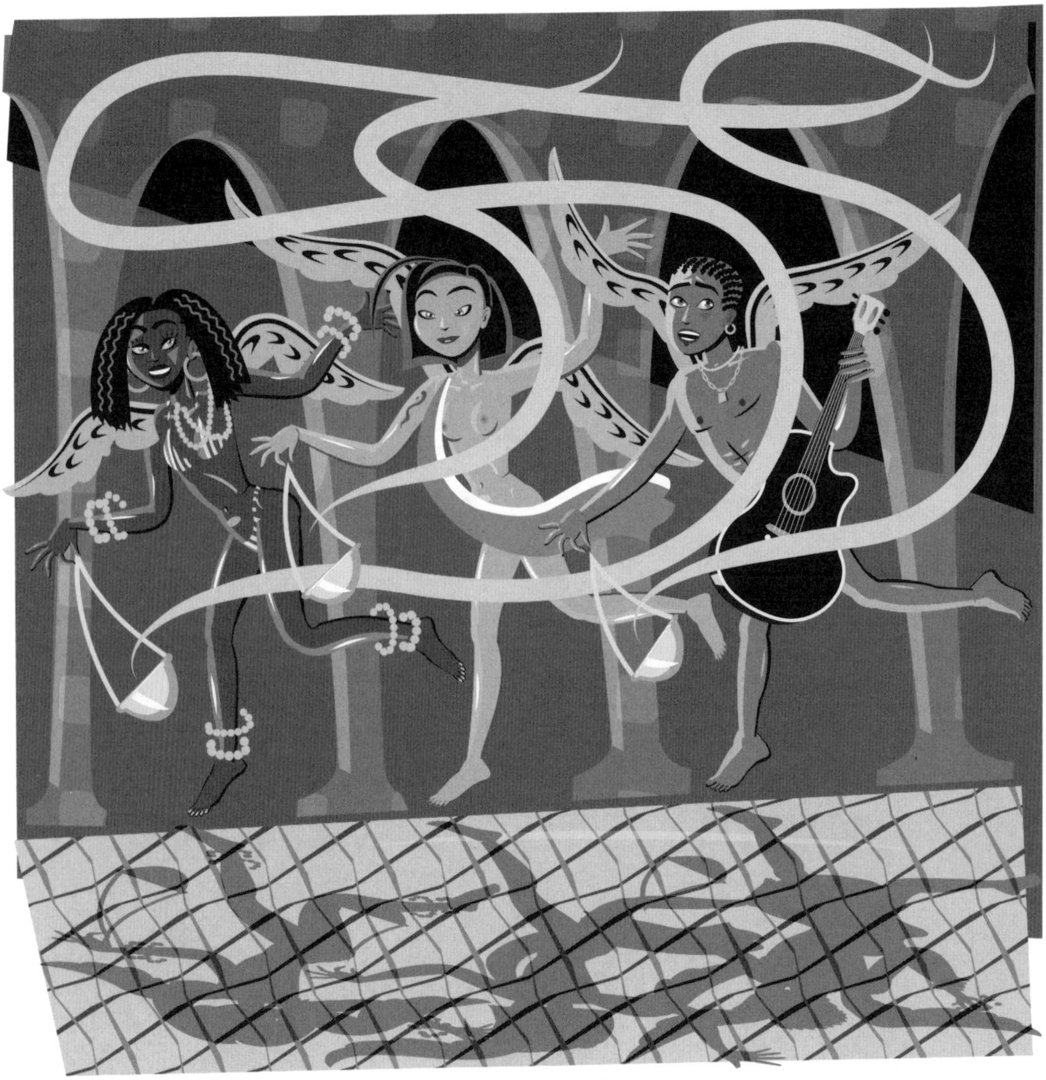

ILLUSTRATION ©2006 EVERT GERADTS

Then, methought, the air grew denser, perfumed from an unseen censer
Swung by Angels whose faint foot-falls tinkled on the tufted floor.
"Wretch," I cried, "thy God hath lent thee — by these angels he hath sent thee
Respite — respite and nepenthe from thy memories of Lenore;
Quaff, oh quaff this kind nepenthe and forget this lost Lenore!"
Quoth the raven, "Nevermore."

"Prophet!" said I, "thing of evil! — prophet still, if bird or devil! —
Whether Tempter sent, or whether tempest tossed thee here ashore,
Desolate yet all undaunted, on this desert land enchanted —
On this home by Horror haunted — tell me truly, I implore —
Is there — *is* there balm in Gilead? — tell me — tell me, I implore!"
Quoth the raven, "Nevermore."

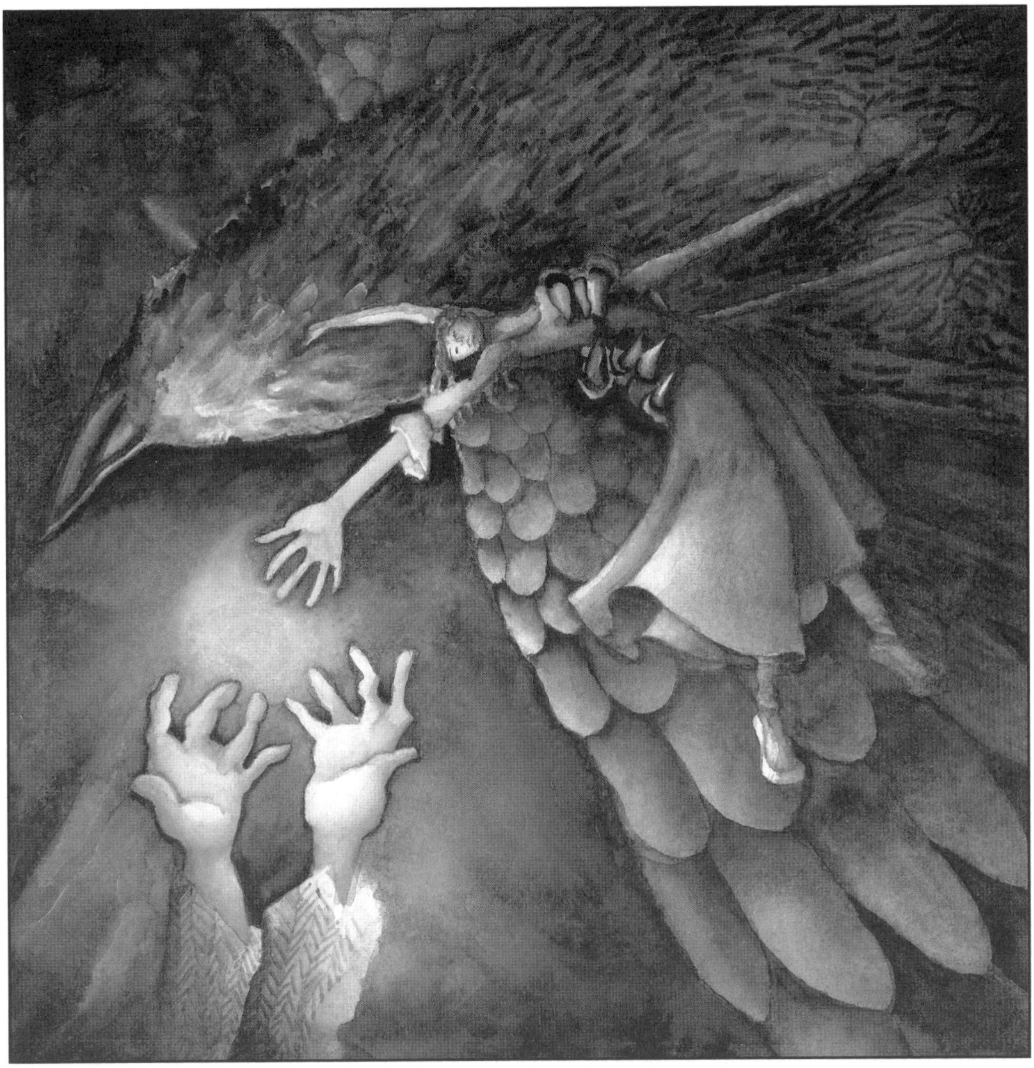

ILLUSTRATION ©2006 TONI PAWLOWSKY

"Prophet!" said I, "thing of evil! — prophet still, if bird or devil!
By that Heaven that bends above us — by that God we both adore —
Tell this soul with sorrow laden if, within the distant Aidenn,
It shall clasp a sainted maiden whom the angels name Lenore —
Clasp a rare and radiant maiden whom the angels name Lenore."
Quoth the raven, "Nevermore."

"Be that word our sign of parting, bird or fiend!" I shrieked, upstarting —
"Get thee back into the tempest and the Night's Plutonian shore!
Leave no black plume as a token of that lie thy soul hath spoken!
Leave my loneliness unbroken! — quit the bust above my door!
Take thy beak from out my heart, and take thy form from off my door!"
Quoth the raven, "Nevermore."

And the raven, never flitting, still is sitting, still is sitting
On the pallid bust of Pallas just above my chamber door;
And his eyes have all the seeming of a demon's that is dreaming,
And the lamp-light o'er him streaming throws his shadow on the floor;
And my soul from out that shadow that lies floating on the floor
Shall be lifted — nevermore!

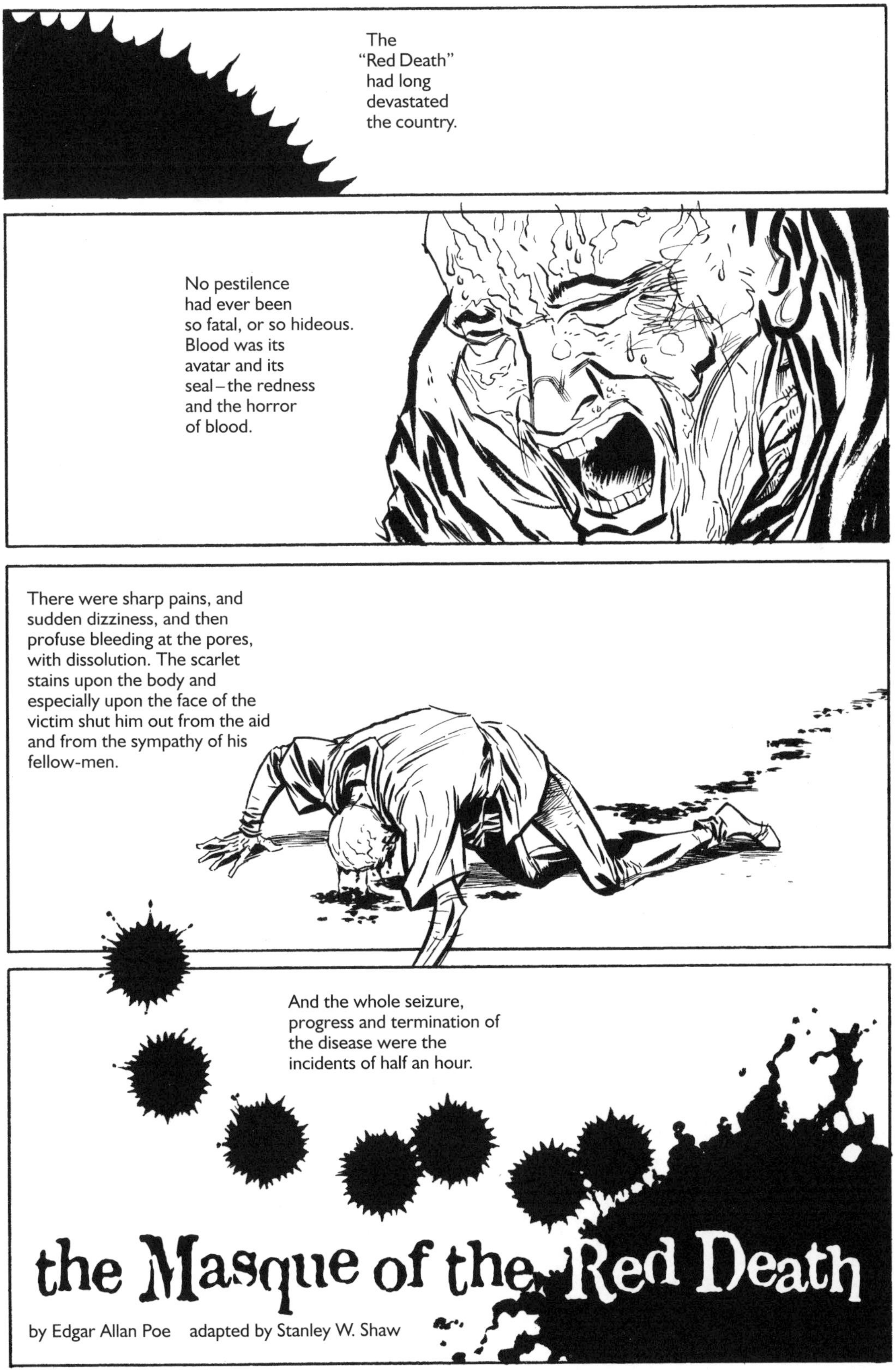
The "Red Death" had long devastated the country.
No pestilence had ever been so fatal, or so hideous. Blood was its avatar and its seal – the redness and the horror of blood.
There were sharp pains, and sudden dizziness, and then profuse bleeding at the pores, with dissolution. The scarlet stains upon the body and especially upon the face of the victim shut him out from the aid and from the sympathy of his fellow-men.
And the whole seizure, progress and termination of the disease were the incidents of half an hour.
the Masque of the Red Death
by Edgar Allan Poe adapted by Stanley W. Shaw

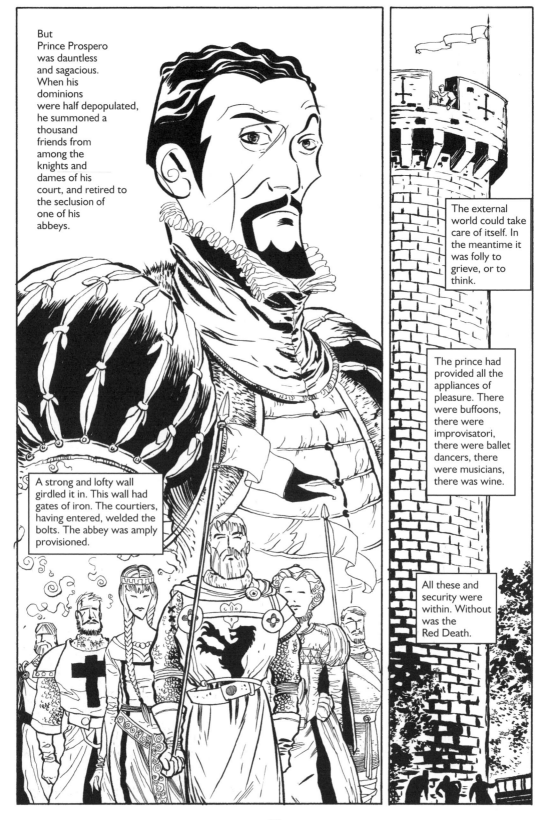

But Prince Prospero was dauntless and sagacious. When his dominions were half depopulated, he summoned a thousand friends from among the knights and dames of his court, and retired to the seclusion of one of his abbeys.

A strong and lofty wall girdled it in. This wall had gates of iron. The courtiers, having entered, welded the bolts. The abbey was amply provisioned.

The external world could take care of itself. In the meantime it was folly to grieve, or to think.

The prince had provided all the appliances of pleasure. There were buffoons, there were improvisatori, there were ballet dancers, there were musicians, there was wine.

All these and security were within. Without was the Red Death.

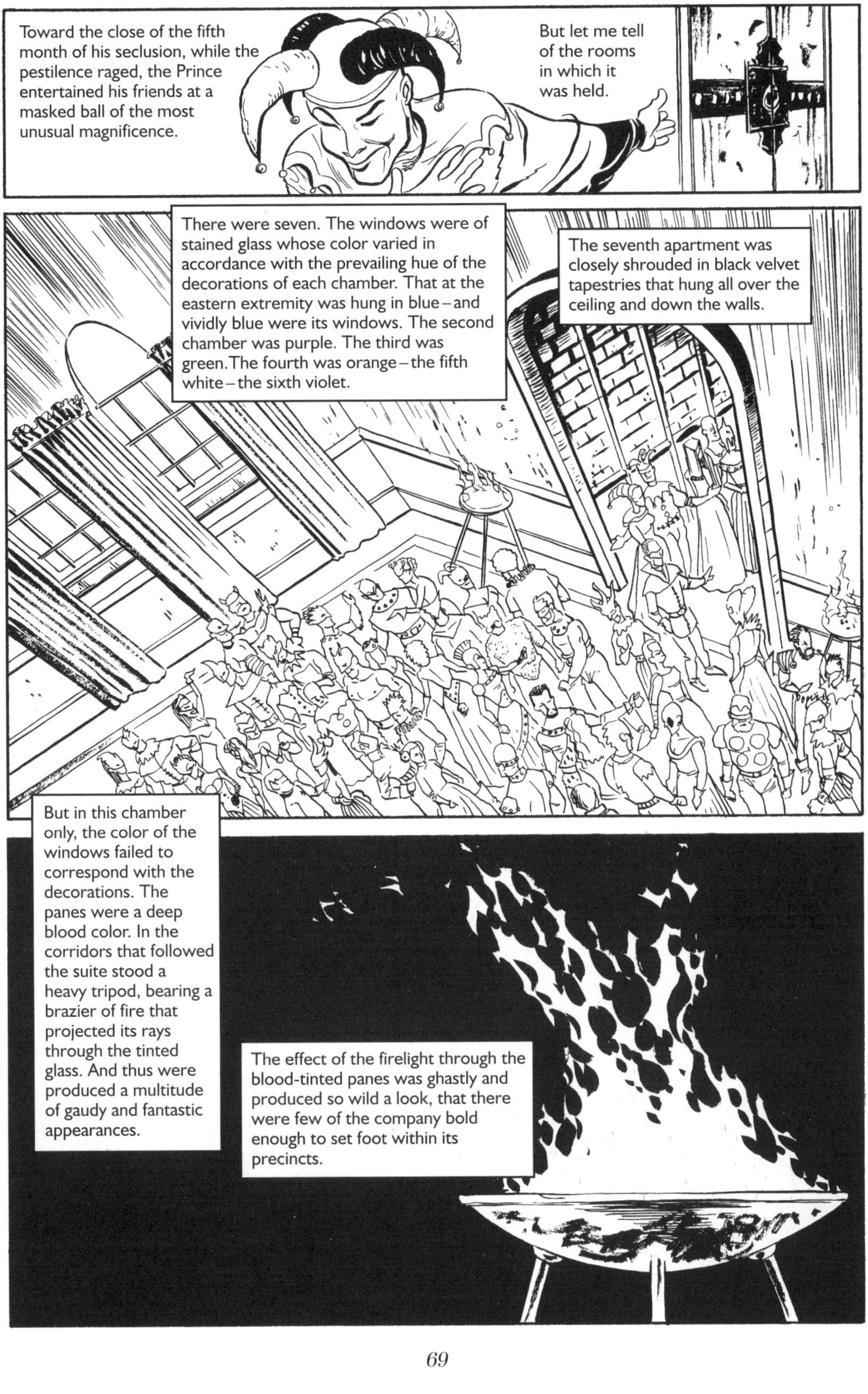
Toward the close of the fifth month of his seclusion, while the pestilence raged, the Prince entertained his friends at a masked ball of the most unusual magnificence.
But let me tell of the rooms in which it was held.
There were seven. The windows were of stained glass whose color varied in accordance with the prevailing hue of the decorations of each chamber. That at the eastern extremity was hung in blue–and vividly blue were its windows. The second chamber was purple. The third was green. The fourth was orange–the fifth white–the sixth violet.
The seventh apartment was closely shrouded in black velvet tapestries that hung all over the ceiling and down the walls.
But in this chamber only, the color of the windows failed to correspond with the decorations. The panes were a deep blood color. In the corridors that followed the suite stood a heavy tripod, bearing a brazier of fire that projected its rays through the tinted glass. And thus were produced a multitude of gaudy and fantastic appearances.
The effect of the firelight through the blood-tinted panes was ghastly and produced so wild a look, that there were few of the company bold enough to set foot within its precincts.

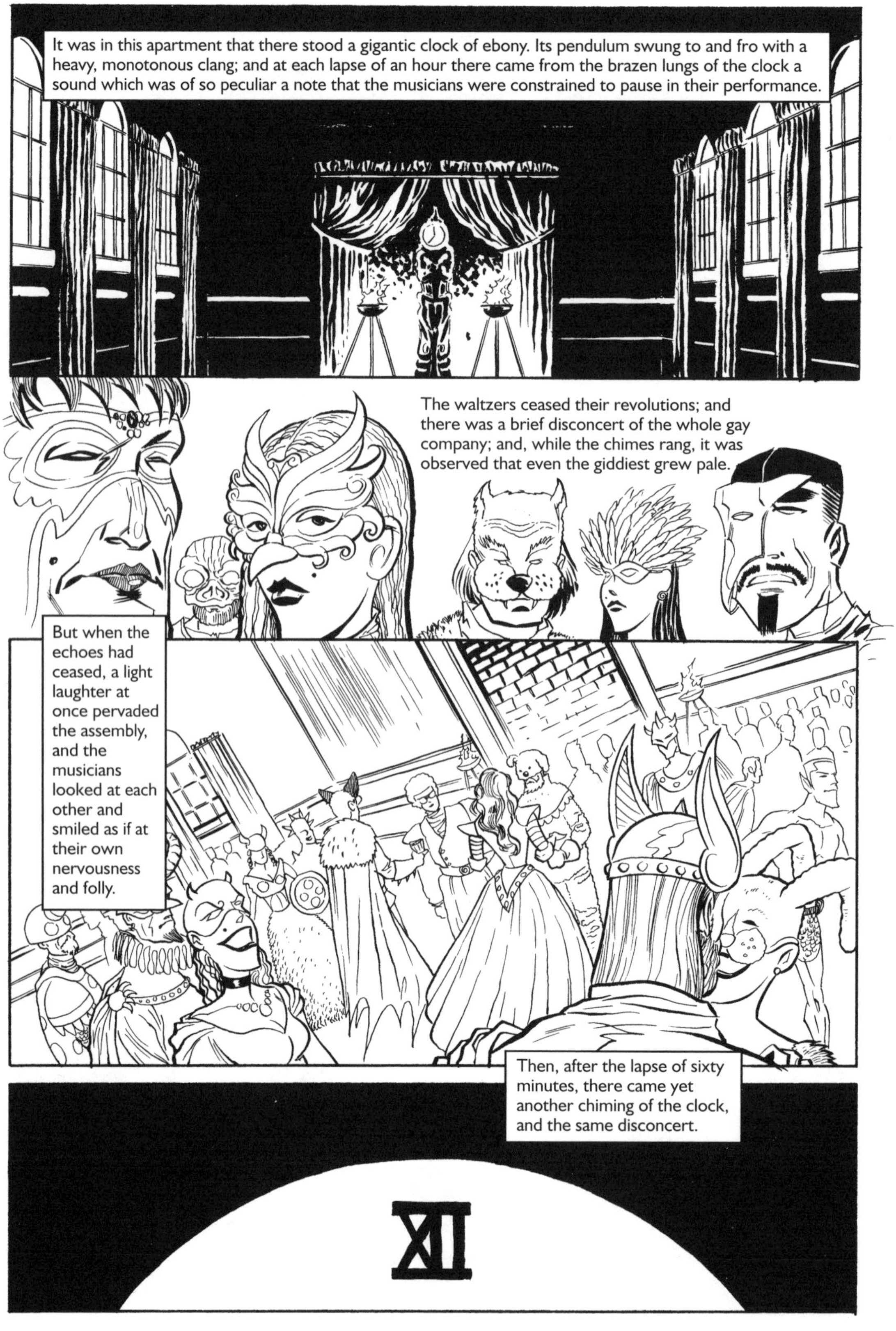
It was in this apartment that there stood a gigantic clock of ebony. Its pendulum swung to and fro with a heavy, monotonous clang; and at each lapse of an hour there came from the brazen lungs of the clock a sound which was of so peculiar a note that the musicians were constrained to pause in their performance.
The waltzers ceased their revolutions; and there was a brief disconcert of the whole gay company; and, while the chimes rang, it was observed that even the giddiest grew pale.
But when the echoes had ceased, a light laughter at once pervaded the assembly, and the musicians looked at each other and smiled as if at their own nervousness and folly.
Then, after the lapse of sixty minutes, there came yet another chiming of the clock, and the same disconcert.
XII

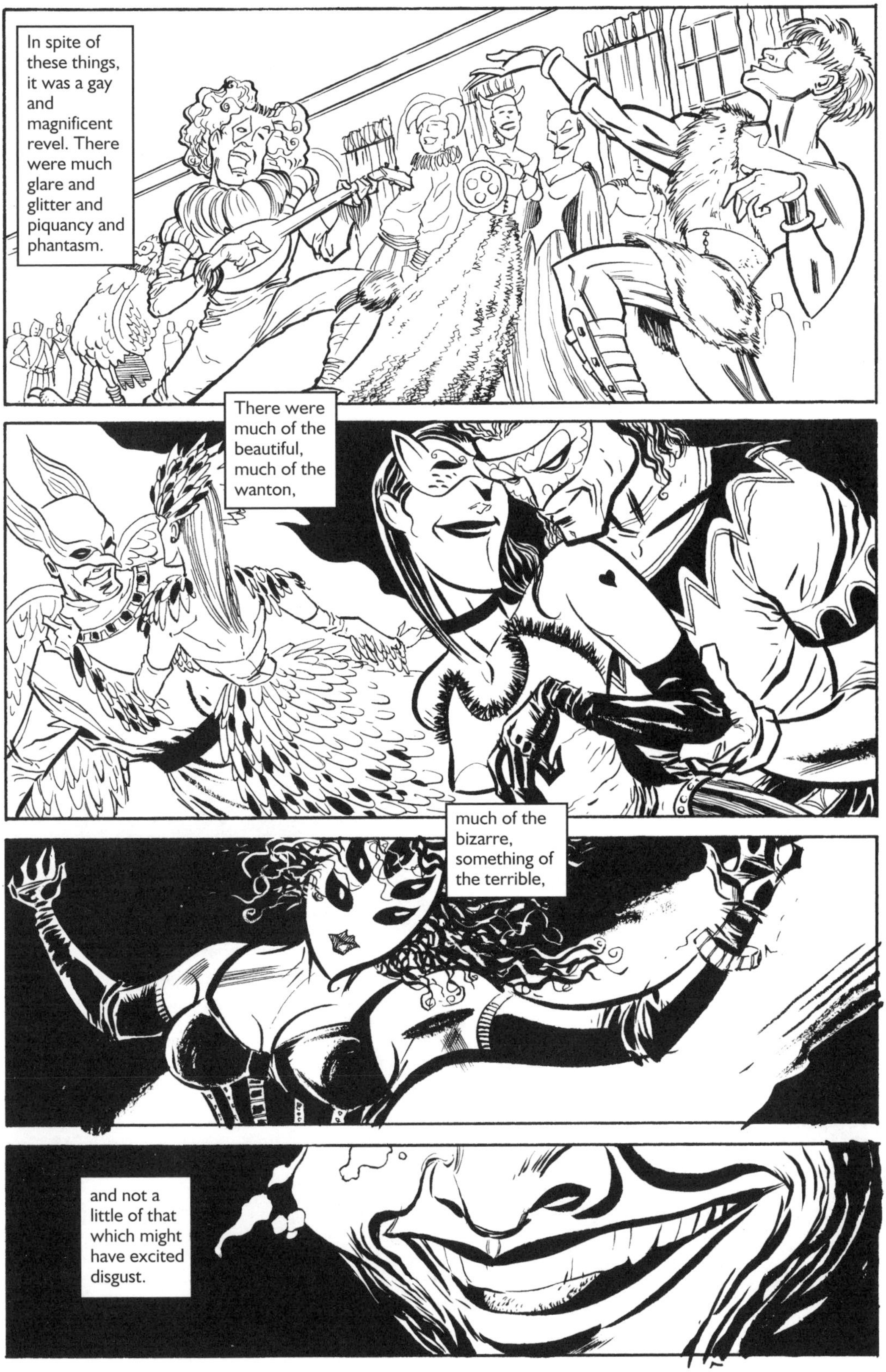
In spite of these things, it was a gay and magnificent revel. There were much glare and glitter and piquancy and phantasm.
There were much of the beautiful, much of the wanton,
much of the bizarre, something of the terrible,
and not a little of that which might have excited disgust.

Excepting the black seventh chamber, the apartments were crowded, and in them beat feverishly the heart of life. And the revel went whirlingly on,

until there commenced the sounding of midnight upon the clock.

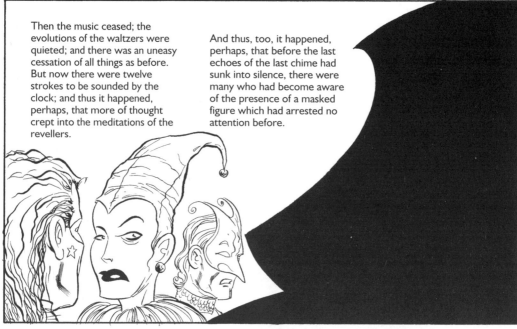

Then the music ceased; the evolutions of the waltzers were quieted; and there was an uneasy cessation of all things as before. But now there were twelve strokes to be sounded by the clock; and thus it happened, perhaps, that more of thought crept into the meditations of the revellers.

And thus, too, it happened, perhaps, that before the last echoes of the last chime had sunk into silence, there were many who had become aware of the presence of a masked figure which had arrested no attention before.

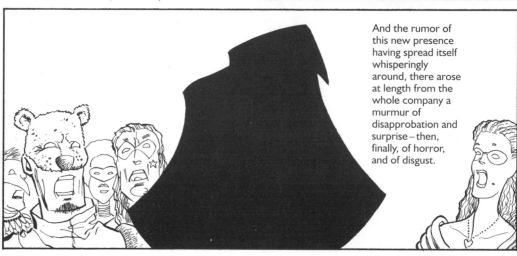

And the rumor of this new presence having spread itself whisperingly around, there arose at length from the whole company a murmur of disapprobation and surprise—then, finally, of horror, and of disgust.

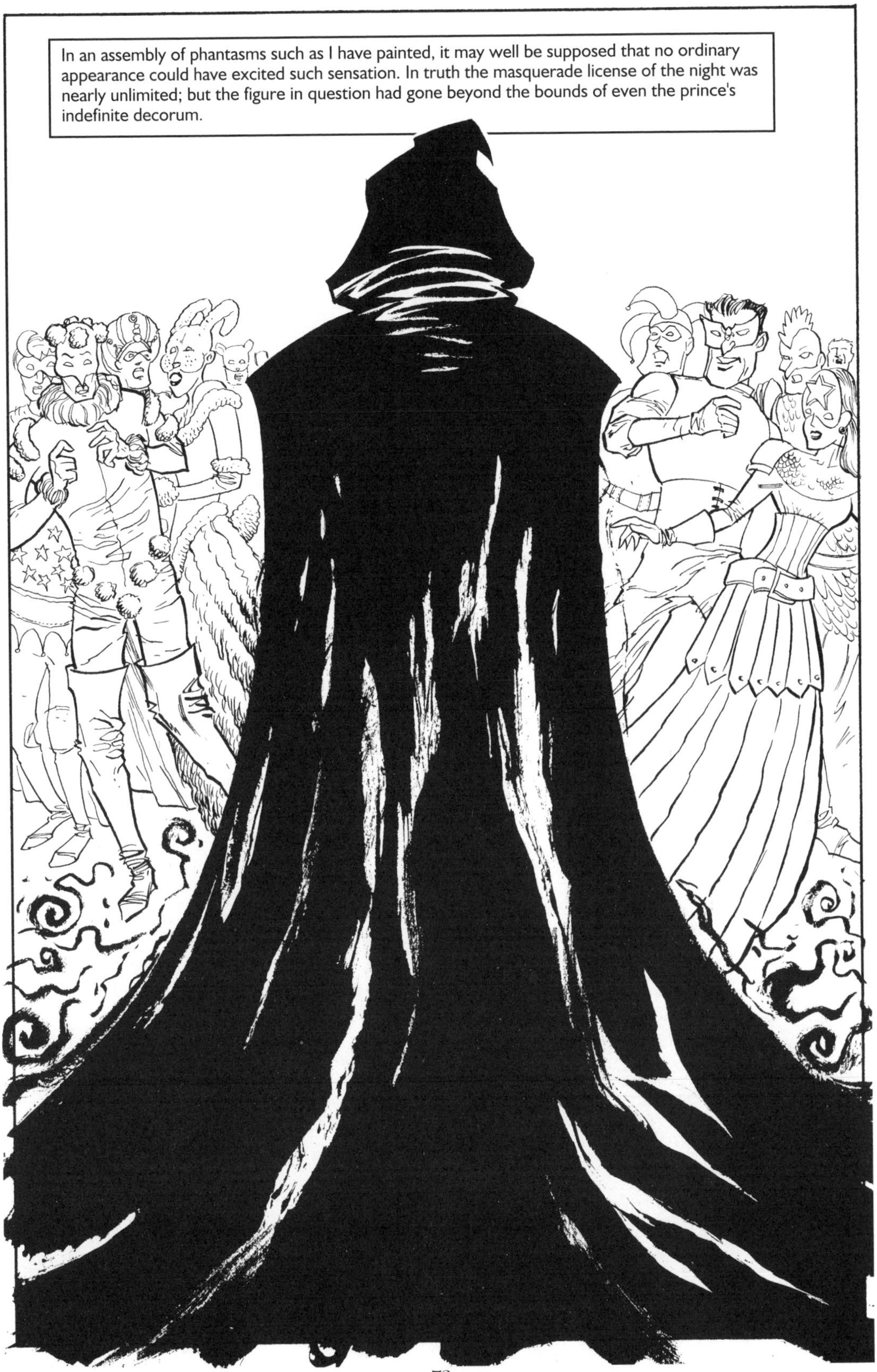
In an assembly of phantasms such as I have painted, it may well be supposed that no ordinary appearance could have excited such sensation. In truth the masquerade license of the night was nearly unlimited; but the figure in question had gone beyond the bounds of even the prince's indefinite decorum.

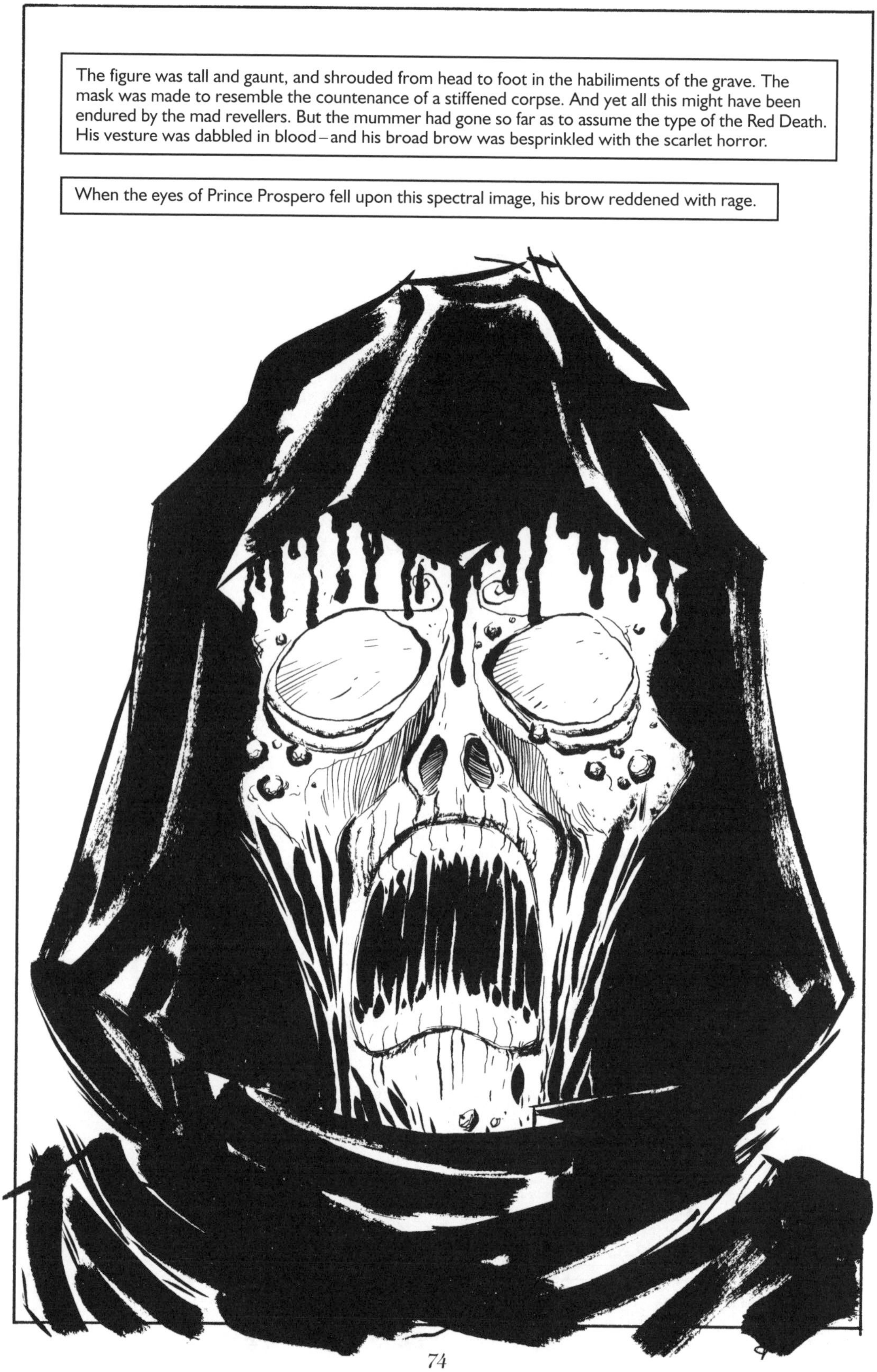
The figure was tall and gaunt, and shrouded from head to foot in the habiliments of the grave. The mask was made to resemble the countenance of a stiffened corpse. And yet all this might have been endured by the mad revellers. But the mummer had gone so far as to assume the type of the Red Death. His vesture was dabbled in blood–and his broad brow was besprinkled with the scarlet horror.
When the eyes of Prince Prospero fell upon this spectral image, his brow reddened with rage.

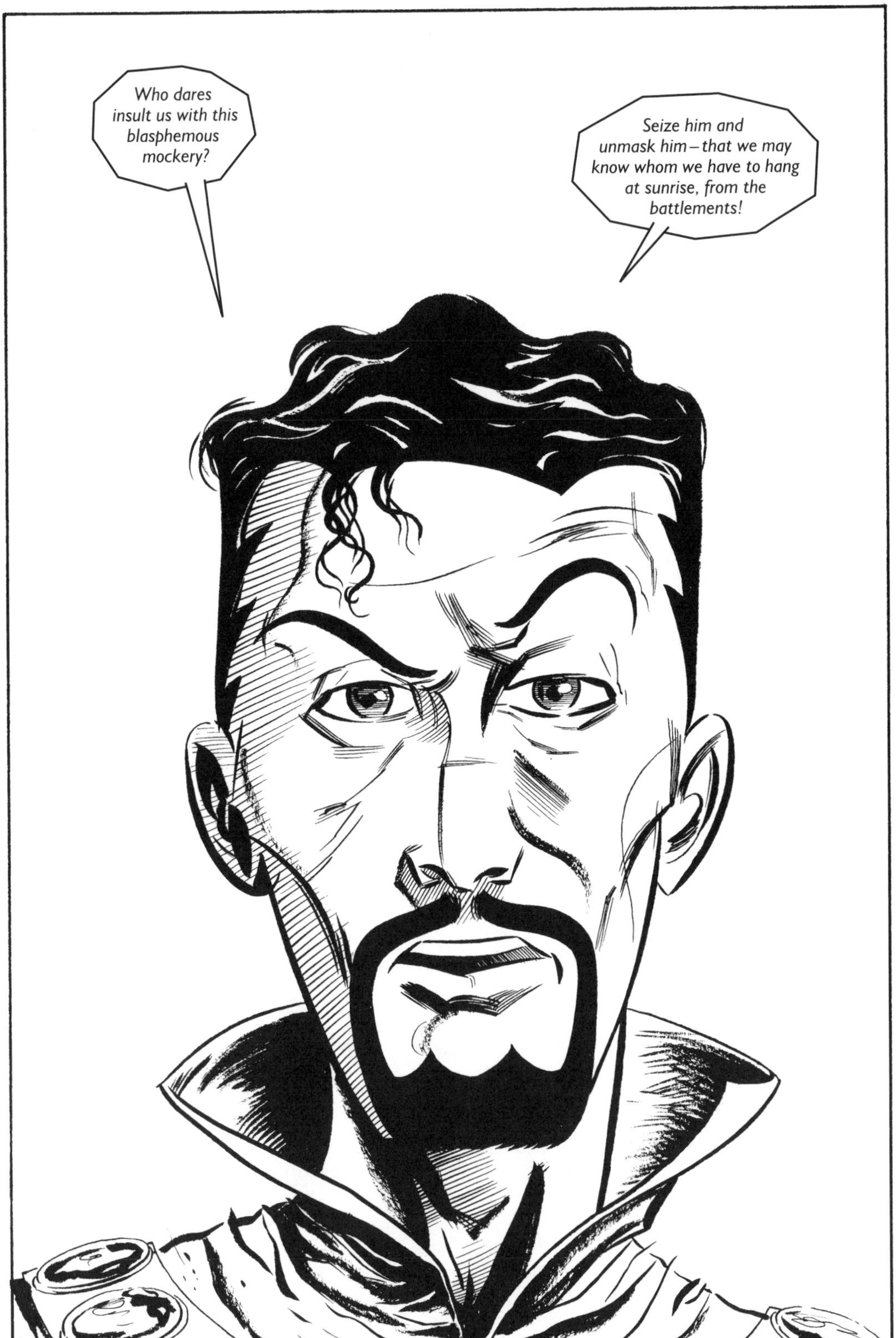
Who dares insult us with this blasphemous mockery?
Seize him and unmask him—that we may know whom we have to hang at sunrise, from the battlements!

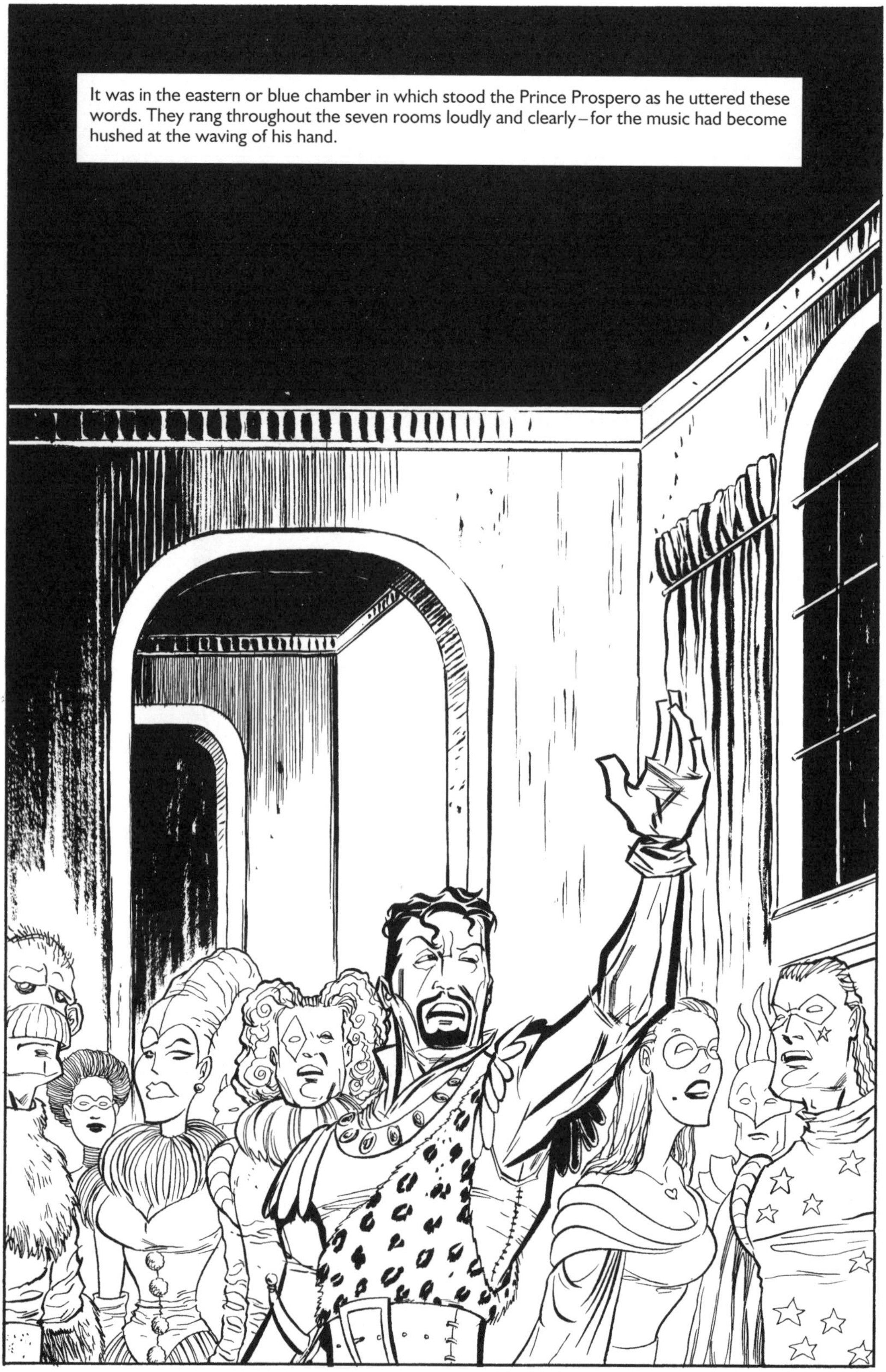
It was in the eastern or blue chamber in which stood the Prince Prospero as he uttered these words. They rang throughout the seven rooms loudly and clearly – for the music had become hushed at the waving of his hand.

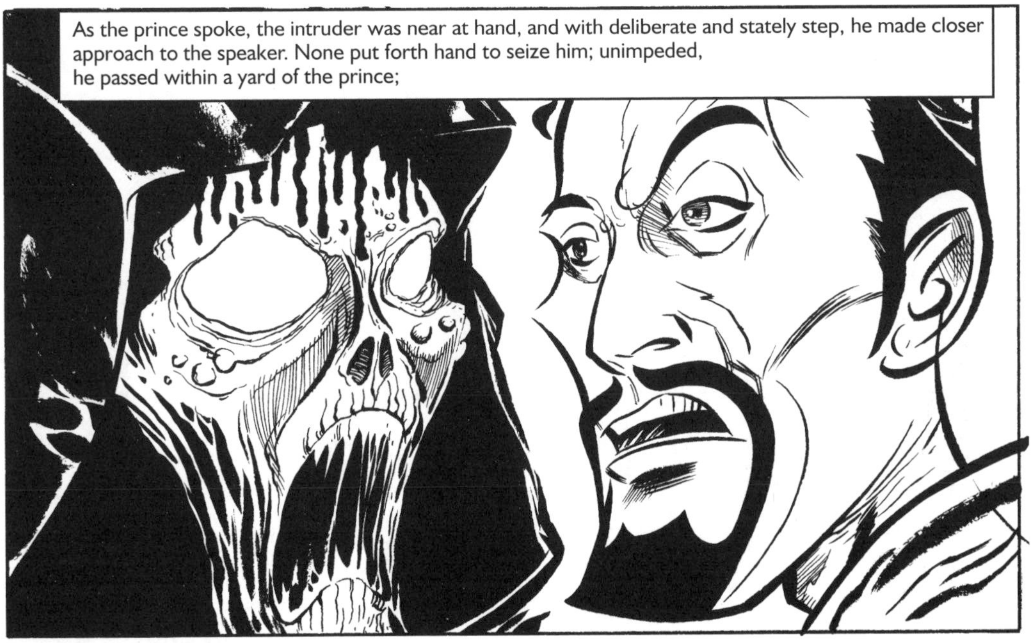
As the prince spoke, the intruder was near at hand, and with deliberate and stately step, he made closer approach to the speaker. None put forth hand to seize him; unimpeded,
he passed within a yard of the prince;

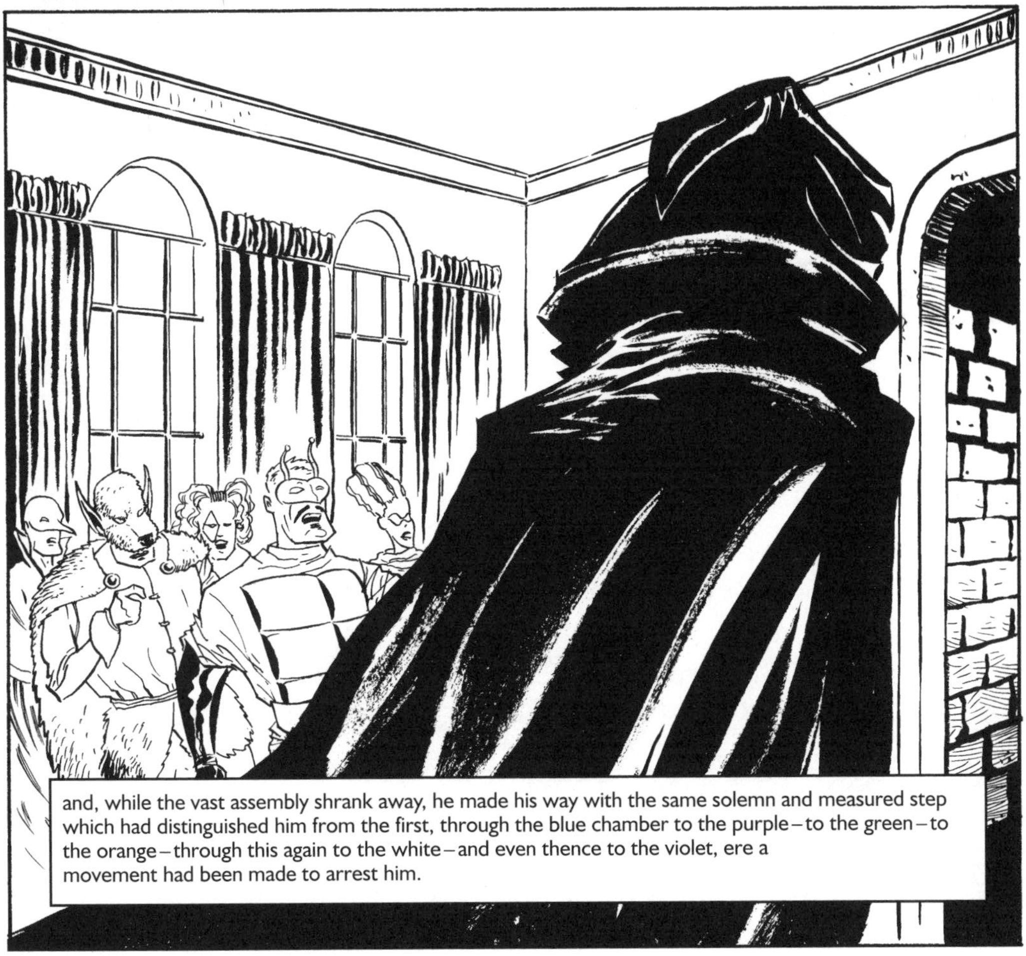
and, while the vast assembly shrank away, he made his way with the same solemn and measured step which had distinguished him from the first, through the blue chamber to the purple–to the green–to the orange–through this again to the white–and even thence to the violet, ere a movement had been made to arrest him.

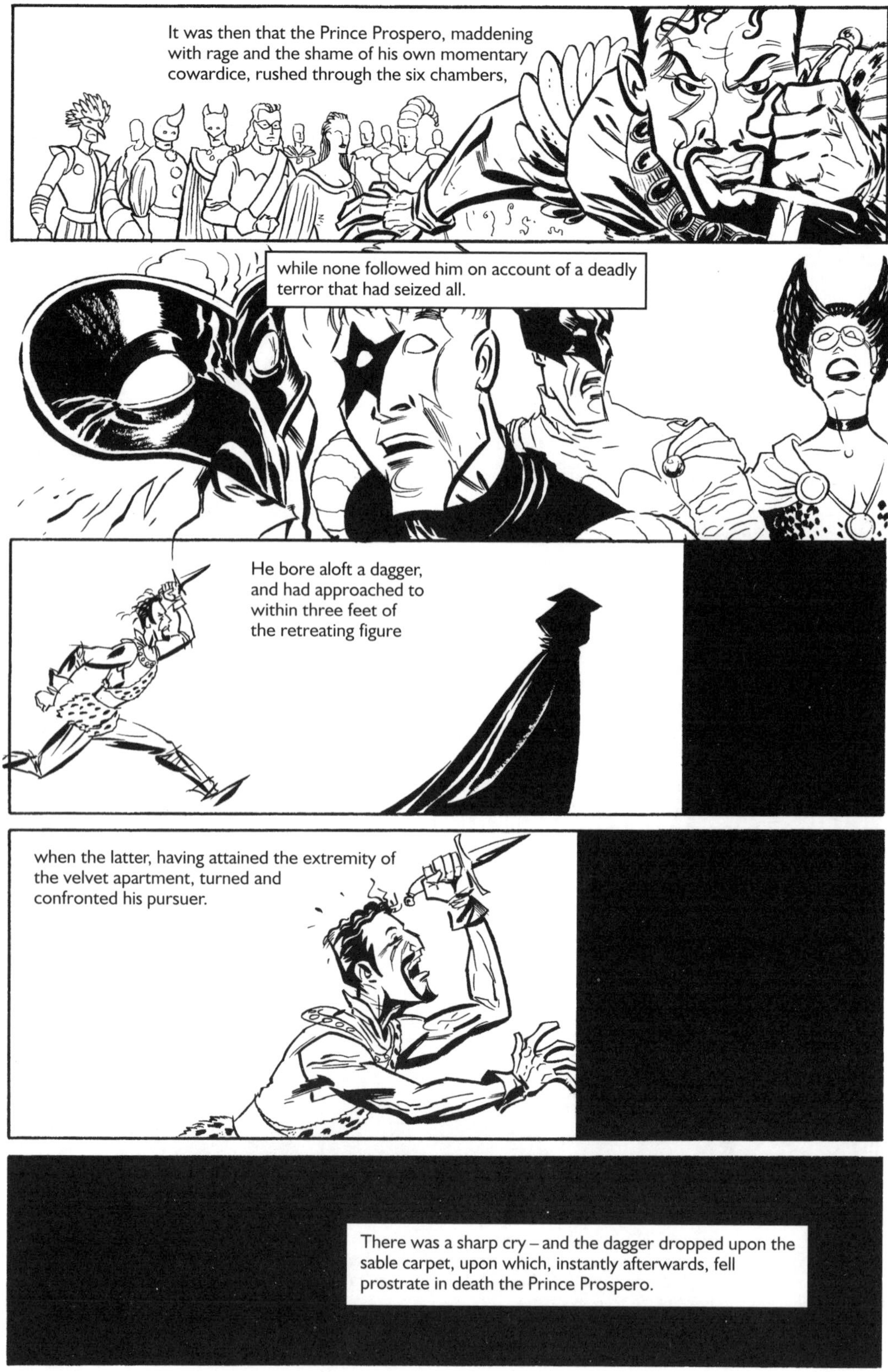
It was then that the Prince Prospero, maddening with rage and the shame of his own momentary cowardice, rushed through the six chambers,
while none followed him on account of a deadly terror that had seized all.
He bore aloft a dagger, and had approached to within three feet of the retreating figure
when the latter, having attained the extremity of the velvet apartment, turned and confronted his pursuer.
There was a sharp cry – and the dagger dropped upon the sable carpet, upon which, instantly afterwards, fell prostrate in death the Prince Prospero.

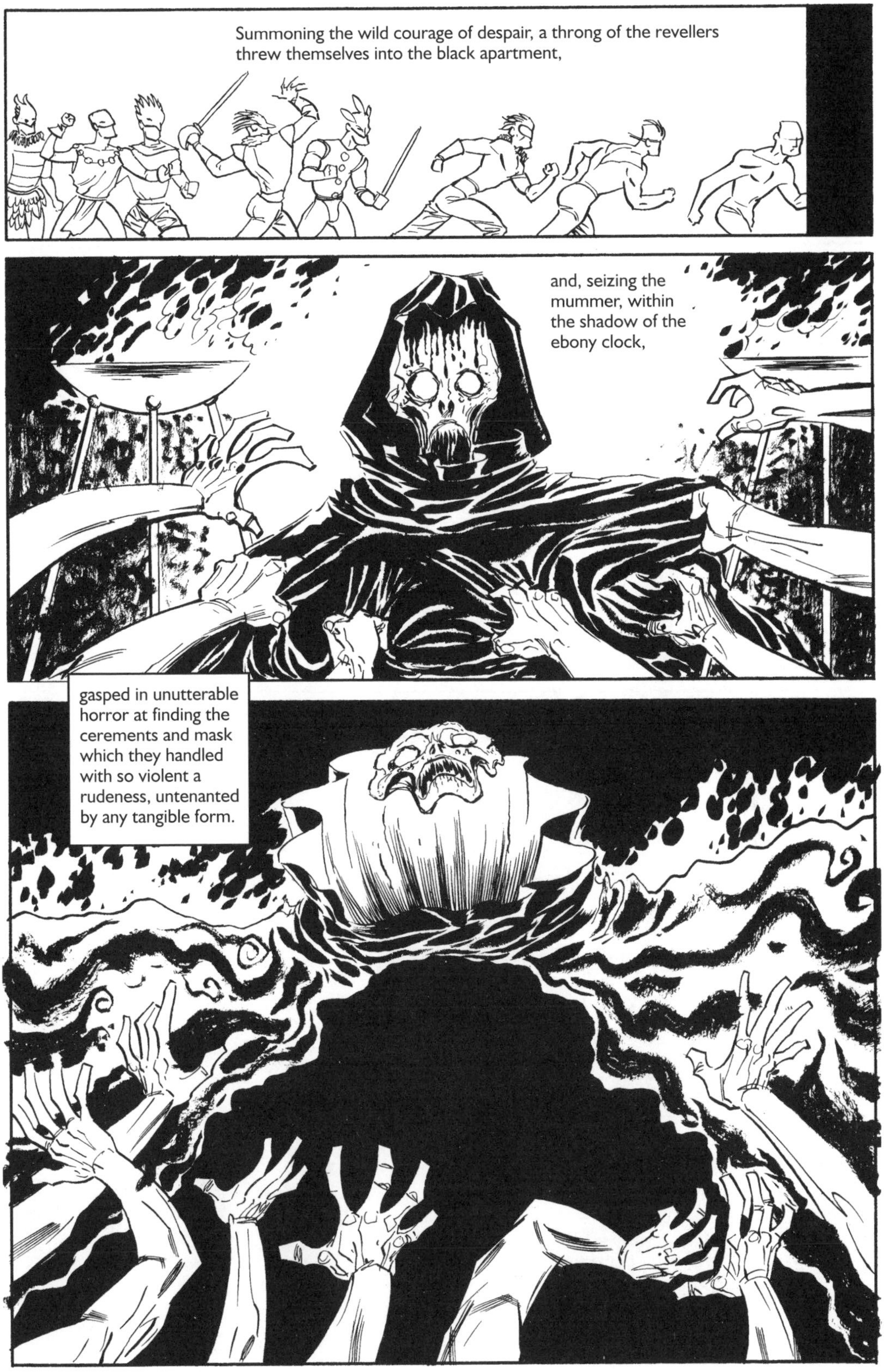
Summoning the wild courage of despair, a throng of the revellers threw themselves into the black apartment,
and, seizing the mummer, within the shadow of the ebony clock,
gasped in unutterable horror at finding the cerements and mask which they handled with so violent a rudeness, untenanted by any tangible form.

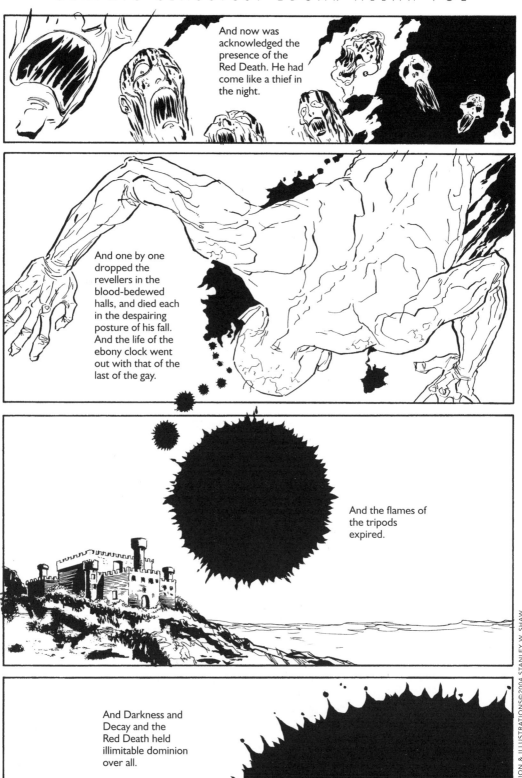

And now was acknowledged the presence of the Red Death. He had come like a thief in the night.

And one by one dropped the revellers in the blood-bedewed halls, and died each in the despairing posture of his fall. And the life of the ebony clock went out with that of the last of the gay.

And the flames of the tripods expired.

And Darkness and Decay and the Red Death held illimitable dominion over all.

STORY BY EDGAR ALLAN POE • ADAPTATION BY MILTON KNIGHT

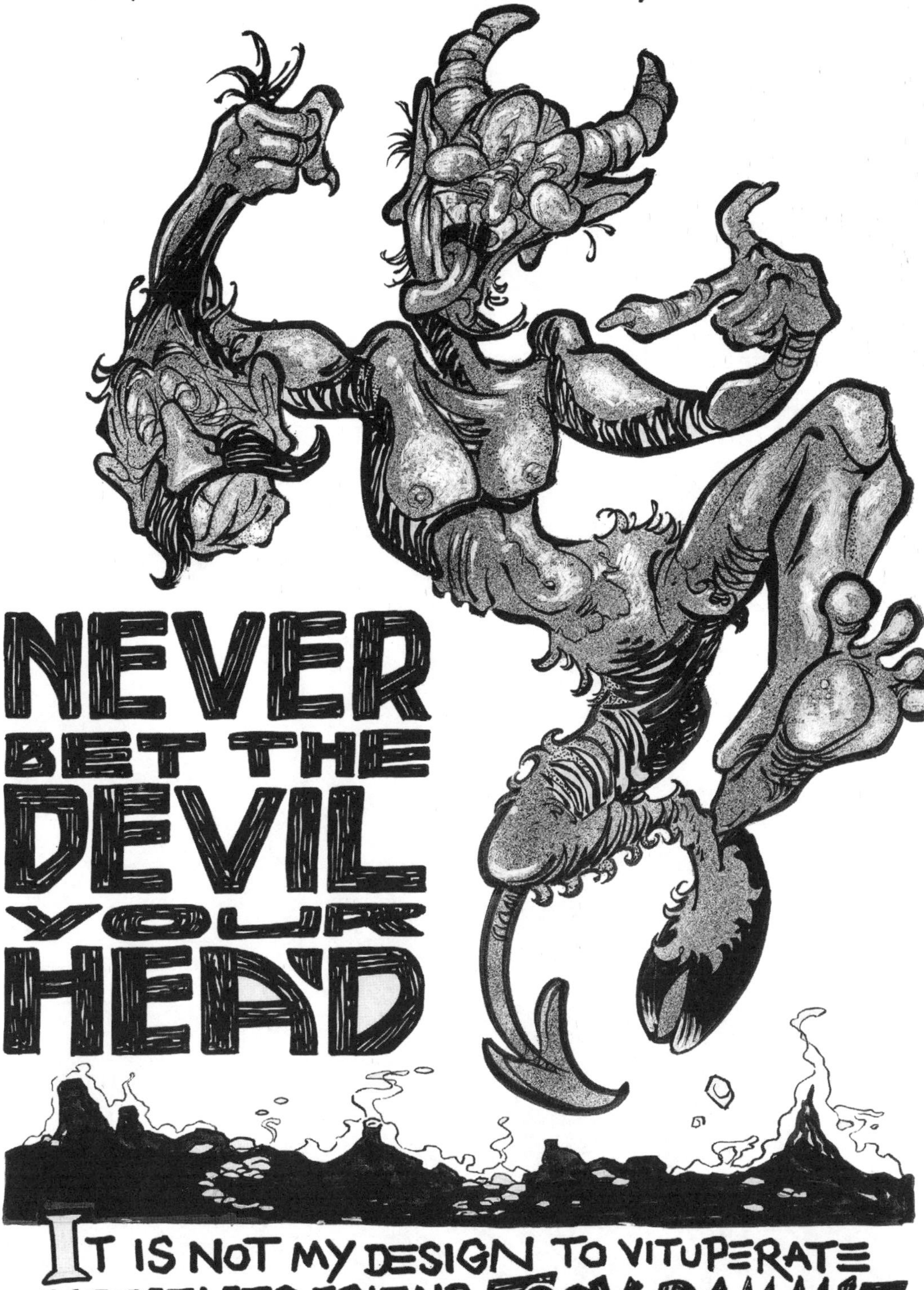
NEVER
BET THE
DEVIL
YOUR
HEAD

IT IS NOT MY DESIGN TO VITUPERATE MY DECEASED FRIEND, **TOBY DAMMIT..**

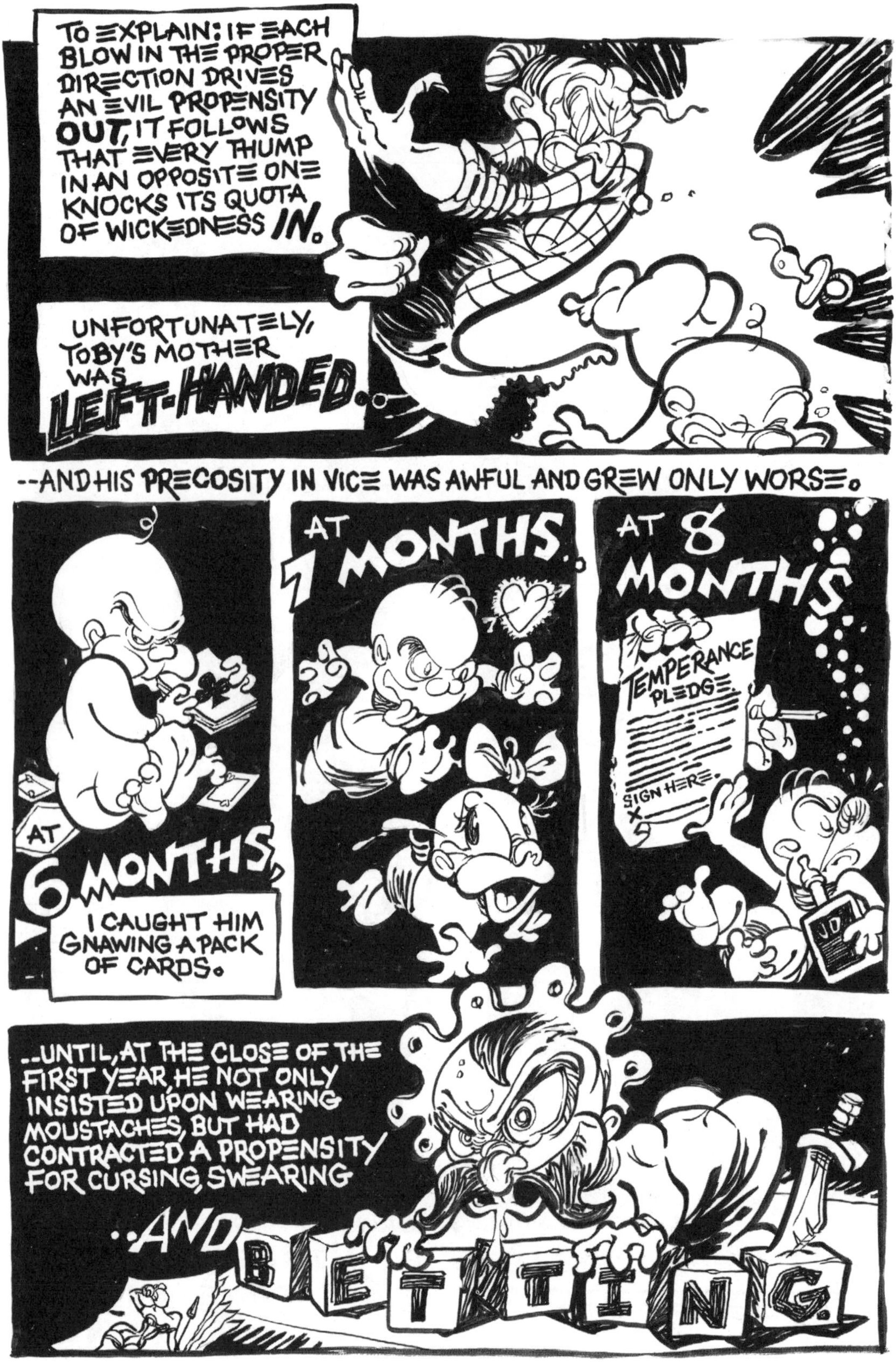
TO EXPLAIN: IF EACH BLOW IN THE PROPER DIRECTION DRIVES AN EVIL PROPENSITY OUT, IT FOLLOWS THAT EVERY THUMP IN AN OPPOSITE ONE KNOCKS ITS QUOTA OF WICKEDNESS IN.
UNFORTUNATELY, TOBY'S MOTHER WAS LEFT-HANDED..
--AND HIS PRECOSITY IN VICE WAS AWFUL AND GREW ONLY WORSE.
AT 6 MONTHS,
I CAUGHT HIM GNAWING A PACK OF CARDS.
AT 7 MONTHS..
AT 8 MONTHS
TEMPERANCE PLEDGE
SIGN HERE.
..UNTIL, AT THE CLOSE OF THE FIRST YEAR, HE NOT ONLY INSISTED UPON WEARING MOUSTACHES, BUT HAD CONTRACTED A PROPENSITY FOR CURSING, SWEARING
..AND BETTING.

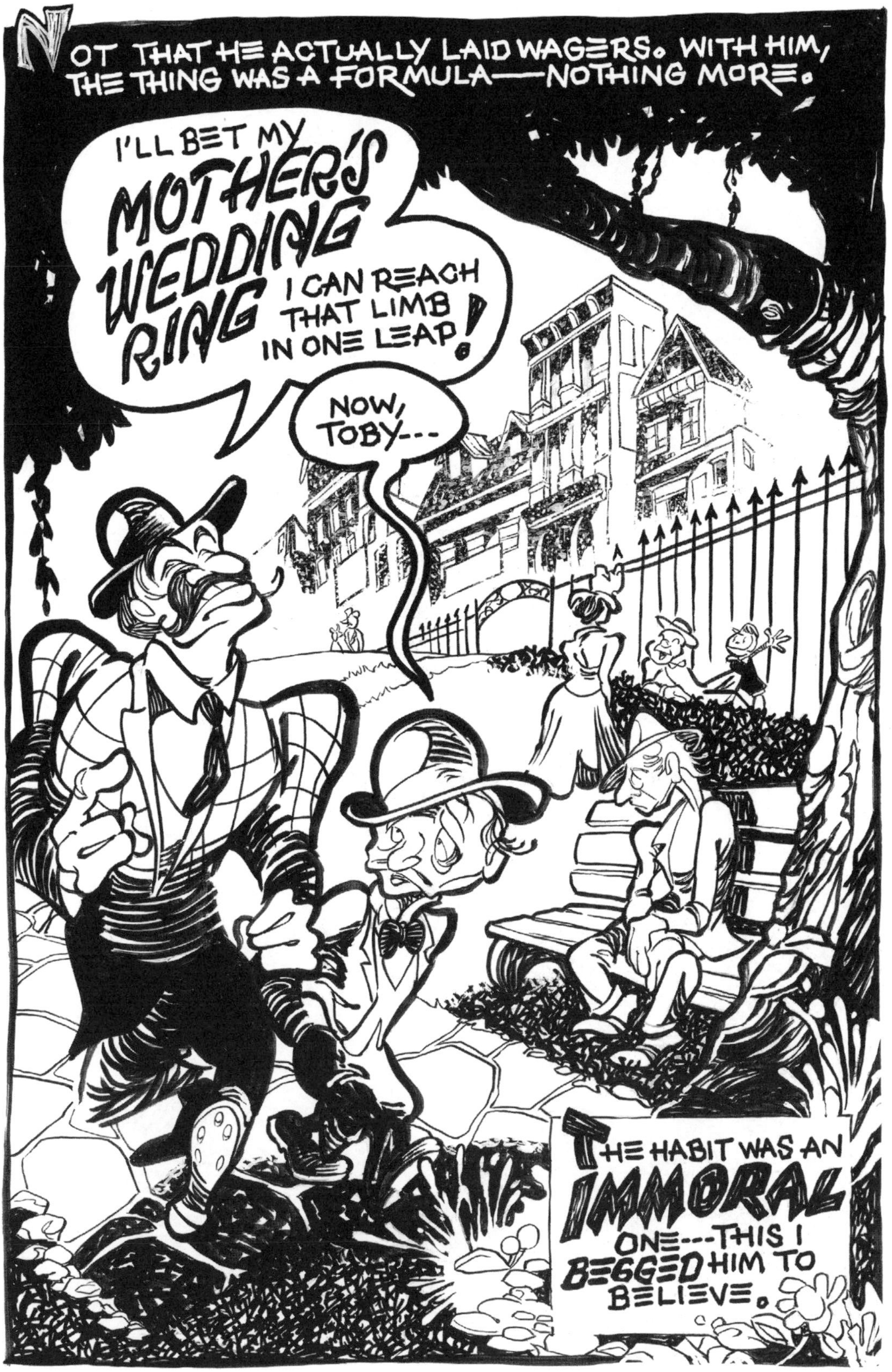
NOT THAT HE ACTUALLY LAID WAGERS. WITH HIM, THE THING WAS A FORMULA—NOTHING MORE.
I'LL BET MY MOTHER'S WEDDING RING I CAN REACH THAT LIMB IN ONE LEAP!
NOW, TOBY---
THE HABIT WAS AN IMMORAL ONE---THIS I BEGGED HIM TO BELIEVE.

HE SAID HE WOULD BE OBLIGED TO ME IF I HELD MY TONGUE.

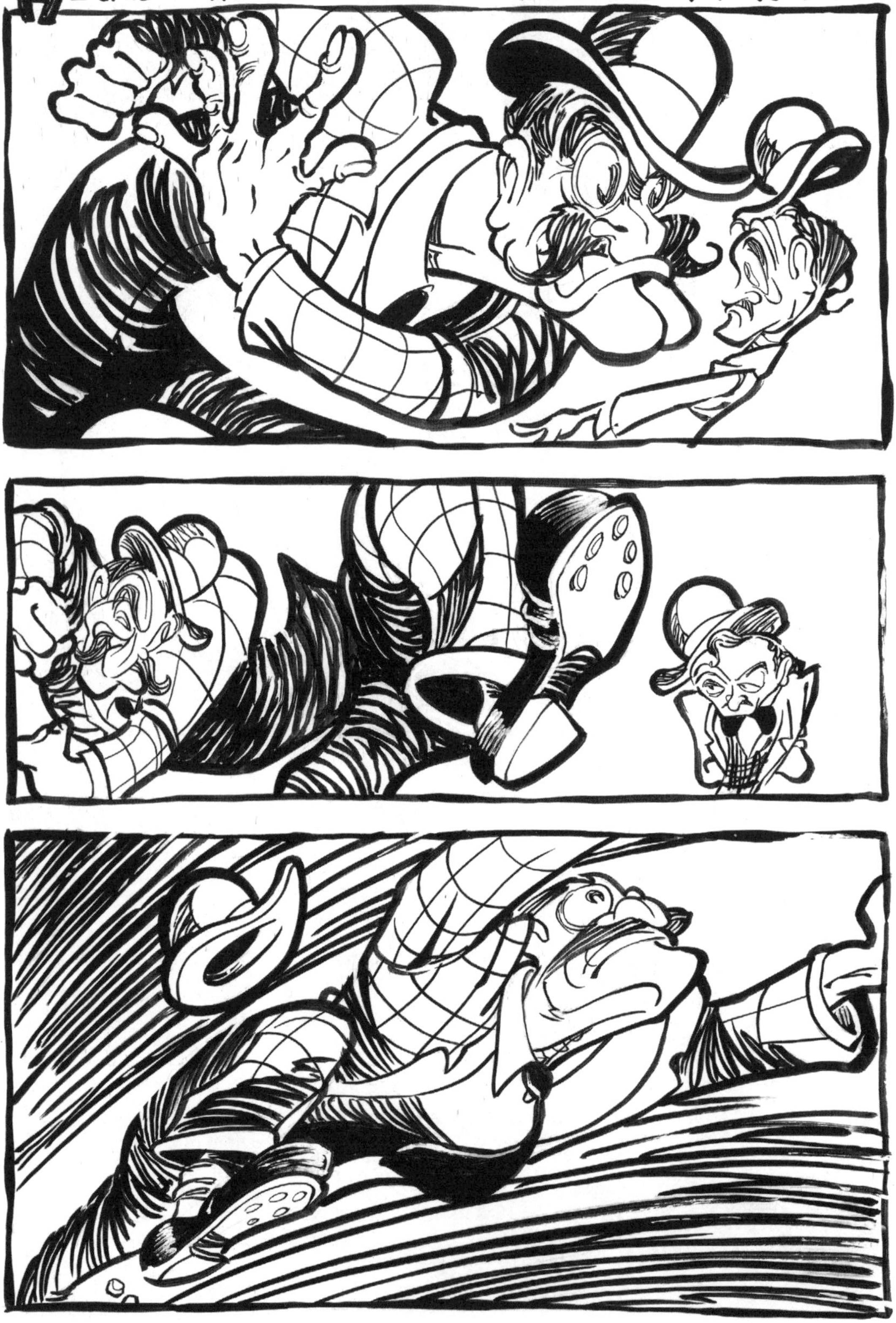

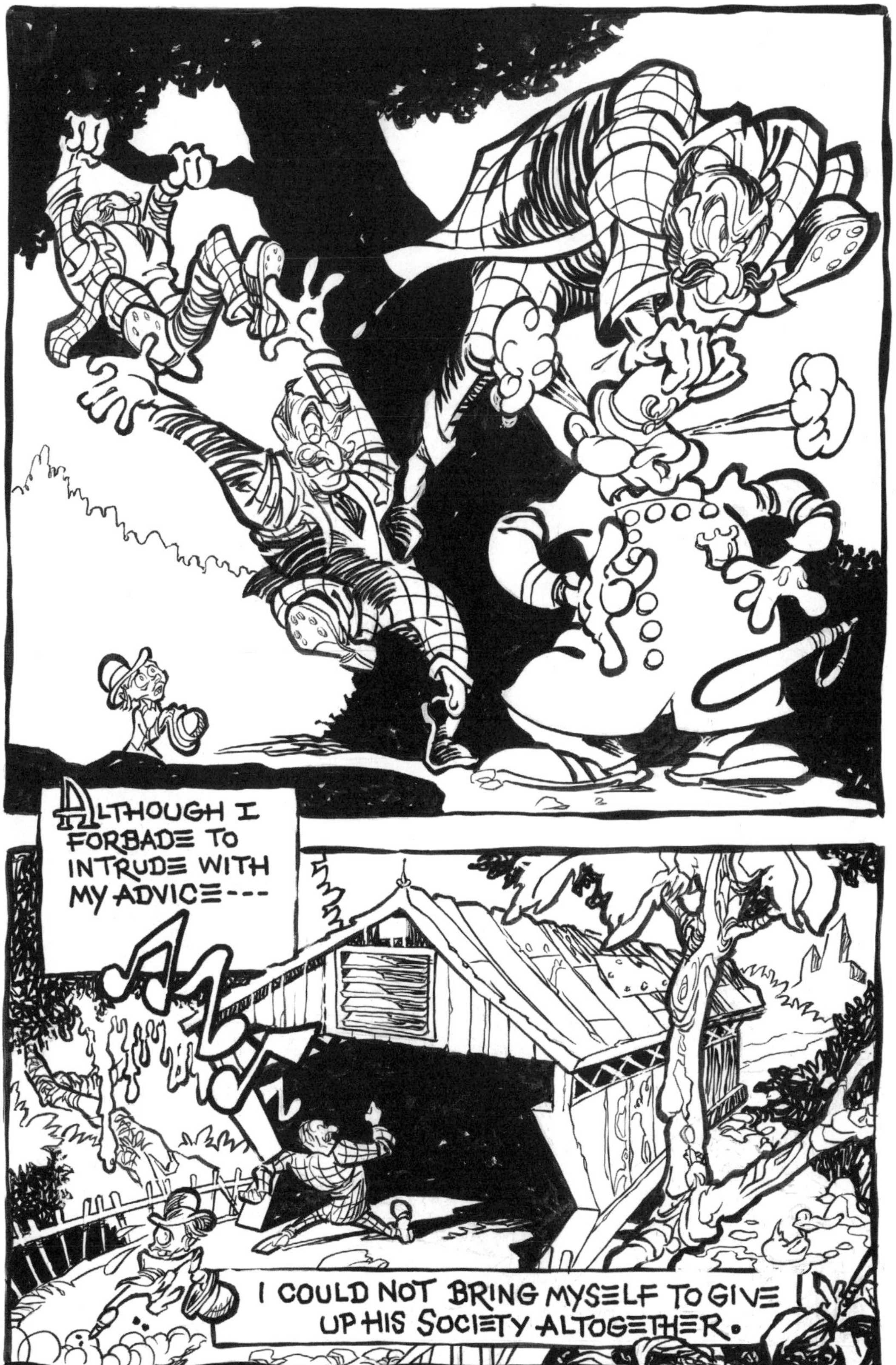
ALTHOUGH I FORBADE TO INTRUDE WITH MY ADVICE---
I COULD NOT BRING MYSELF TO GIVE UP HIS SOCIETY ALTOGETHER.

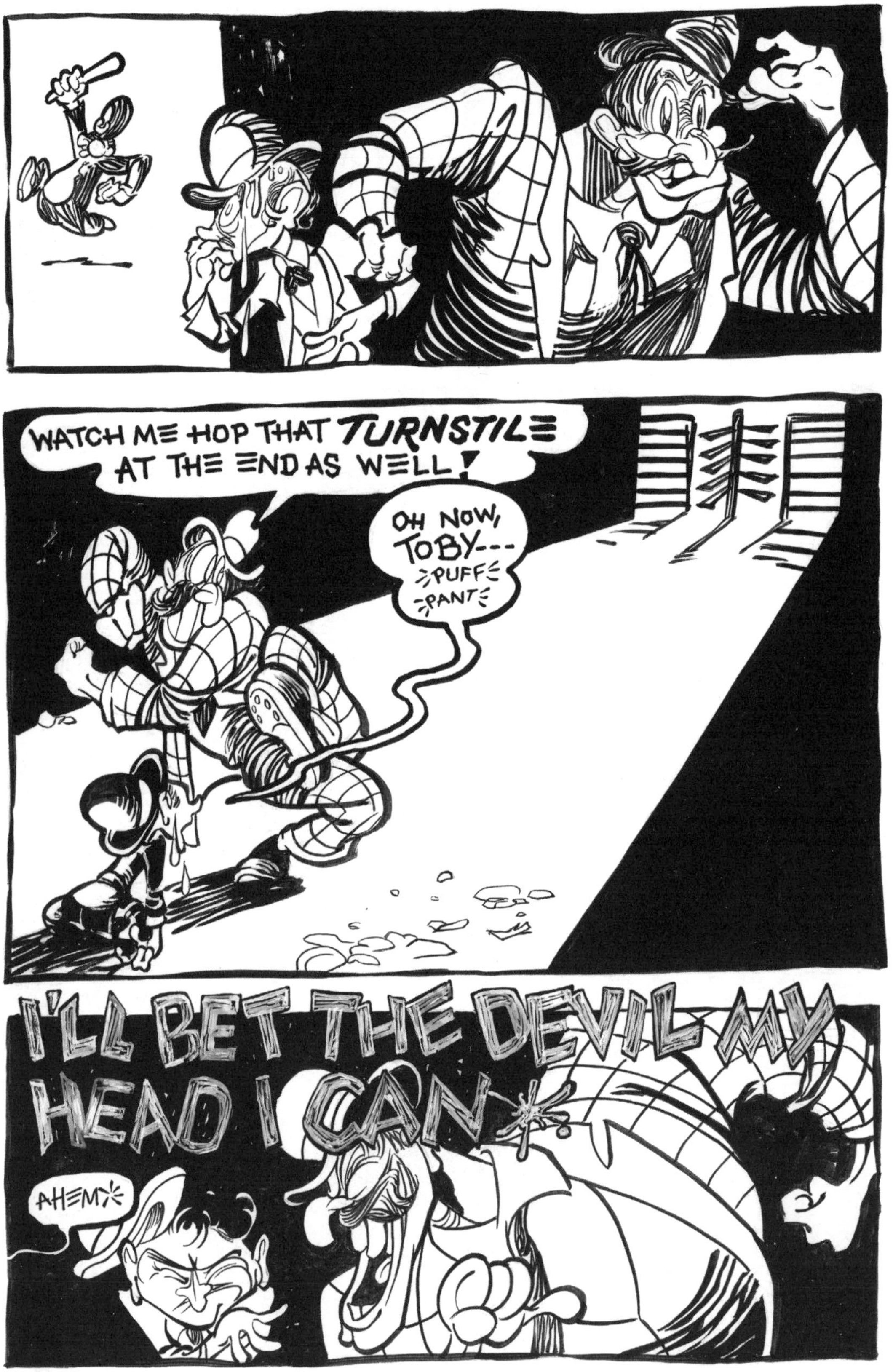
WATCH ME HOP THAT TURNSTILE AT THE END AS WELL!
OH NOW, TOBY---
PUFF
PANT
I'LL BET THE DEVIL MY HEAD I CAN!
AHEM!

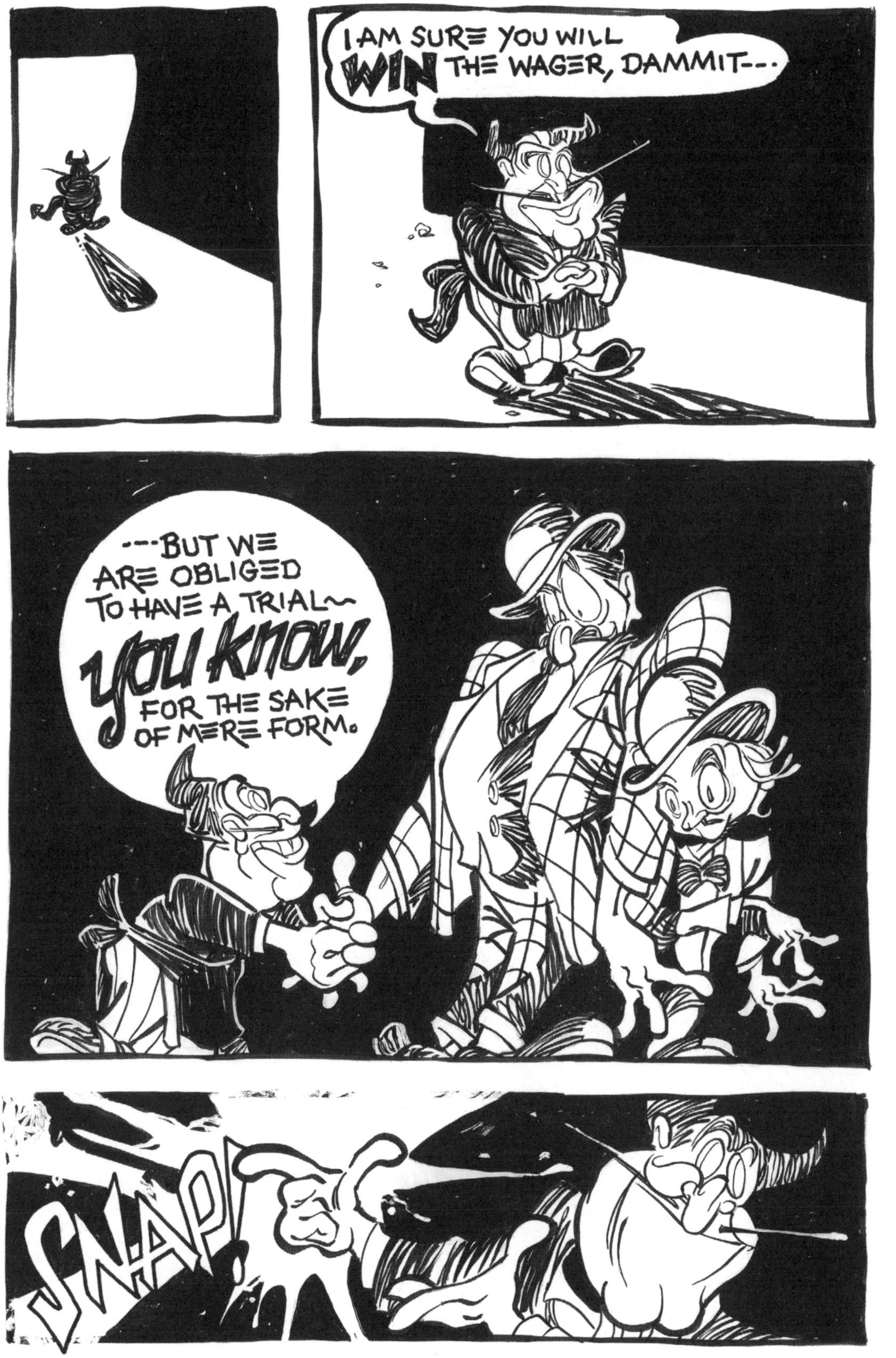
I AM SURE YOU WILL WIN THE WAGER, DAMMIT---
---BUT WE ARE OBLIGED TO HAVE A TRIAL~ YOU KNOW, FOR THE SAKE OF MERE FORM.
SNAP!

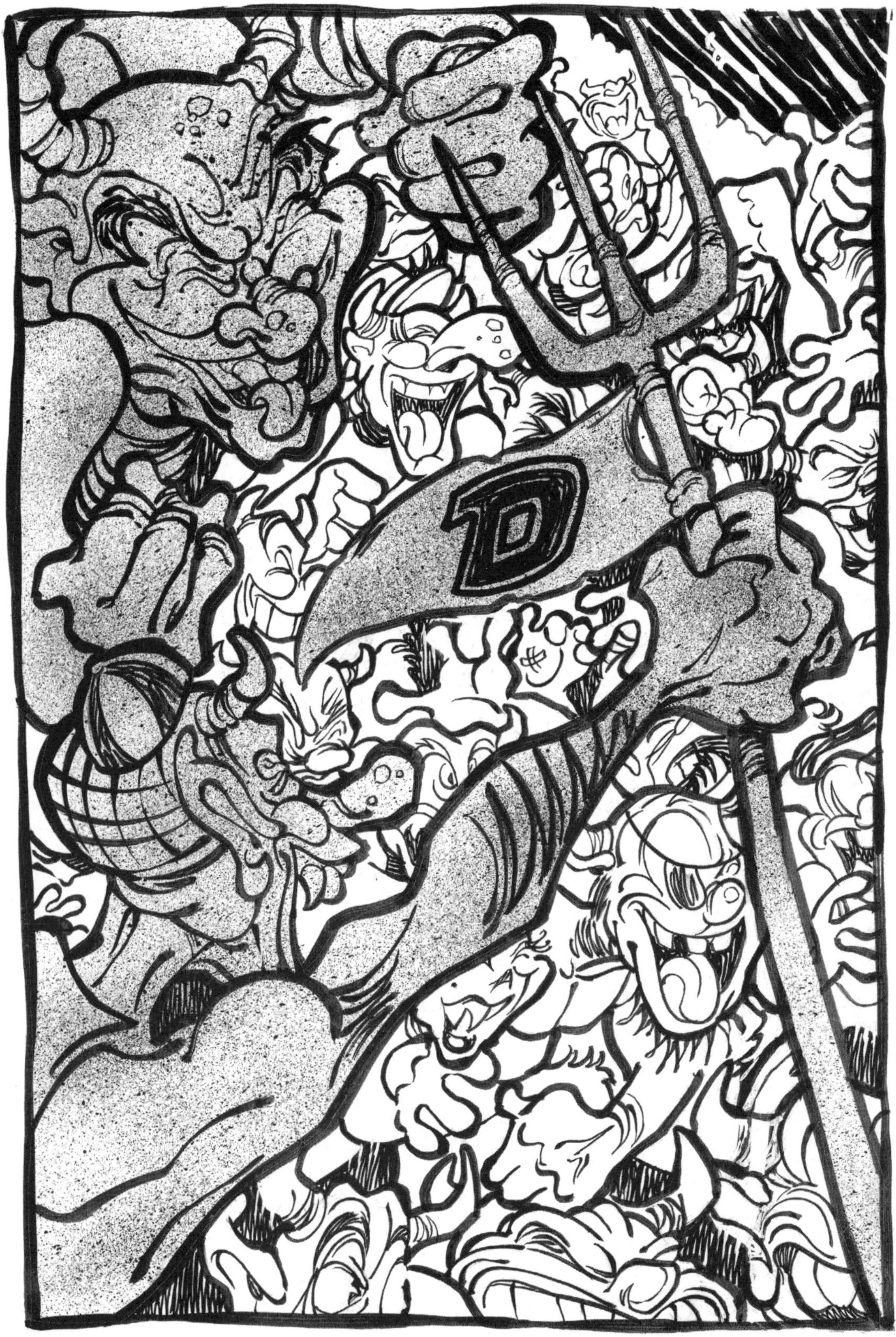

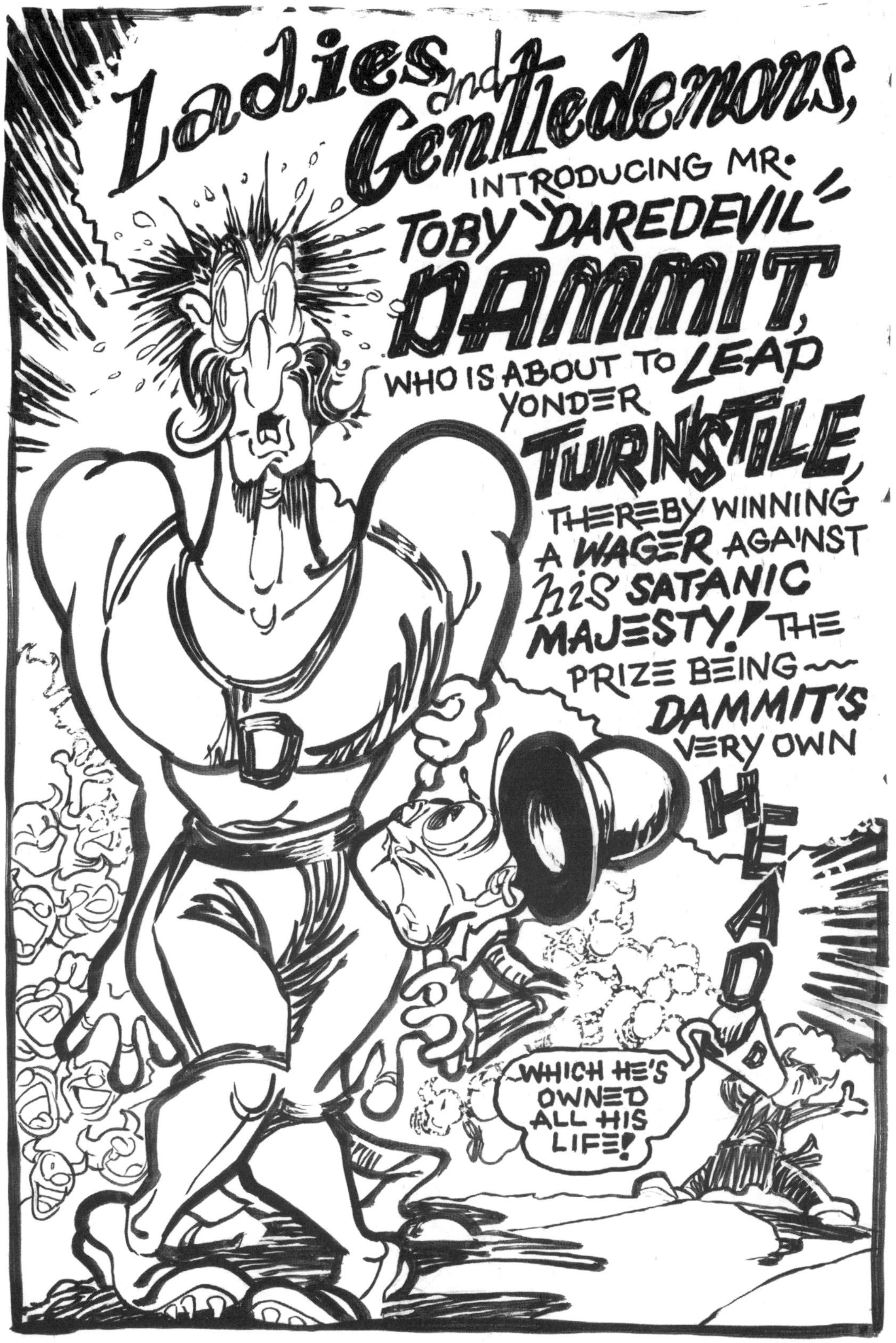
Ladies and Gentledemons,
INTRODUCING MR. TOBY "DAREDEVIL" DAMMIT,
WHO IS ABOUT TO LEAP YONDER TURNSTILE,
THEREBY WINNING A WAGER AGAINST his SATANIC MAJESTY! THE PRIZE BEING~~ DAMMIT'S VERY OWN HEAD
WHICH HE'S OWNED ALL HIS LIFE!

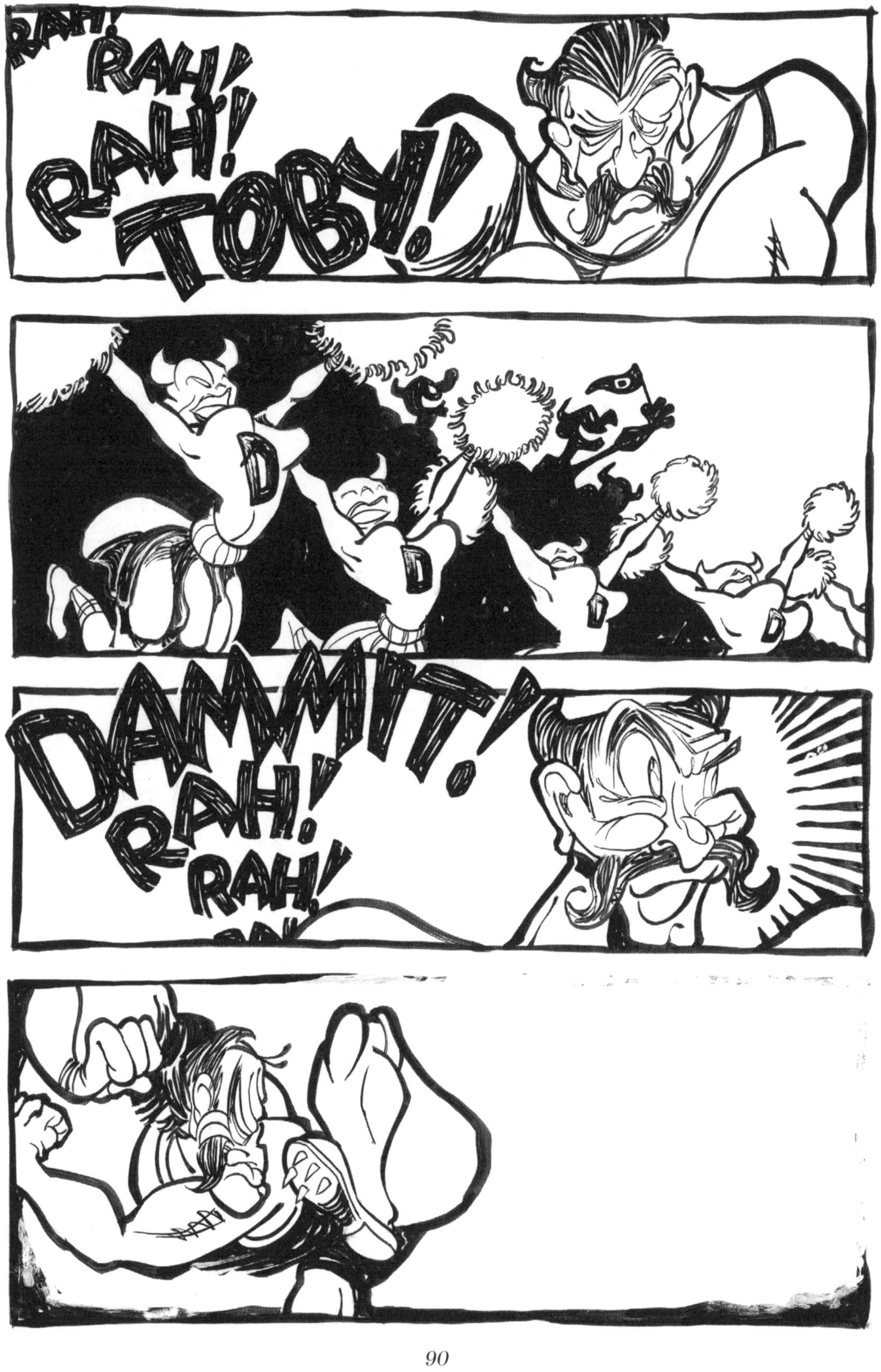
RAH!
RAH!
TOBY!
DAMMIT!
RAH!
RAH!

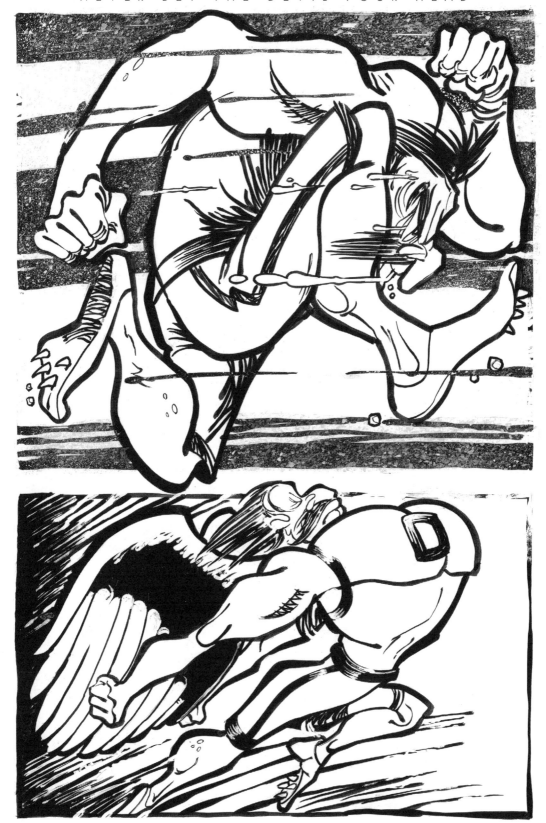

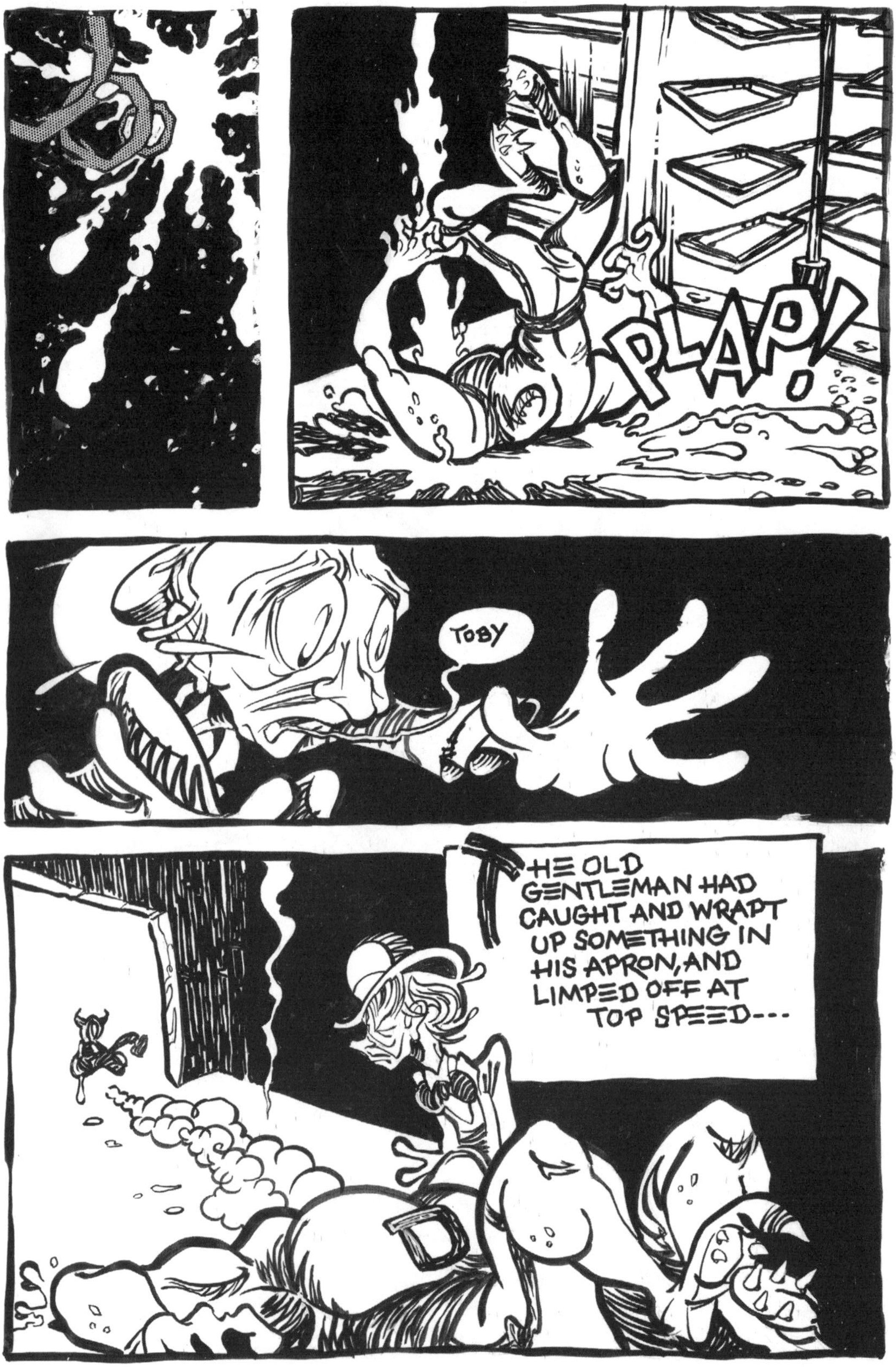
PLAP!
TOBY
THE OLD GENTLEMAN HAD CAUGHT AND WRAPT UP SOMETHING IN HIS APRON, AND LIMPED OFF AT TOP SPEED---

THE TRUTH IS, DAMMIT HAD BEEN DEPRIVED OF HIS HEAD---

BY AN IRON BAR SUPPORTING THE TUNNEL---

HE DID NOT LONG SURVIVE HIS TERRIBLE LOSS---

BEDEWING HIS GRAVE WITH MY TEARS, I BILLED HIS SURVIVORS FOR THE FUNERAL EXPENSES---

Mr. DAMMIT a LESSON to all RIOTOUS LIVERS

WHEN THE SCOUNDRELS REFUSED TO PAY THEM, I HAD MR. DAMMIT DUG UP AT ONCE---

TO LET.

--AND SOLD HIM FOR DOG'S MEAT.

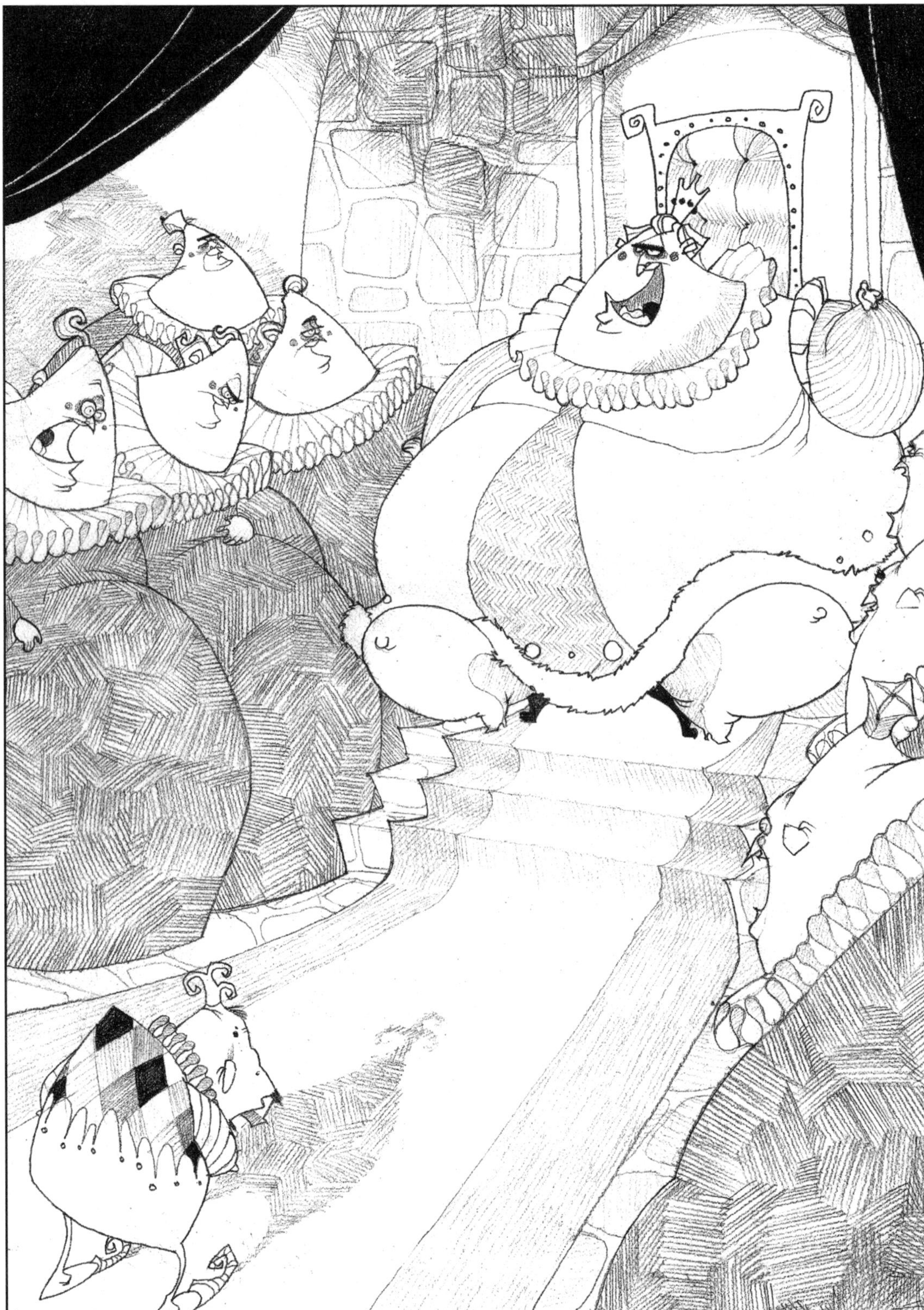

Hop-Frog

story by EDGAR ALLAN POE
illustrated by LISA K. WEBER

I never knew anyone so keenly alive to a joke as the king was. He seemed to live only for joking. To tell a good story of the joke kind, and to tell it well, was the surest road to his favor. Thus it happened that his seven ministers were all noted for their accomplishments as jokers. They all took after the king, too, in being large, corpulent, oily men, as well as inimitable jokers. Whether people grow fat by joking, or whether there is something in fat itself which predisposes to a joke, I have never been quite able to determine; but certain it is that a lean joker is a *rara avis in terris.*

About the refinements, or, as he called them, the "ghosts" of wit, the king troubled himself very little. He had an especial admiration for *breadth* in a jest, and would often put up with *length,* for the sake of it. Over-niceties wearied him. He would have preferred Rabelais' *Gargantua* to the *Zadig* of Voltaire; and, upon the whole, practical jokes suited his taste far better than verbal ones.

At the date of my narrative, professing jesters had not altogether gone out of fashion at court. Several of the great continental "powers" still retained their "fools," who wore motley, with caps and bells, and who were expected to be always ready with sharp witticisms, at a moment's notice, in consideration of the crumbs that fell from the royal table.

Our king, as a matter of course, retained his "fool." The fact is, he *required* something in the way of folly — if only to counterbalance the heavy wisdom of the seven wise men who were his ministers — not to mention himself.

His fool, or professional jester, was not *only* a fool, however. His value was trebled in the eyes of the king, by the fact of his being also a dwarf and a cripple. Dwarfs were as common at court, in those days, as fools; and many monarchs would have found it difficult to get through their days (days are rather longer at court than elsewhere) without both a jester to laugh *with,* and a dwarf to laugh *at.* But, as I have already

with great pain and difficulty along a road or floor, the prodigious muscular power which nature seemed to have bestowed upon his arms, by way of compensation for deficiency in the lower limbs, enabled him to perform many feats of wonderful dexterity, where trees or ropes were in question, or any thing else to climb. At such exercises he certainly much more resembled a squirrel, or a small monkey, than a frog.

I am not able to say, with precision, from what country Hop-Frog originally came. It was from some barbarous region, however, that no person ever heard of — a vast distance from the court of our king. Hop-Frog, and a young girl very little less dwarfish than himself (although of exquisite proportions, and a marvellous dancer), had been forcibly carried off from their respective homes in adjoining provinces, and sent as presents to the king, by one of his ever-victorious generals.

Under these circumstances, it is not to be wondered at that a close intimacy arose between the two little captives. Indeed, they soon became sworn friends. Hop-Frog, who, although he made a great deal of sport, was by no means popular, had it not in his power to render Trippetta many services; but *she*, on account of her grace and exquisite beauty (although a dwarf), was universally admired and petted; so she possessed much influence; and never failed to use it, whenever she could, for the benefit of Hop-Frog.

observed, your jesters, in ninety-nine cases out of a hundred, are fat, round, and unwieldy — so that it was no small source of self-gratulation with our king that, in Hop-Frog (this was the fool's name), he possessed a triplicate treasure in one person.

I believe the name "Hop-Frog" was *not* that given to the dwarf by his sponsors at baptism, but it was conferred upon him, by general consent of the several ministers, on account of his inability to walk as other men do. In fact, Hop-Frog could only get along by a sort of interjectional gait — something between a leap and a wriggle — a movement that afforded illimitable amusement, and of course consolation, to the king, for (notwithstanding the protuberance of his stomach and a constitutional swelling of the head) the king, by his whole court, was accounted a capital figure.

But although Hop-Frog, through the distortion of his legs, could move only

On some grand state occasion — I forgot what — the king determined to have a masquerade, and whenever a masquerade or any thing of that kind occurred at our court, then the talents both of Hop-Frog and Trippetta were sure to be called into play. Hop-Frog, in especial, was so inventive in the way of getting up pageants, suggesting novel characters, and arranging costumes for masked balls, that nothing could be done, it seems, without his assistance.

The night appointed for the *fête* had arrived. A gorgeous hall had been fitted up, under Trippetta's eye, with every kind of device which could possibly give *éclat* to a masquerade. The whole court was in a fever of expectation. As for costumes and characters, it might well be supposed that everybody had come to a decision on such points. Many had made up their minds (as to what *rôles* they should assume) a week, or even a month, in advance; and, in fact, there was not a particle of indecision anywhere — except in the case of the king and his seven minsters. Why *they* hesitated I never could tell, unless they did it by way of a joke. More probably, they found it difficult, on account of being so fat, to make up their minds. At all events, time flew; and, as a last resort they sent for Trippetta and Hop-Frog.

When the two little friends obeyed the summons of the king they found him sitting at his wine with the seven members of his cabinet council; but the monarch appeared to be in a very ill humor. He knew that Hop-Frog was not fond of wine, for it excited the poor cripple almost to madness; and madness is no comfortable feeling. But the king loved his practical jokes, and took pleasure in forcing Hop-Frog to drink and (as the king called it) "to be merry."

"Come here, Hop-Frog," said he, as the jester and his friend entered the room;

"swallow this bumper to the health of your absent friends [here Hop-Frog sighed] and then let us have the benefit of your invention. We want characters — *characters*, man — something novel — out of the way. We are wearied with this everlasting sameness. Come, drink! the wine will brighten your wits."

Hop-Frog endeavored, as usual, to get up a jest in reply to these advances from the king; but the effort was too much. It happened to be the poor dwarf's birthday, and the command to drink to his "absent friends" forced the tears to his eyes. Many large, bitter drops fell into the goblet as he took it, humbly, from the hand of the tyrant.

"Ah! ha! ha!" roared the latter, as the dwarf reluctantly drained the beaker — "See what a glass of good wine can do! Why, your eyes are shining already!"

Poor fellow! his large eyes *gleamed,* rather than shone; for the effect of wine on his excitable brain was not more powerful than instantaneous. He placed the goblet nervously on the table, and looked round upon the company with a half-insane stare. They all seemed highly amused at the success of the king's *"joke."*

"And now to business," said the prime minister, a *very* fat man.

"Yes," said the King; "come lend us your assistance. Characters, my fine fellow; we stand in need of characters — all of us — ha! ha! ha!" and as this was seriously meant for a joke, his laugh was chorused by the seven.

Hop-Frog also laughed although feebly and somewhat vacantly.

"Come, come," said the king, impatiently, "have you nothing to suggest?"

"I am endeavoring to think of something *novel,*" replied the dwarf, abstractedly, for he was quite bewildered by the wine.

"Endeavoring!" cried the tyrant, fiercely; "what do you mean by *that?* Ah, I perceive. You are sulky, and want more wine. Here,

drink this!" and he poured out another goblet full and offered it to the cripple, who merely gazed at it, gasping for breath.

"Drink, I say!" shouted the monster, "or by the fiends —"

The dwarf hesitated. The king grew purple with rage. The courtiers smirked. Trippetta, pale as a corpse, advanced to the monarch's seat, and, falling on her knees before him, implored him to spare her friend.

The tyrant regarded her, for some moments, in evident wonder at her audacity. He seemed quite at a loss what to do or say — how most becomingly to express his indignation. At last, without uttering a syllable, he pushed her violently from him, and threw the contents of the brimming goblet in her face.

The poor girl got up the best she could, and, not daring even to sigh, resumed her position at the foot of the table.

There was a dead silence for about half a minute, during which the falling of a leaf, or of a feather, might have been heard. It was interrupted by a low, but harsh and protracted *grating* sound which seemed to come at once from every corner of the room.

"What — what — *what* are you making that noise for?" demanded the king, turning furiously to the dwarf.

The latter seemed to have recovered, in great measure, from his intoxication, and looking fixedly but quietly into the tyrant's face, merely ejaculated:

"I — I? How could it have been me?"

"The sound appeared to come from without," observed one of the courtiers. "I fancy it was the parrot at the window, whetting his bill upon his cage-wires."

"True," replied the monarch, as if much relieved by the suggestion; "but, on the honor of a knight, I could have sworn that it was the gritting of this vagabond's teeth."

Hereupon the dwarf laughed (the king was too confirmed a joker to object to any one's laughing), and displayed a set of large, powerful, and very repulsive teeth. Moreover, he avowed his perfect willingness to swallow as much wine as desired. The monarch was pacified; and having drained another bumper with no very perceptible ill effect, Hop-Frog entered at once, and with spirit, into the plans for the masquerade.

"I cannot tell what was the association of idea," observed he, very tranquilly, and as if he had never tasted wine in his life, "but *just after* your majesty had struck the girl and thrown the wine in her face — *just after* your majesty had done this, and while the parrot was making that odd noise outside the window, there came into my mind a capital diversion — one of my own country frolics — often enacted among us, at our masquerades: but here it will be new altogether. Unfortunately, however, it requires a company of eight persons and —"

"Here we *are!*" cried the king, laughing at his acute discovery of the coincidence; "eight to a fraction — I and my seven ministers. Come! what is the diversion?"

"We call it," replied the cripple, "the Eight Chained Ourang-Outangs, and it really is excellent sport if well enacted."

"*We* will enact it," remarked the king, drawing himself up, and lowering his eyelids.

"The beauty of the game," continued Hop-Frog, "lies in the fright it occasions among the women."

"Capital!" roared in chorus the monarch and his ministry.

"I will equip you as ourang-outangs," proceeded the dwarf; "leave all that to me. The resemblance shall be so striking, that the company of masqueraders will take you for real beasts — and of course, they will be as much terrified as astonished."

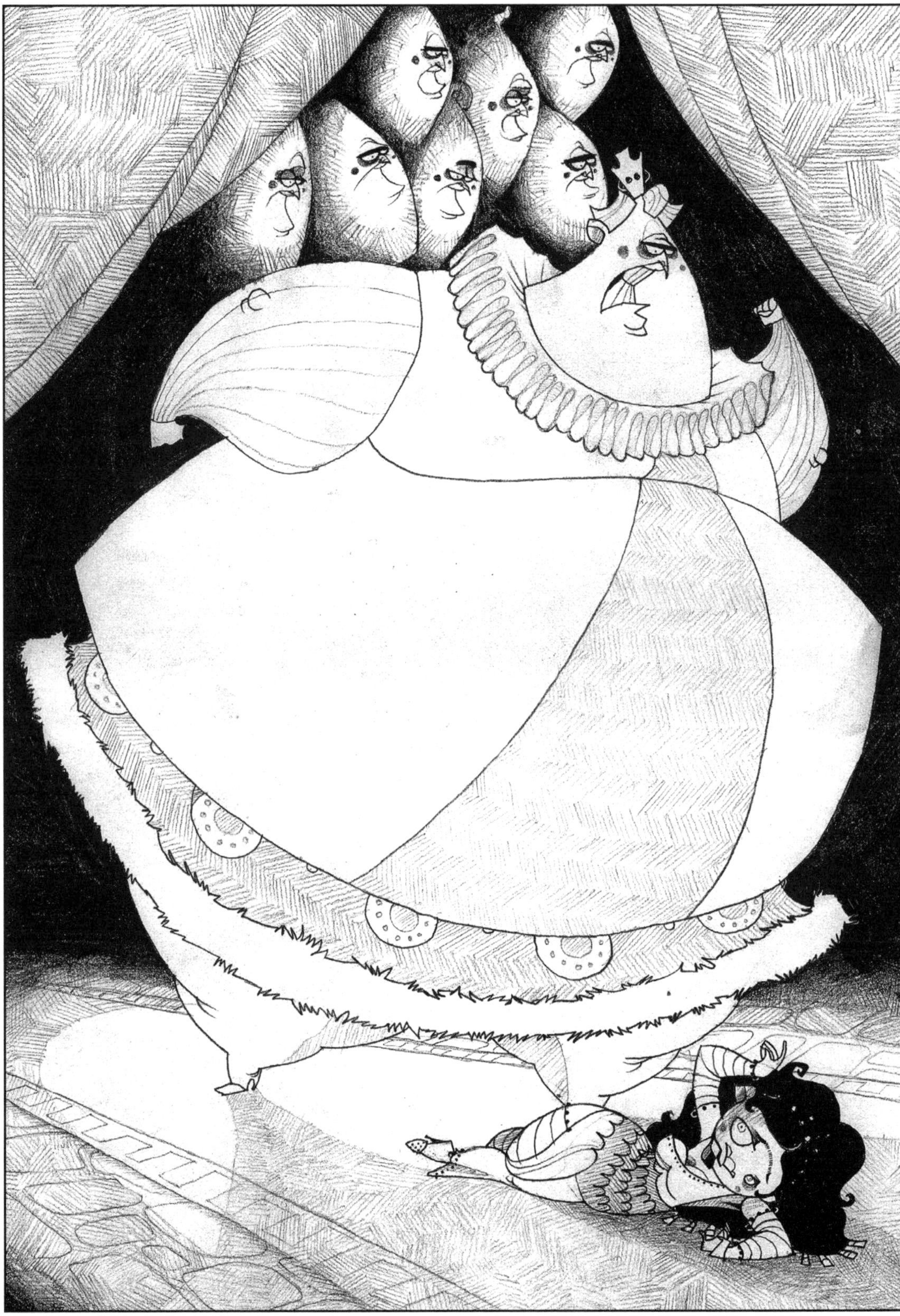

"Oh, this is exquisite!" exclaimed the king. "Hop-Frog! I will make a man of you."

"The chains are for the purpose of increasing the confusion by their jangling. You are supposed to have escaped, *en masse*, from your keepers. Your majesty cannot conceive the *effect* produced, at a masquerade, by eight chained ourang-outangs, imagined to be real ones by most of the company; and rushing in with savage cries, among the crowd of delicately and gorgeously habited men and women. The *contrast* is inimitable!"

"It *must* be," said the king: and the council arose hurriedly (as it was growing late), to put in execution the scheme of Hop-Frog.

His mode of equipping the party as ourang-outangs was very simple, but effective enough for his purposes. The animals in question had, at the epoch of my story, very rarely been seen in any part of the civilized world; and as the imitations made by the dwarf were sufficiently beast-like and more than sufficiently hideous, their truthfulness to nature was thus thought to be secured.

The king and his ministers were first encased in tight-fitting stockinet shirts and drawers. They were then saturated with tar. At this stage of the process, some one of the party suggested feathers; but the suggestion was at once overruled by the dwarf, who soon convinced the eight, by ocular demonstration, that the hair of such a brute as the ourang-outang was much more efficiently represented by *flax*. A thick coating of the latter was accordingly plastered upon the coating of tar. A long chain was now procured. First, it was passed about the waist of the king, *and tied,* then about another of the party, and also tied; then about all successively, in the same manner. When this chaining arrangement was complete, and the party stood as far apart from each other as possible, they formed a circle; and to make all things appear natural, Hop-Frog passed the residue of the chain in two diameters, at right angles, across the circle, after the fashion adopted, at the present day, by those who capture Chimpanzees, or other large apes, in Borneo.

The grand saloon in which the masquerade was to take place was a circular room, very lofty, and receiving the light of the sun only through a single window at top. At night

(the season for which the apartment was especially designed) it was illuminated principally by a large chandelier, depending by a chain from the centre of the sky-light, and lowered, or elevated, by means of a counter-balance as usual; but (in order not to look unsightly) this latter passed outside the cupola and over the roof.

The arrangements of the room had been left to Trippetta's superintendence; but, in some particulars, it seems, she had been guided by the calmer judgment of her friend the dwarf. At his suggestion it was that, on this occasion, the chandelier was removed. Its waxen drippings (which, in weather so warm, it was quite impossible to prevent) would have been seriously detrimental to the rich dresses of the guests, who, on account of the crowded state of the saloon, could not *all* be expected to keep from out its center—that is to say, from under the chandelier. Additional sconces were set in various parts of the hall, out of the way, and a flambeau, emitting sweet odor, was placed in the right hand of each of the caryatides that stood against the wall—some fifty or sixty altogether.

The eight ourang-outangs, taking Hop-Frog's advice, waited patiently until midnight (when the room was thoroughly filled with masqueraders) before making their appearance. No sooner had the clock ceased striking, however, than they rushed, or rather rolled in, all together—for the impediments of their chains caused most of the party to fall, and all to stumble as they entered.

The excitement among the masqueraders was prodigious, and filled the heart of the king with glee. As had been anticipated, there were not a few of the guests who supposed the ferocious-looking creatures to be beasts of *some* kind in reality, if not precisely ourang-outangs. Many of the women swooned with affright; and had not the king taken the precaution to exclude all weapons from the saloon, his party might soon have expiated their frolic in their blood. As it was, a general rush was made for the doors; but the king had ordered them to be locked immediately upon his entrance; and, at the dwarf's suggestion, the keys had been deposited with *him*.

While the tumult was at its height, and each masquerader attentive only to his own safety (for, in fact, there was much real danger from the pressure of the excited crowd), the chain by which the chandelier ordinarily hung, and which had been drawn up on its removal, might have been seen very gradually to descend, until its hooked extremity came within three feet of the floor.

Soon after this, the king and his seven friends having reeled about the hall in all directions, found themselves, at length, in its centre, and, of course, in immediate contact with the chain. While they were thus situated, the dwarf, who had followed noiselessly at their heels, inciting them to keep up the commotion, took hold of their own chain at the intersection of the two portions which crossed the circle diametrically and at right angles. Here, with the rapidity of thought, he inserted the hook from which the chandelier had been wont to depend; and, in an instant, by some unseen agency, the chandelier-chain was drawn so far upward as to take the hook out of reach, and, as an inevitable consequence, to drag the ourang-outangs together in close connection, and face to face.

The masqueraders, by this time, had recovered, in some measure, from their alarm; and, beginning to regard the whole matter as a well-contrived pleasantry, set up a loud shout of laughter at the predicament of the apes.

"Leave them to *me!*" now screamed Hop-Frog, his shrill voice making itself easily heard through all the din. "Leave them to *me*. I fancy *I* know them. If I can only get a good look at them, *I* can soon tell who they are."

Here, scrambling over the heads of the crowd, he managed to get to the wall; when, seizing a flambeau from one of the caryatides, he returned, as he went, to the center of the room—leaping, with the agility of a monkey, upon the king's head, and thence clambered a few feet up the chain; holding down the torch to examine the group of ourang-outangs, and still screaming: "I shall soon find out who they are!"

And now, while the whole assembly (the apes included) were convulsed with

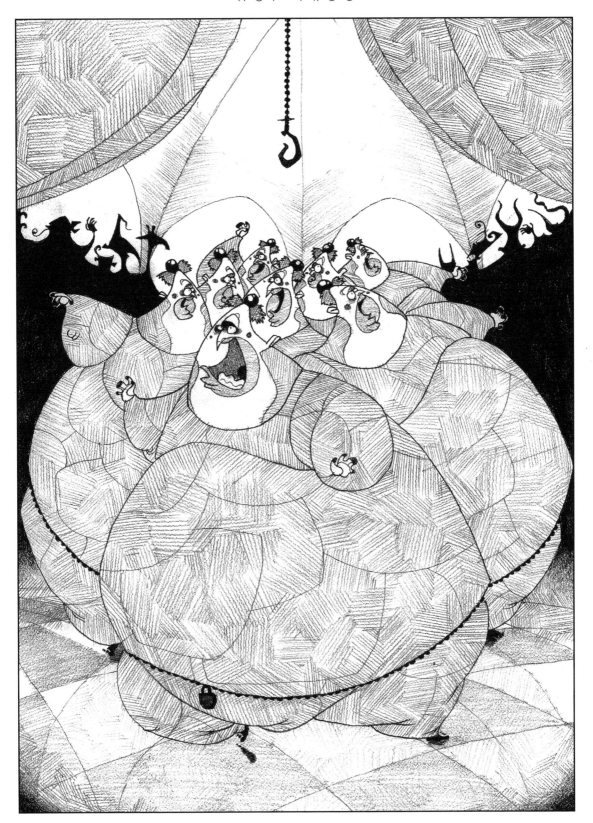

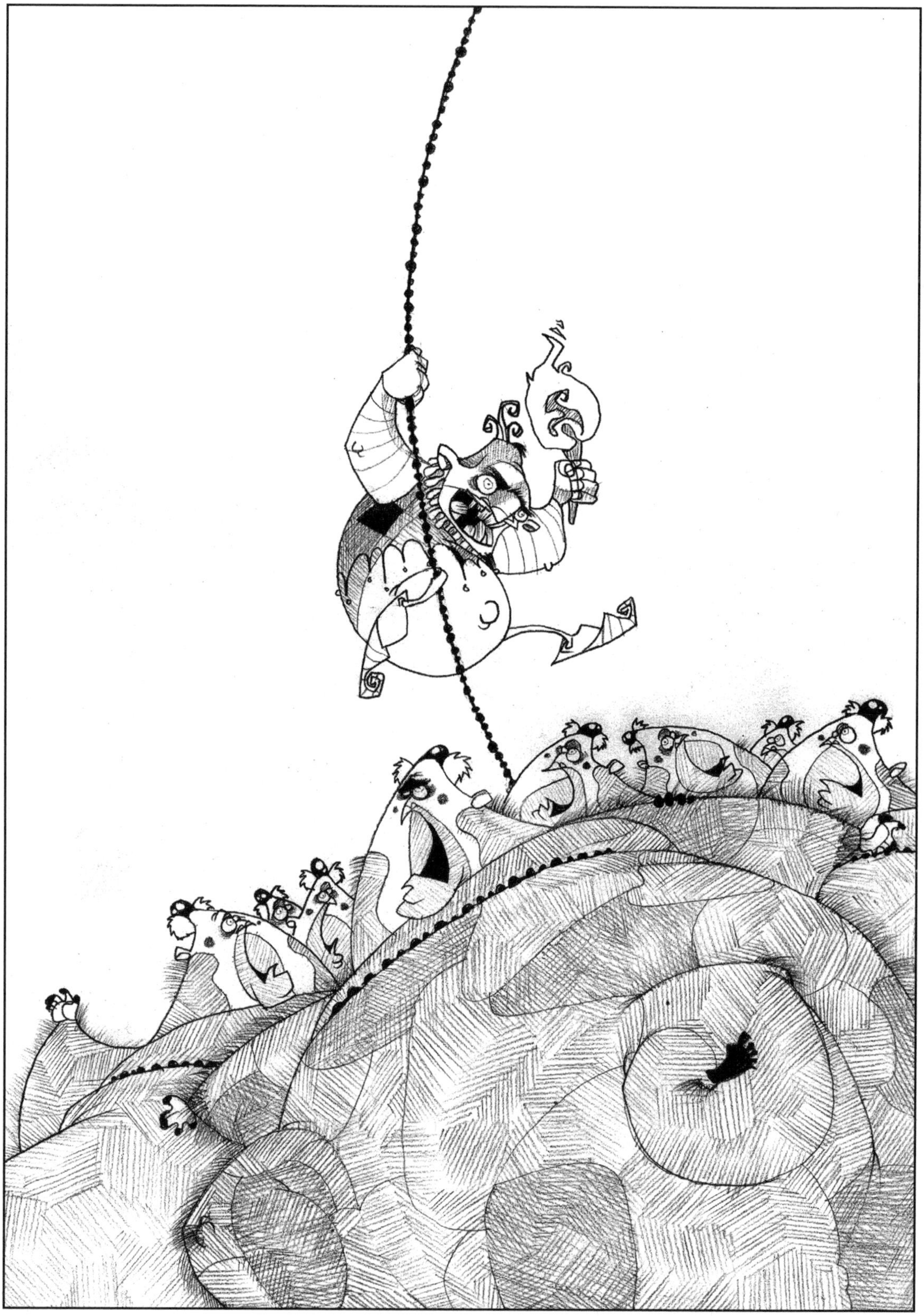

laughter, the jester suddenly uttered a shrill whistle; when the chain flew violently up for about thirty feet — dragging with it the dismayed and struggling ourang-outangs, and leaving them suspended in mid-air between the sky-light and the floor. Hop-Frog, clinging to the chain as it rose, still maintained his relative position in respect to the eight maskers, and still (as if nothing were the matter) continued to thrust his torch down toward them, as though endeavoring to discover who they were.

So thoroughly astonished was the whole company at this ascent, that a dead silence, of about a minute's duration, ensued. It was broken by just such a low, harsh, *grating* sound, as had before attracted the attention of the king and his councillors when the former threw the wine in the face of Trippetta. But, on the present occasion, there could be no question as to *whence* the sound issued. It came from the fang-like teeth of the dwarf, who ground them and gnashed them as he foamed at the mouth, and glared, with an expression of maniacal rage, into the upturned countenances of the king and his seven companions.

"Ah, ha!" said at length the infuriated jester. "Ah, ha! I begin to see who these people *are* now!" Here, pretending to scrutinize the king more closely, he held the flambeau to the flaxen coat which enveloped him, and which instantly burst into a sheet of vivid flame. In less than half a minute the whole eight ourang-outangs were blazing fiercely, amid the shrieks of the multitude who gazed at them from below, horror-stricken, and without the power to render them the slightest assistance.

At length the flames, suddenly increasing in virulence, forced the jester to climb higher up the chain, to be out of their reach; and, as he made this movement, the crowd again sank, for a brief instant, into silence. The dwarf seized his opportunity, and once more spoke:

"I now see *distinctly,*" he said, "what manner of people these maskers are. They are a great king and his seven privy-councillors, — a king who does not scruple to strike a defenseless girl and his seven councillors who abet him in the outrage. As for myself, I am simply Hop-Frog, the jester — *and this is my last jest.*"

Owing to the high combustibility of both the flax and the tar to which it adhered, the dwarf had scarcely made an end of his brief speech before the work of vengeance was complete. The eight corpses swung in their chains, a fetid, blackened, hideous, and indistinguishable mass. The cripple hurled his torch at them, clambered leisurely to the ceiling, and disappeared through the skylight.

It is supposed that Trippetta, stationed on the roof of the saloon, had been the accomplice of her friend in his fiery revenge, and that, together, they effected their escape to their own country; for neither was seen again.

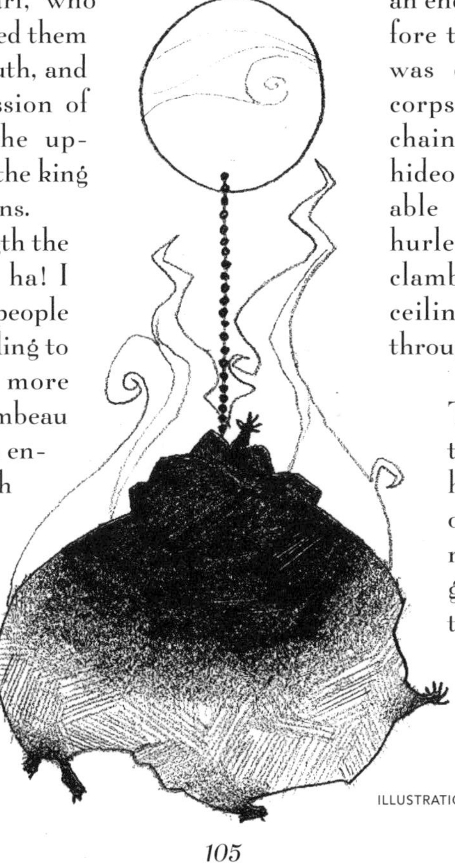

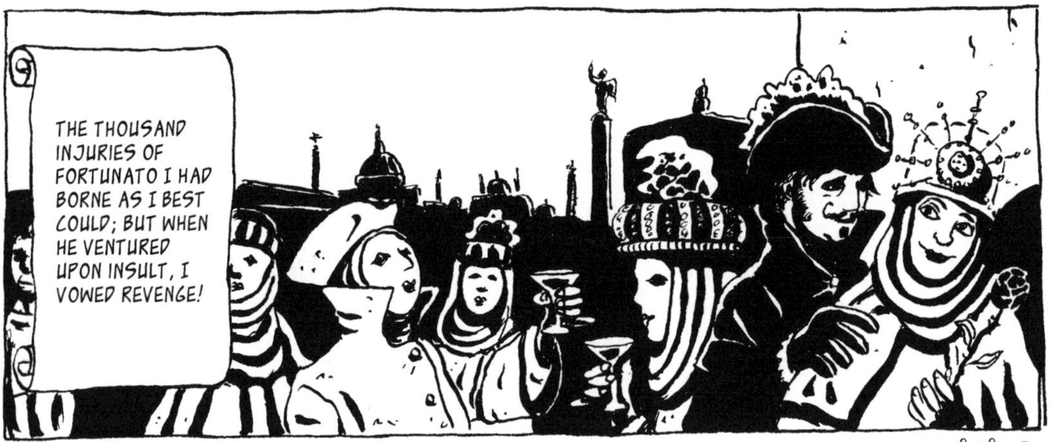
THE THOUSAND INJURIES OF FORTUNATO I HAD BORNE AS I BEST COULD; BUT WHEN HE VENTURED UPON INSULT, I VOWED REVENGE!

EDGAR ALLAN POE PEDRO LOPEZ

The Cask of Amontillado

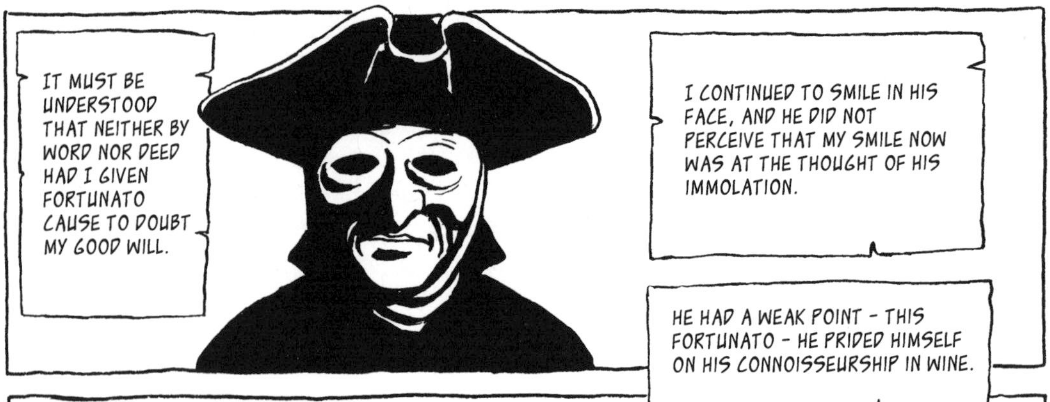
IT MUST BE UNDERSTOOD THAT NEITHER BY WORD NOR DEED HAD I GIVEN FORTUNATO CAUSE TO DOUBT MY GOOD WILL.
I CONTINUED TO SMILE IN HIS FACE, AND HE DID NOT PERCEIVE THAT MY SMILE NOW WAS AT THE THOUGHT OF HIS IMMOLATION.
HE HAD A WEAK POINT - THIS FORTUNATO - HE PRIDED HIMSELF ON HIS CONNOISSEURSHIP IN WINE.

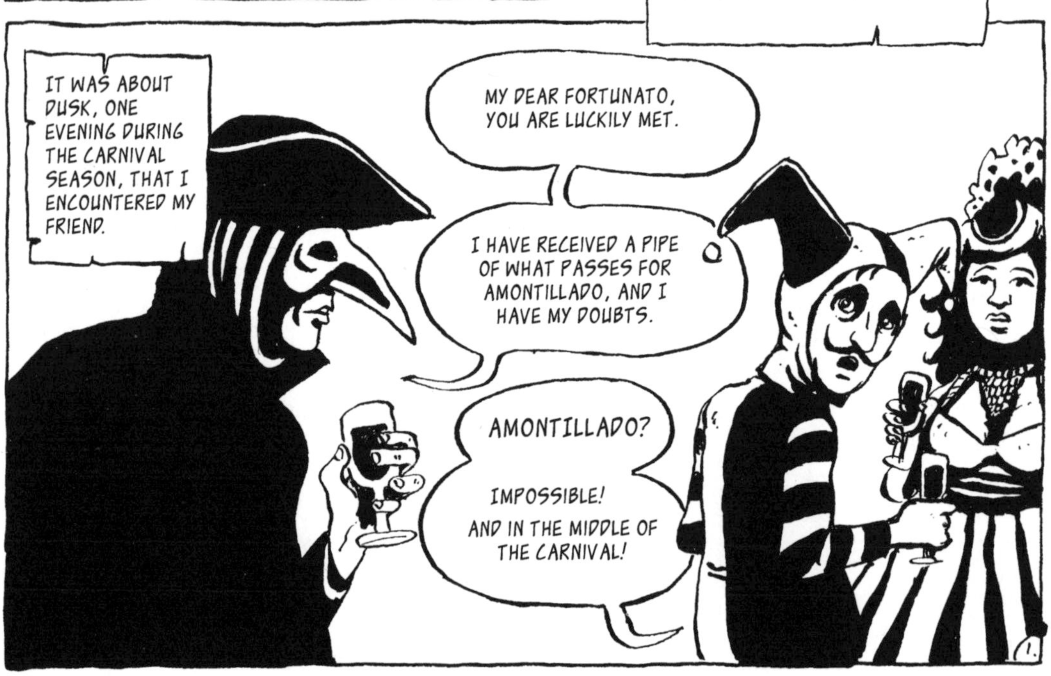
IT WAS ABOUT DUSK, ONE EVENING DURING THE CARNIVAL SEASON, THAT I ENCOUNTERED MY FRIEND.
MY DEAR FORTUNATO, YOU ARE LUCKILY MET.
I HAVE RECEIVED A PIPE OF WHAT PASSES FOR AMONTILLADO, AND I HAVE MY DOUBTS.
AMONTILLADO?
IMPOSSIBLE!
AND IN THE MIDDLE OF THE CARNIVAL!

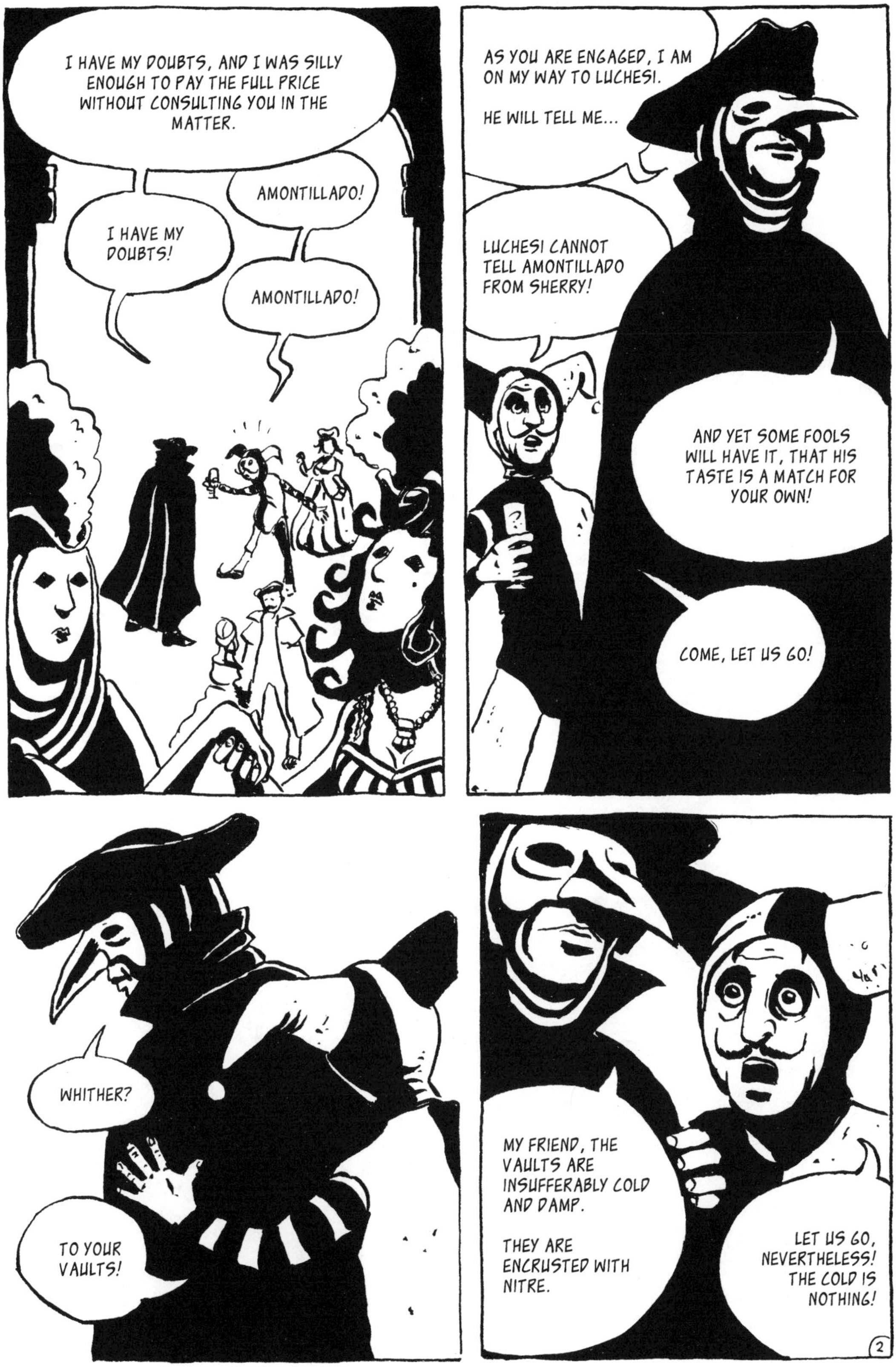
I HAVE MY DOUBTS, AND I WAS SILLY ENOUGH TO PAY THE FULL PRICE WITHOUT CONSULTING YOU IN THE MATTER.
AMONTILLADO!
I HAVE MY DOUBTS!
AMONTILLADO!
AS YOU ARE ENGAGED, I AM ON MY WAY TO LUCHESI.
HE WILL TELL ME...
LUCHESI CANNOT TELL AMONTILLADO FROM SHERRY!
AND YET SOME FOOLS WILL HAVE IT, THAT HIS TASTE IS A MATCH FOR YOUR OWN!
COME, LET US GO!
WHITHER?
TO YOUR VAULTS!
MY FRIEND, THE VAULTS ARE INSUFFERABLY COLD AND DAMP.
THEY ARE ENCRUSTED WITH NITRE.
LET US GO, NEVERTHELESS! THE COLD IS NOTHING!
2

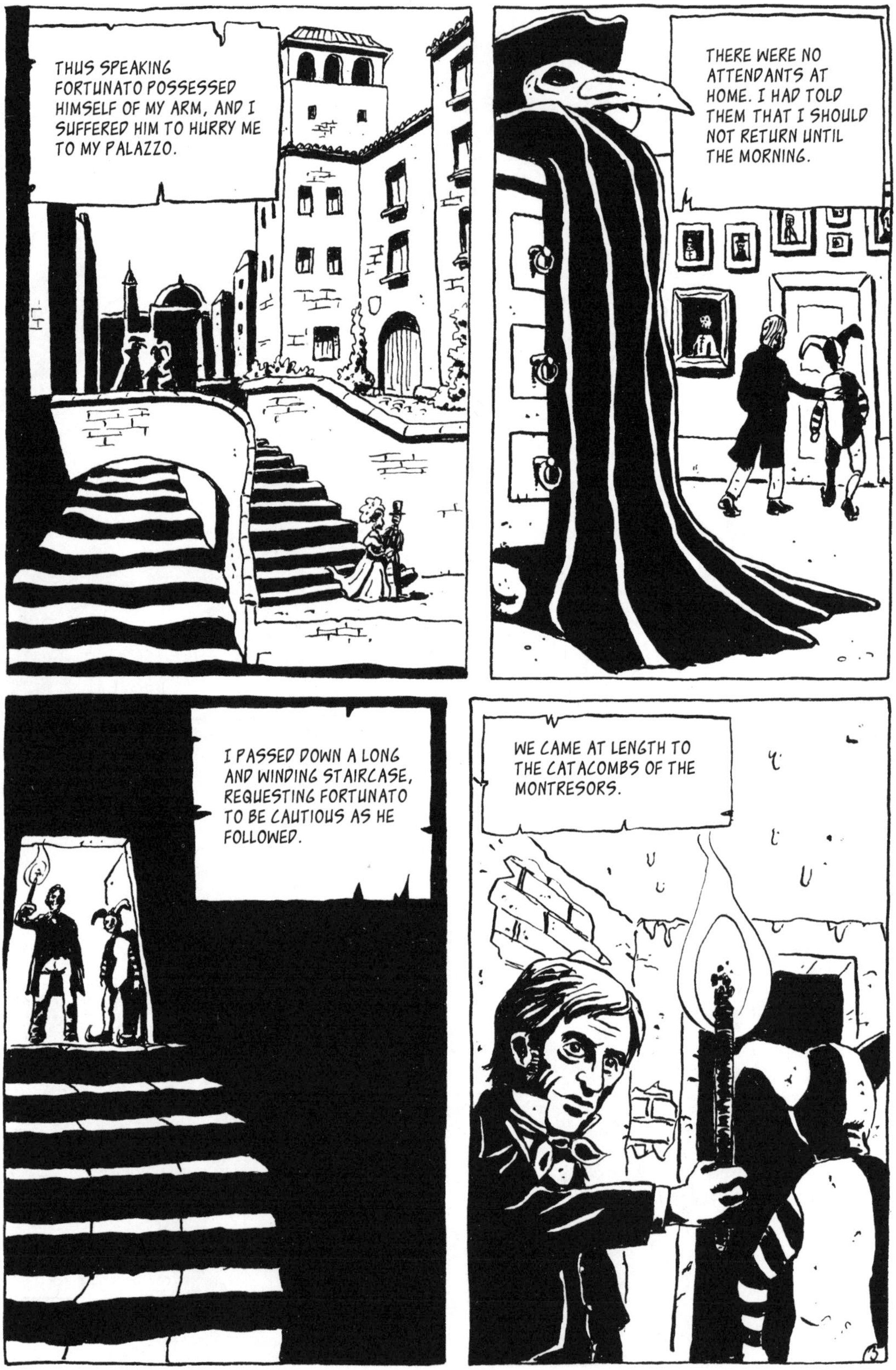
THUS SPEAKING FORTUNATO POSSESSED HIMSELF OF MY ARM, AND I SUFFERED HIM TO HURRY ME TO MY PALAZZO.
THERE WERE NO ATTENDANTS AT HOME. I HAD TOLD THEM THAT I SHOULD NOT RETURN UNTIL THE MORNING.
I PASSED DOWN A LONG AND WINDING STAIRCASE, REQUESTING FORTUNATO TO BE CAUTIOUS AS HE FOLLOWED.
WE CAME AT LENGTH TO THE CATACOMBS OF THE MONTRESORS.

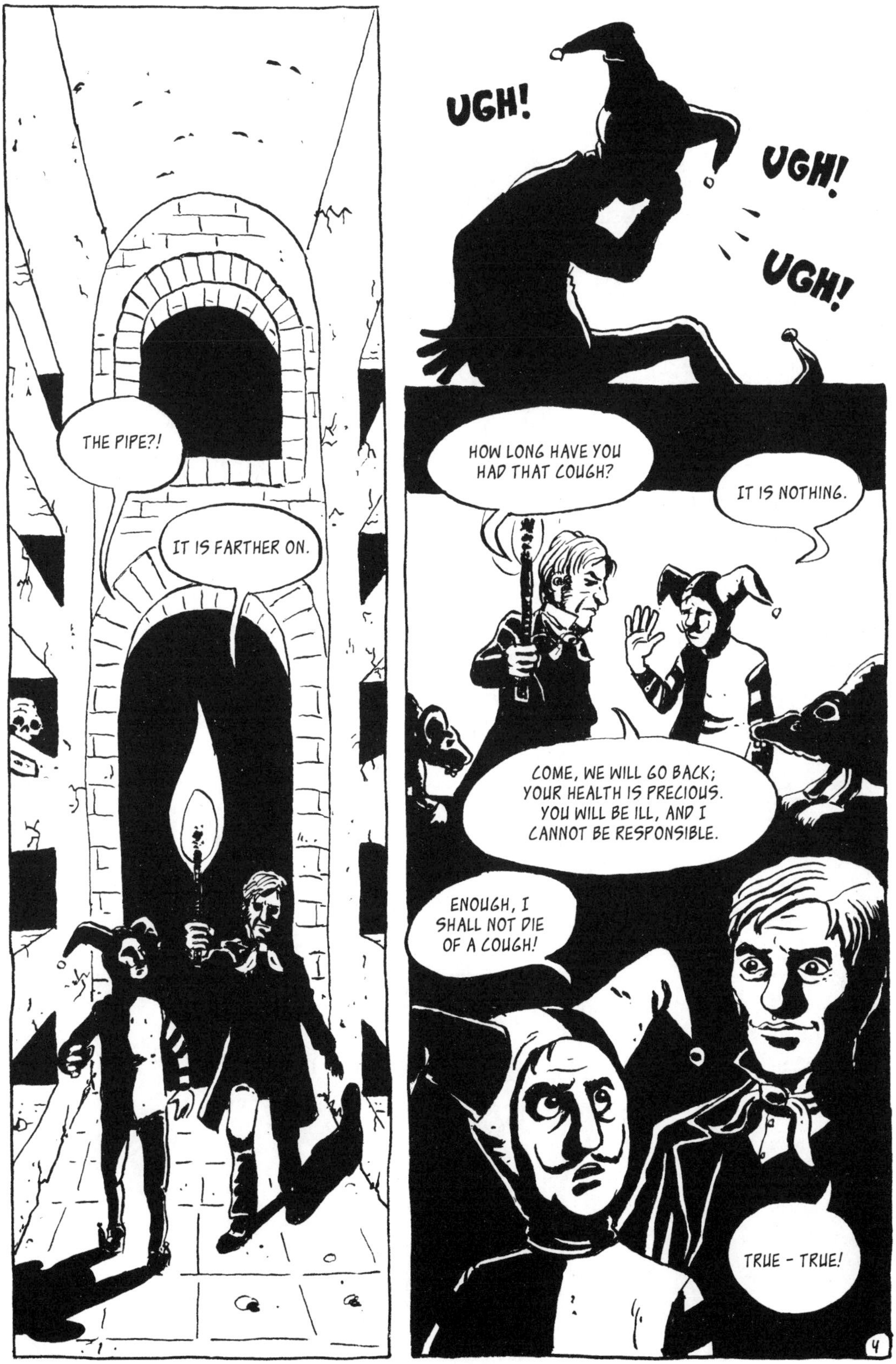
THE PIPE?!
IT IS FARTHER ON.
UGH!
UGH!
UGH!
HOW LONG HAVE YOU HAD THAT COUGH?
IT IS NOTHING.
COME, WE WILL GO BACK; YOUR HEALTH IS PRECIOUS. YOU WILL BE ILL, AND I CANNOT BE RESPONSIBLE.
ENOUGH, I SHALL NOT DIE OF A COUGH!
TRUE - TRUE!
4

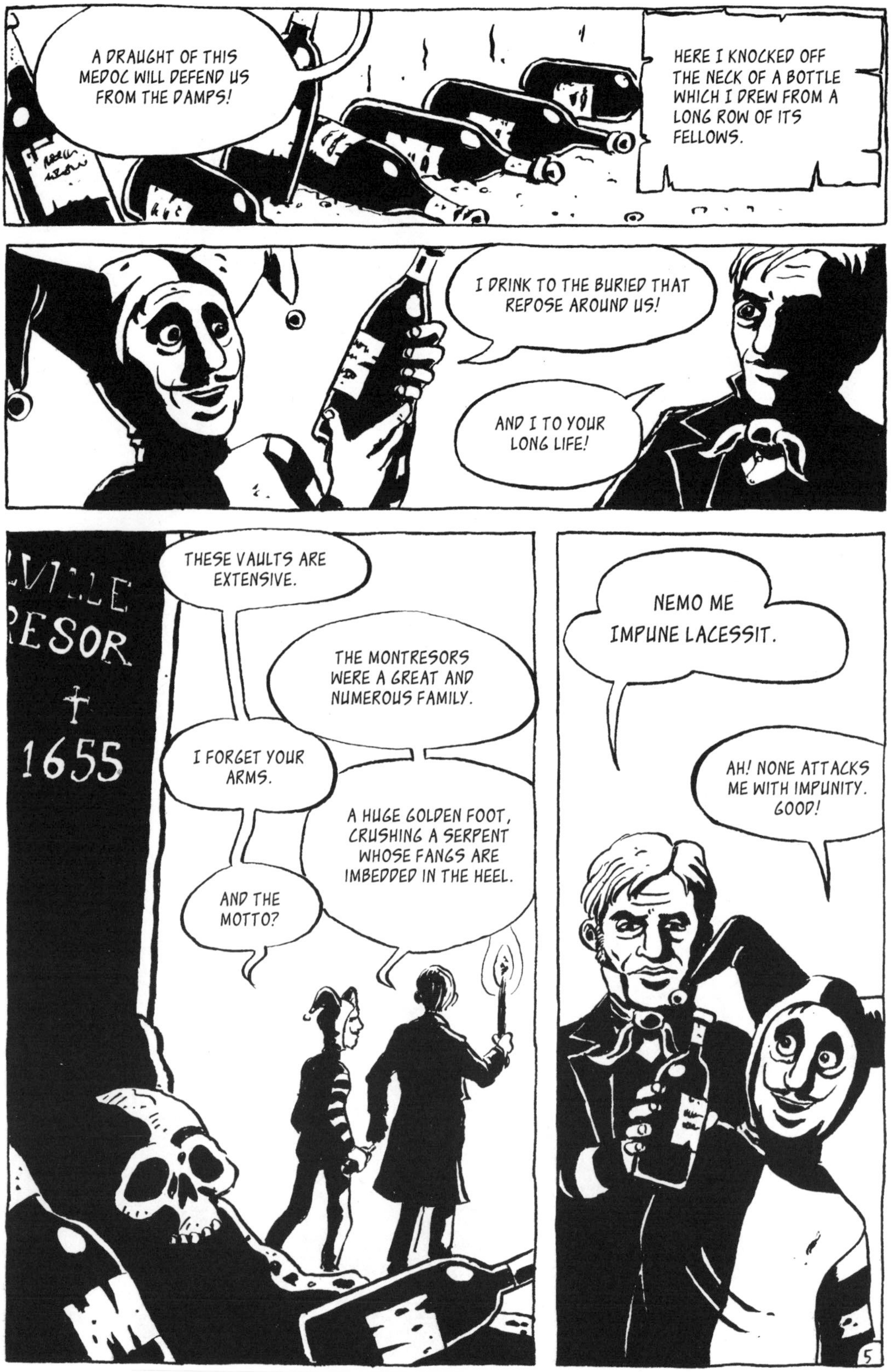
A DRAUGHT OF THIS MEDOC WILL DEFEND US FROM THE DAMPS!
HERE I KNOCKED OFF THE NECK OF A BOTTLE WHICH I DREW FROM A LONG ROW OF ITS FELLOWS.
I DRINK TO THE BURIED THAT REPOSE AROUND US!
AND I TO YOUR LONG LIFE!
LVILLE
RESOR
1655
THESE VAULTS ARE EXTENSIVE.
THE MONTRESORS WERE A GREAT AND NUMEROUS FAMILY.
I FORGET YOUR ARMS.
A HUGE GOLDEN FOOT, CRUSHING A SERPENT WHOSE FANGS ARE IMBEDDED IN THE HEEL.
AND THE MOTTO?
NEMO ME IMPUNE LACESSIT.
AH! NONE ATTACKS ME WITH IMPUNITY. GOOD!
5

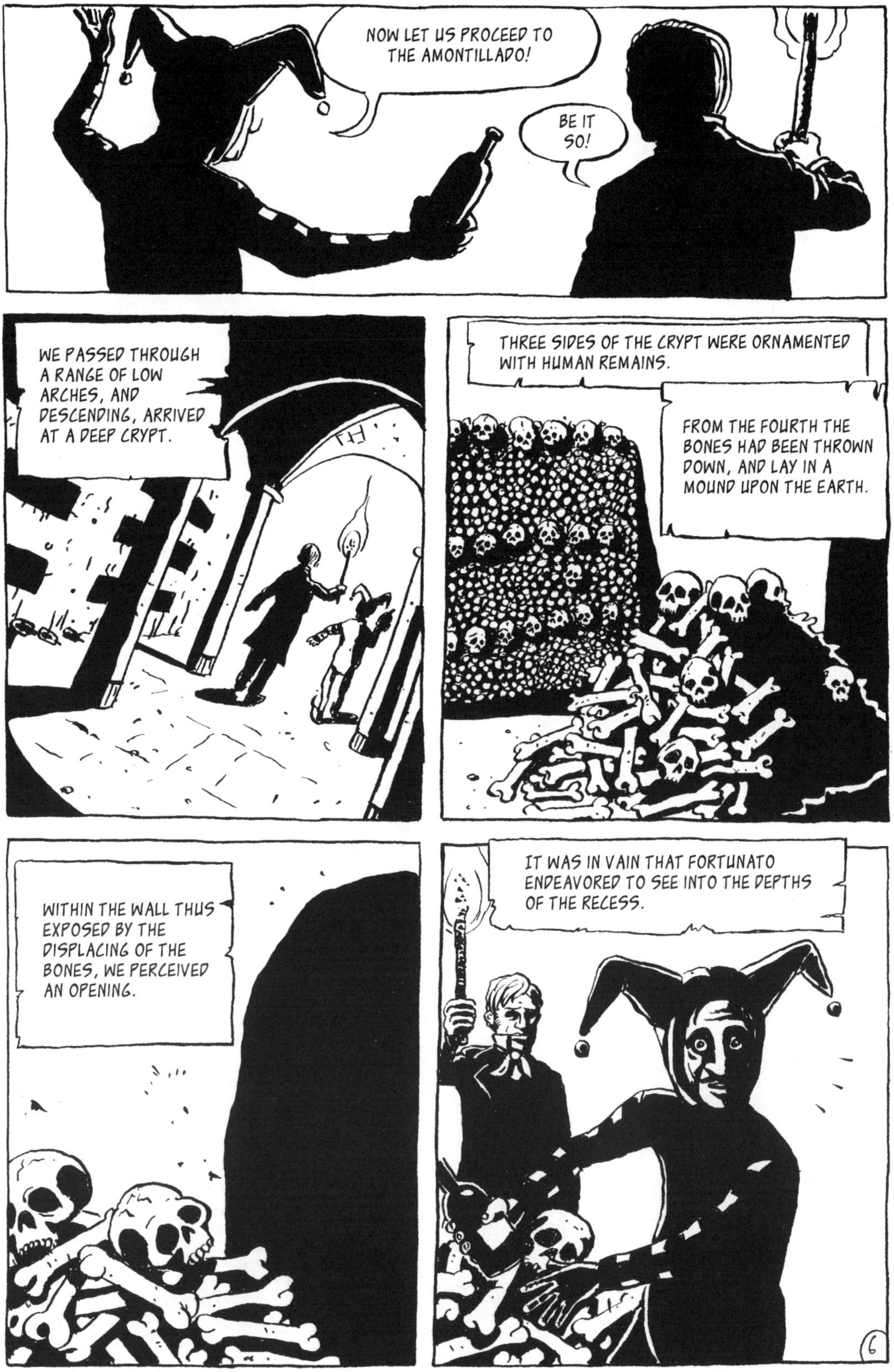
NOW LET US PROCEED TO THE AMONTILLADO!
BE IT SO!
WE PASSED THROUGH A RANGE OF LOW ARCHES, AND DESCENDING, ARRIVED AT A DEEP CRYPT.
THREE SIDES OF THE CRYPT WERE ORNAMENTED WITH HUMAN REMAINS.
FROM THE FOURTH THE BONES HAD BEEN THROWN DOWN, AND LAY IN A MOUND UPON THE EARTH.
WITHIN THE WALL THUS EXPOSED BY THE DISPLACING OF THE BONES, WE PERCEIVED AN OPENING.
IT WAS IN VAIN THAT FORTUNATO ENDEAVORED TO SEE INTO THE DEPTHS OF THE RECESS.
6

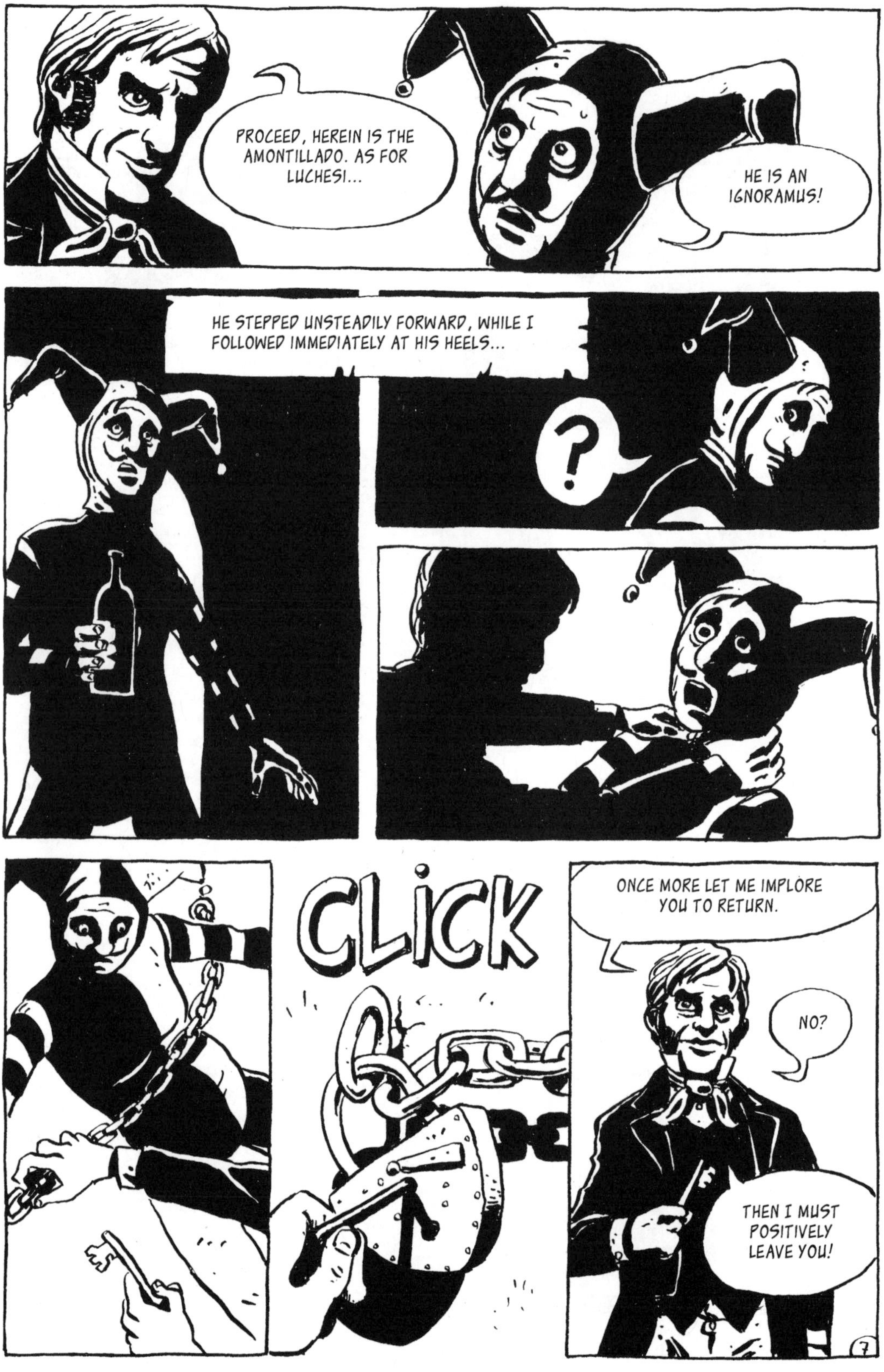
PROCEED, HEREIN IS THE AMONTILLADO. AS FOR LUCHESI...
HE IS AN IGNORAMUS!
HE STEPPED UNSTEADILY FORWARD, WHILE I FOLLOWED IMMEDIATELY AT HIS HEELS...
?
CLICK
ONCE MORE LET ME IMPLORE YOU TO RETURN.
NO?
THEN I MUST POSITIVELY LEAVE YOU!
7

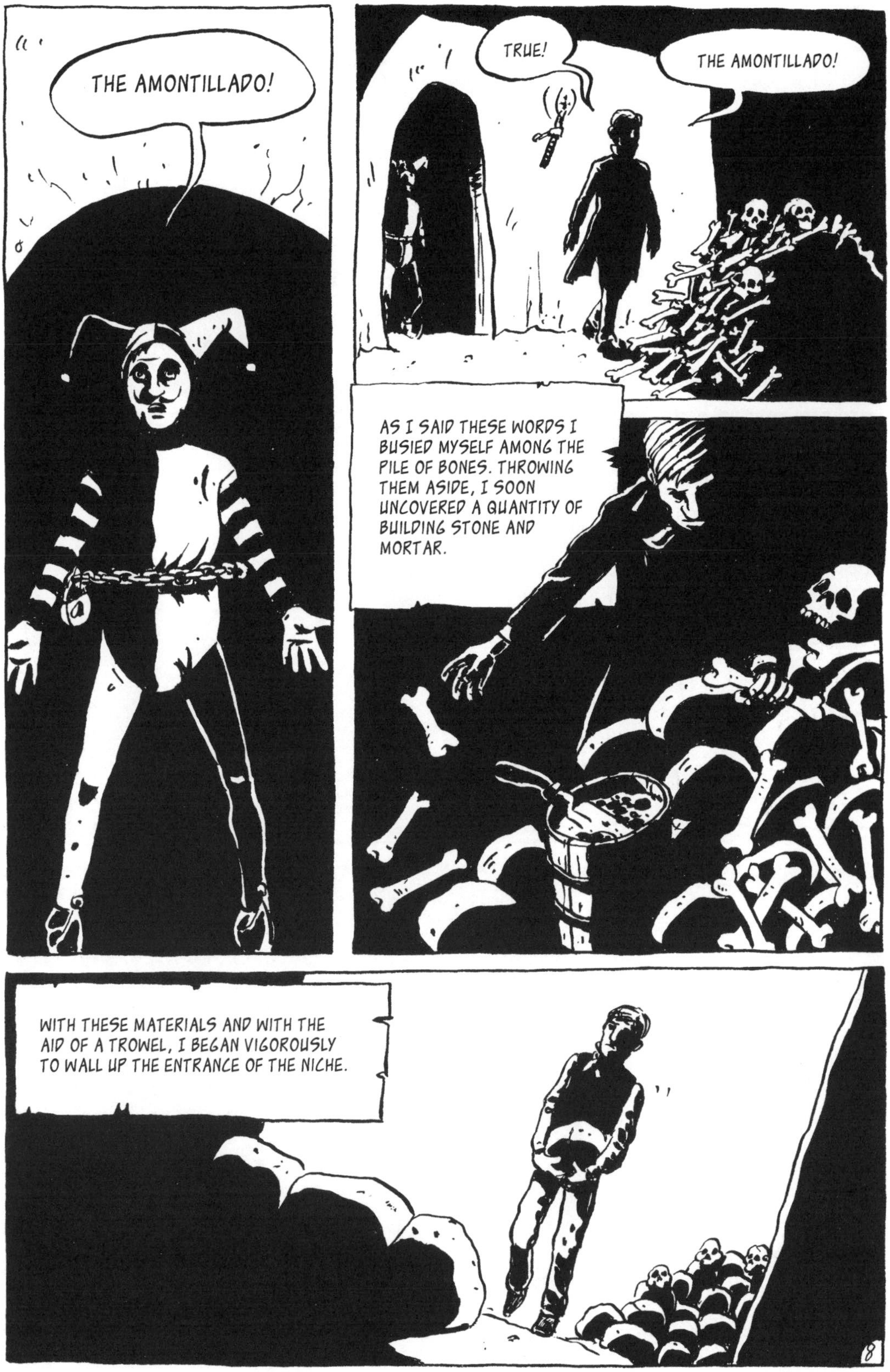
THE AMONTILLADO!
TRUE!
THE AMONTILLADO!
AS I SAID THESE WORDS I BUSIED MYSELF AMONG THE PILE OF BONES. THROWING THEM ASIDE, I SOON UNCOVERED A QUANTITY OF BUILDING STONE AND MORTAR.
WITH THESE MATERIALS AND WITH THE AID OF A TROWEL, I BEGAN VIGOROUSLY TO WALL UP THE ENTRANCE OF THE NICHE.
8

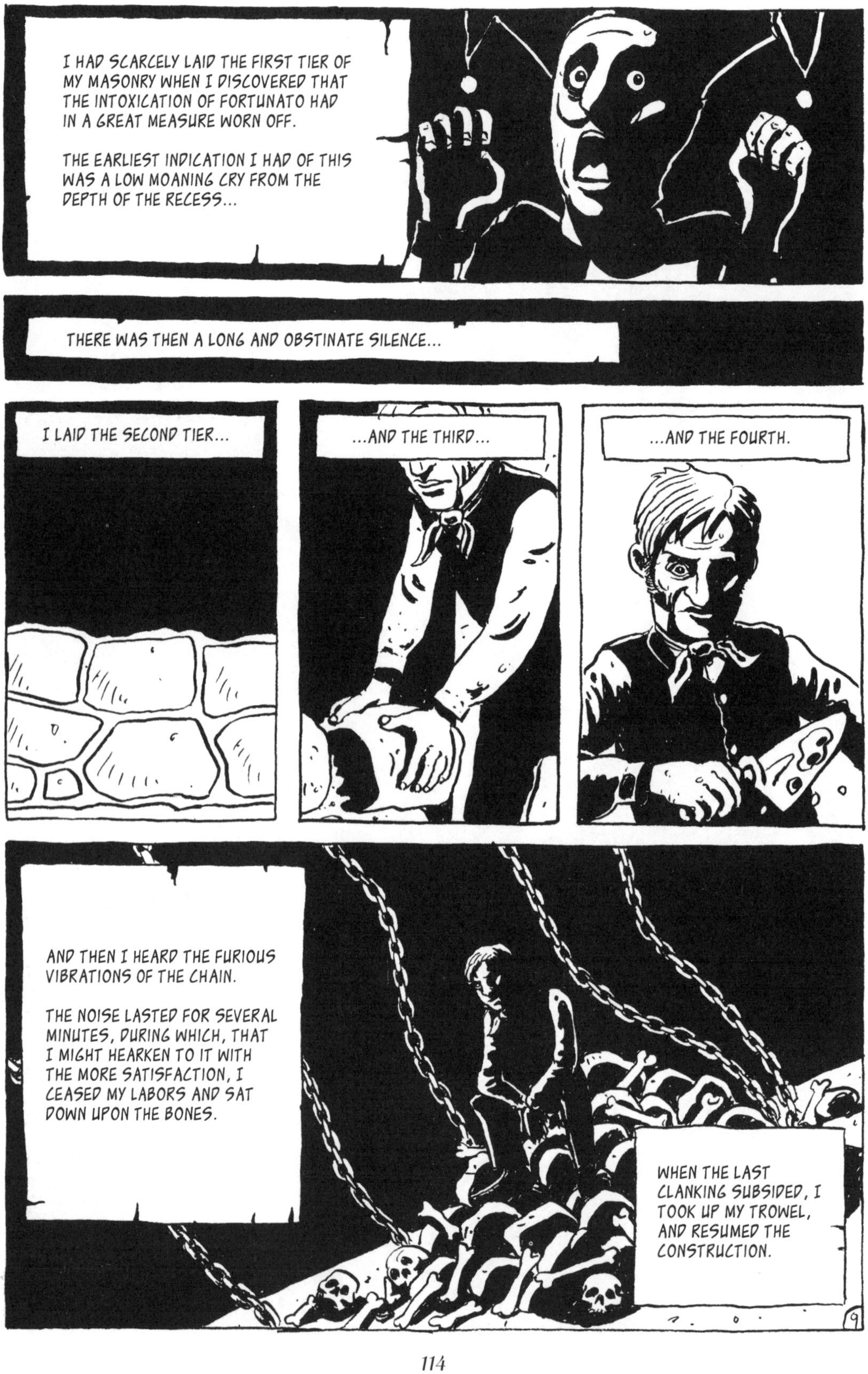
I HAD SCARCELY LAID THE FIRST TIER OF MY MASONRY WHEN I DISCOVERED THAT THE INTOXICATION OF FORTUNATO HAD IN A GREAT MEASURE WORN OFF.
THE EARLIEST INDICATION I HAD OF THIS WAS A LOW MOANING CRY FROM THE DEPTH OF THE RECESS...
THERE WAS THEN A LONG AND OBSTINATE SILENCE...
I LAID THE SECOND TIER...
...AND THE THIRD...
...AND THE FOURTH.
AND THEN I HEARD THE FURIOUS VIBRATIONS OF THE CHAIN.
THE NOISE LASTED FOR SEVERAL MINUTES, DURING WHICH, THAT I MIGHT HEARKEN TO IT WITH THE MORE SATISFACTION, I CEASED MY LABORS AND SAT DOWN UPON THE BONES.
WHEN THE LAST CLANKING SUBSIDED, I TOOK UP MY TROWEL, AND RESUMED THE CONSTRUCTION.
9

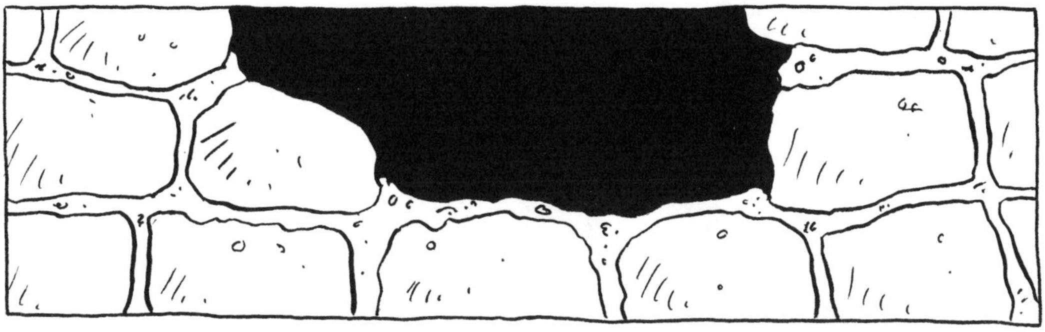

IT WAS NOW MIDNIGHT, AND MY TASK WAS DRAWING TO A CLOSE. I HAD COMPLETED THE TENTH TIER, AND I HAD FINISHED A PORTION OF THE LAST; THERE REMAINED BUT A SINGLE STONE TO BE FITTED AND PLASTERED IN. I STRUGGLED WITH ITS WEIGHT; I PLACED IT PARTIALLY IN ITS DESTINED POSITION.

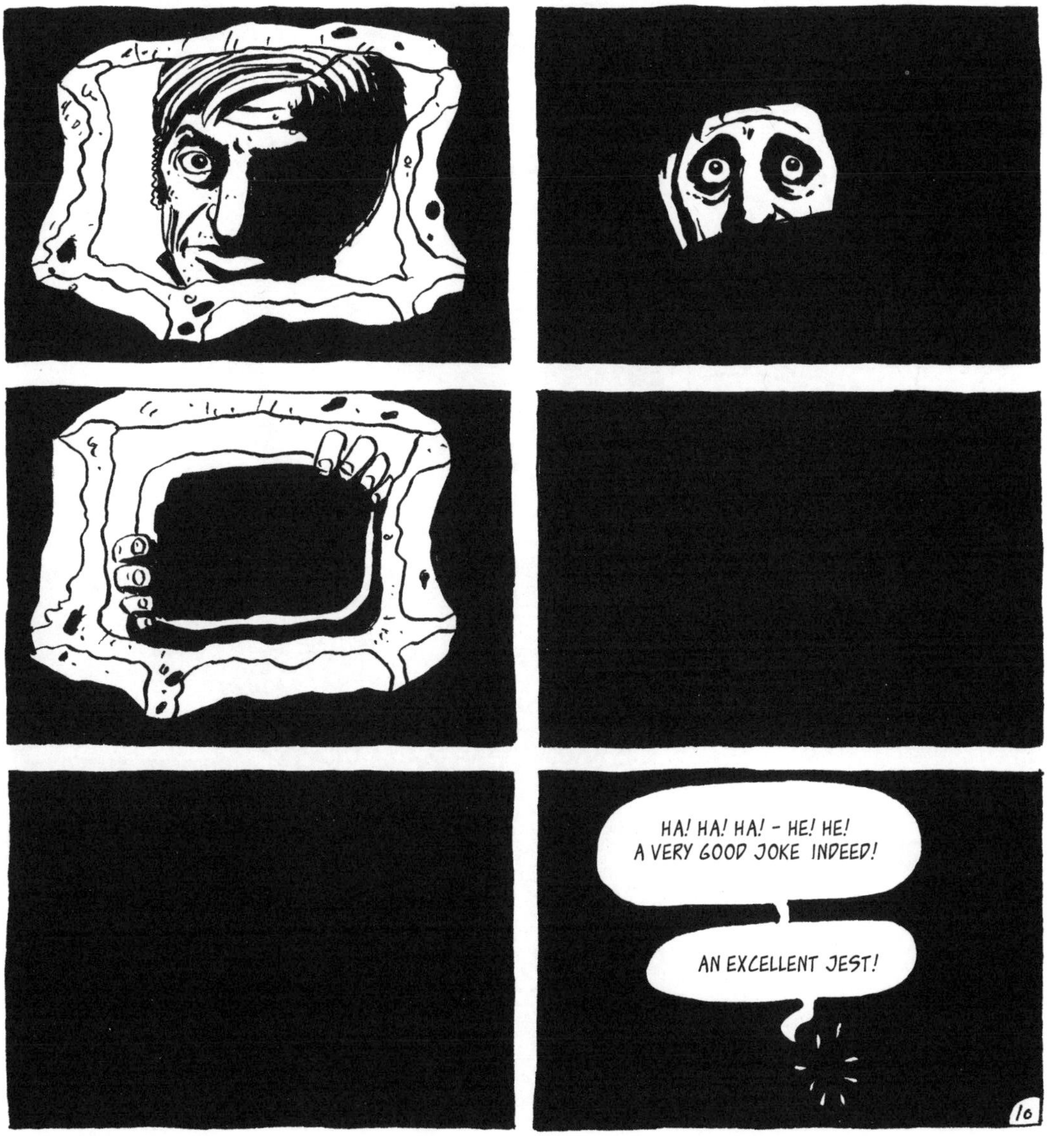
HA! HA! HA! - HE! HE!
A VERY GOOD JOKE INDEED!
AN EXCELLENT JEST!
10

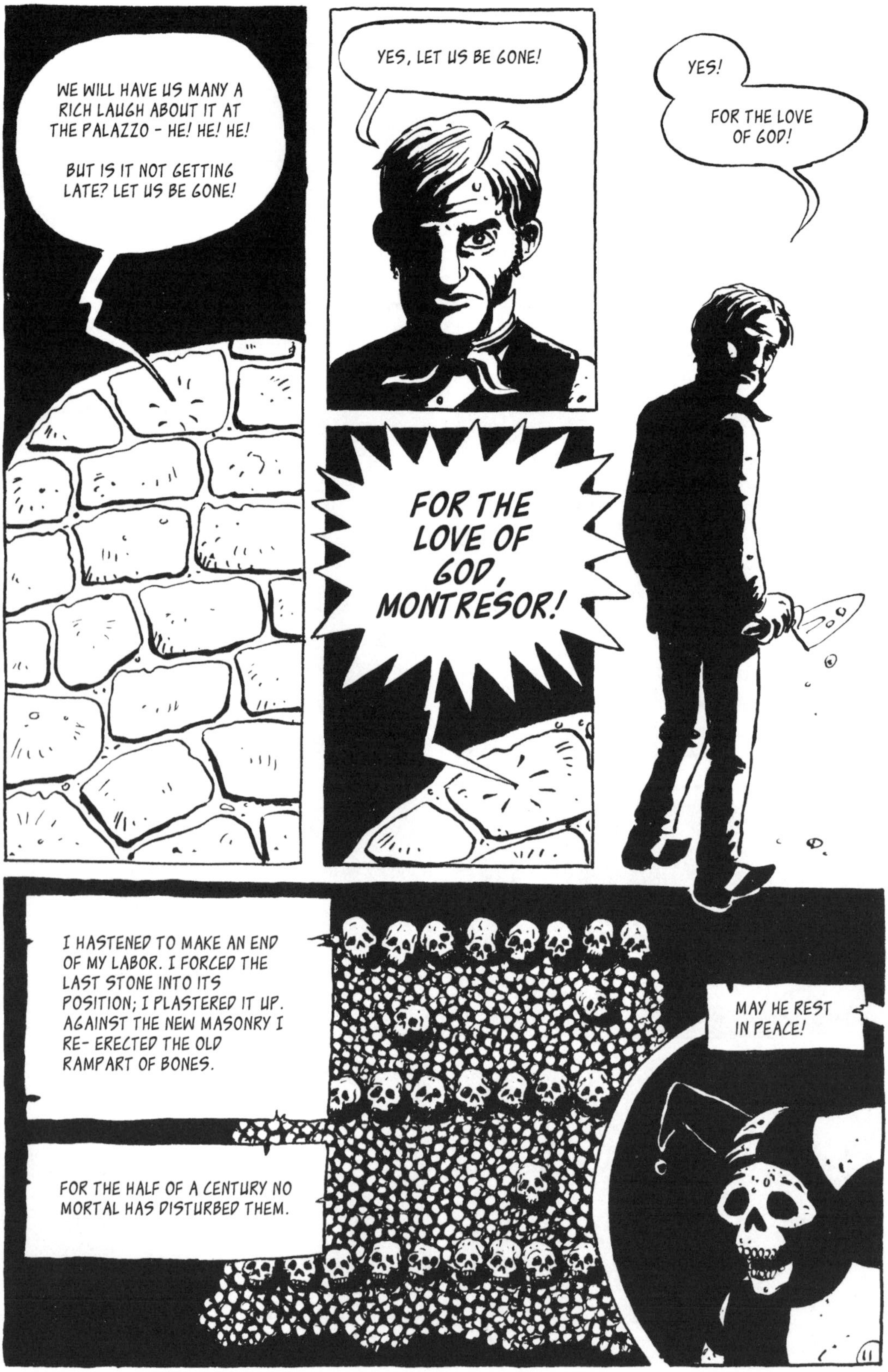
WE WILL HAVE US MANY A RICH LAUGH ABOUT IT AT THE PALAZZO – HE! HE! HE!
BUT IS IT NOT GETTING LATE? LET US BE GONE!
YES, LET US BE GONE!
FOR THE LOVE OF GOD, MONTRESOR!
YES!
FOR THE LOVE OF GOD!
I HASTENED TO MAKE AN END OF MY LABOR. I FORCED THE LAST STONE INTO ITS POSITION; I PLASTERED IT UP. AGAINST THE NEW MASONRY I RE- ERECTED THE OLD RAMPART OF BONES.
FOR THE HALF OF A CENTURY NO MORTAL HAS DISTURBED THEM.
MAY HE REST IN PEACE!

THE FALL OF THE HOUSE OF USHER

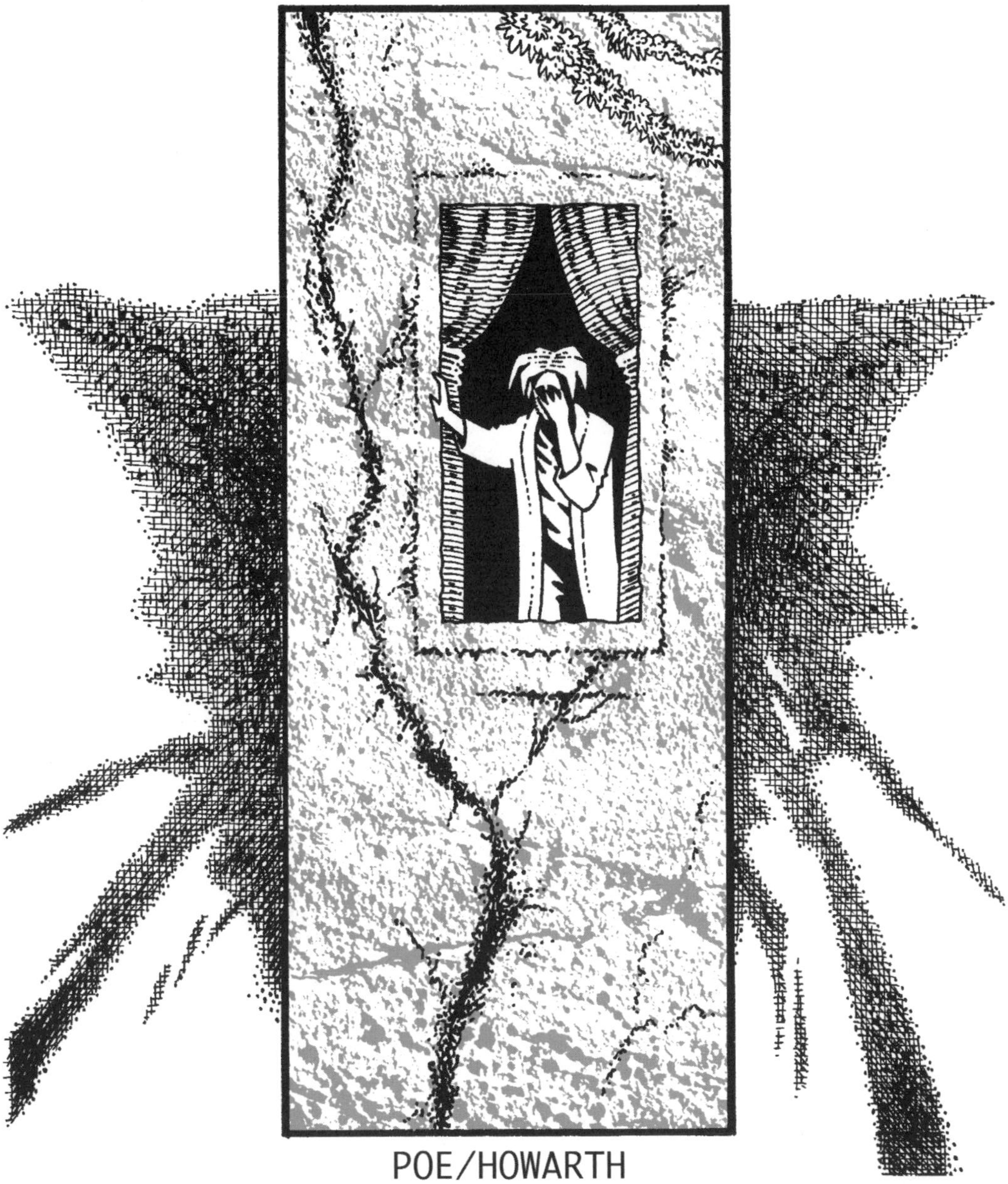

POE/HOWARTH

During the whole of a dark and soundless day in the autumn of the year, I had been passing alone, on horseback, through a singularly dreary tract of country; and at length found myself within view of the melancholy House of Usher. With the first glimpse of the building, a sense of insufferable gloom pervaded my spirit.

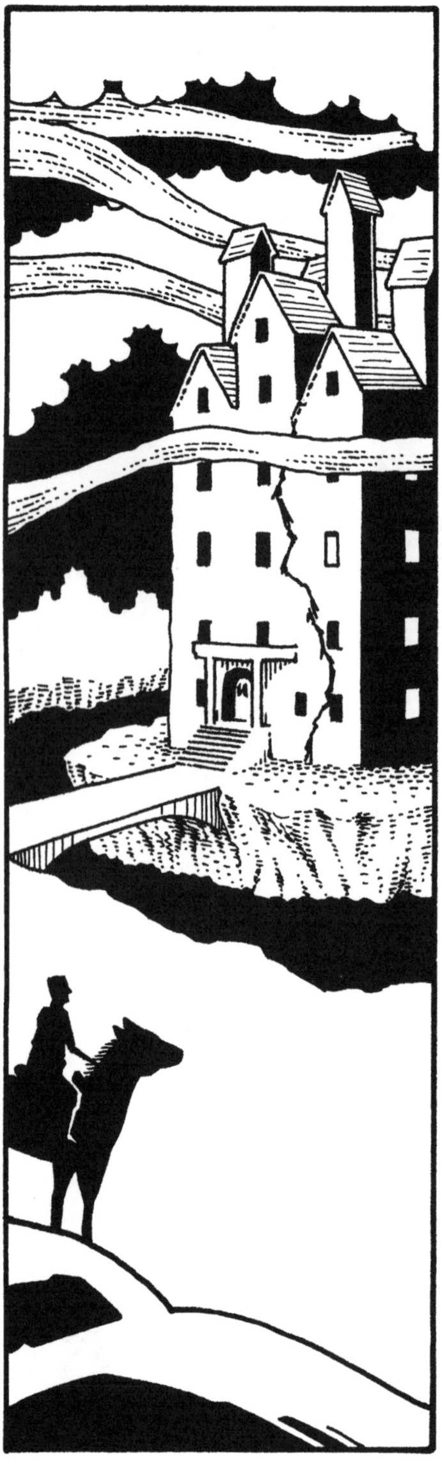

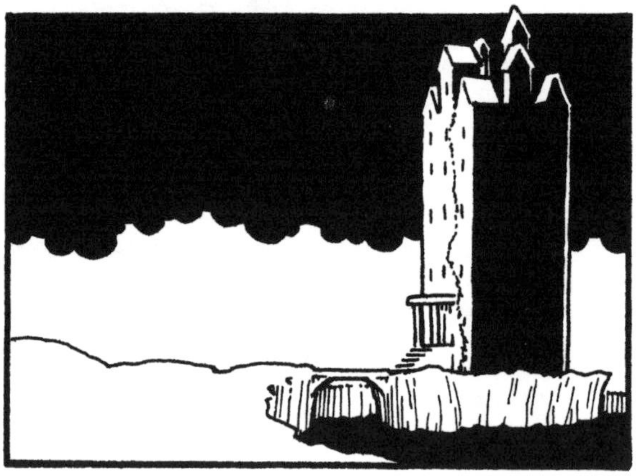

Nevertheless, in this mansion of gloom I now proposed to myself a sojourn of some weeks.

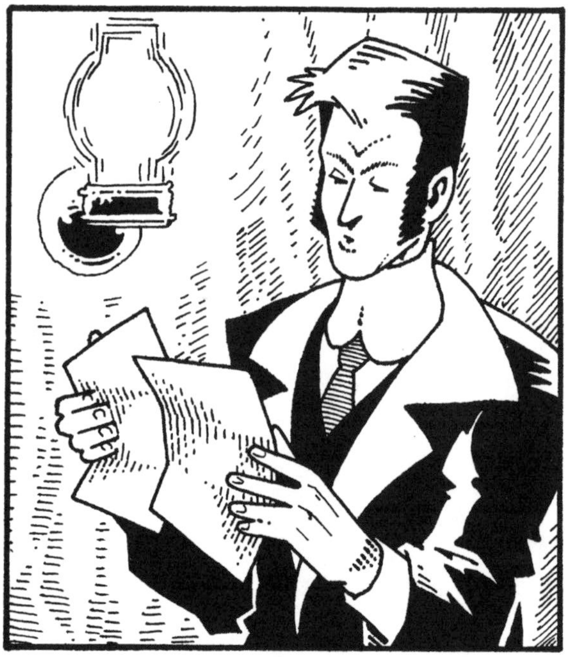

Its proprietor, Roderick Usher, had been one of my companions in boyhood; but many years had elapsed since our last meeting. A letter, however, had lately reached me which, in its wildly importunate nature, had admitted of no other than a personal reply. The writer spoke of acute bodily illness–of a mental disorder which oppressed him–and of an earnest desire to see me, as his best, and indeed his only personal friend. I accordingly obeyed forthwith what I considered a very singular summons.

Although, as boys, we had been intimate associates, I really knew little of my friend. His reserve had been always excessive and habitual.

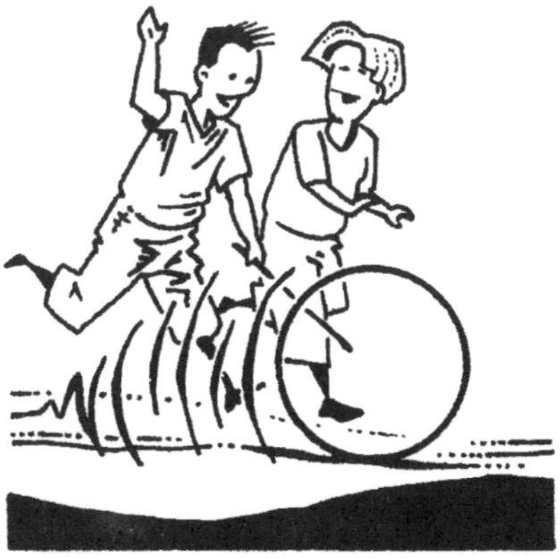

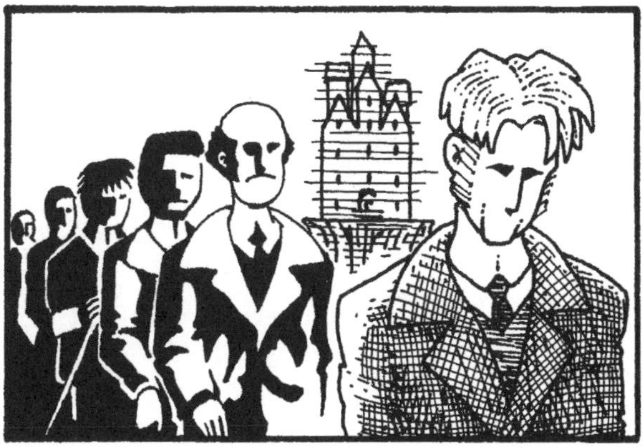

I was aware, however, of the very remarkable fact that the entire Usher family lay in the direct line of descent, and had always so lain. The undeviating transmission, from sire to son, of the patrimony with the name had, at length, merged the two in the quaint appellation of the "House of Usher"– which seemed to include both the family and the mansion.

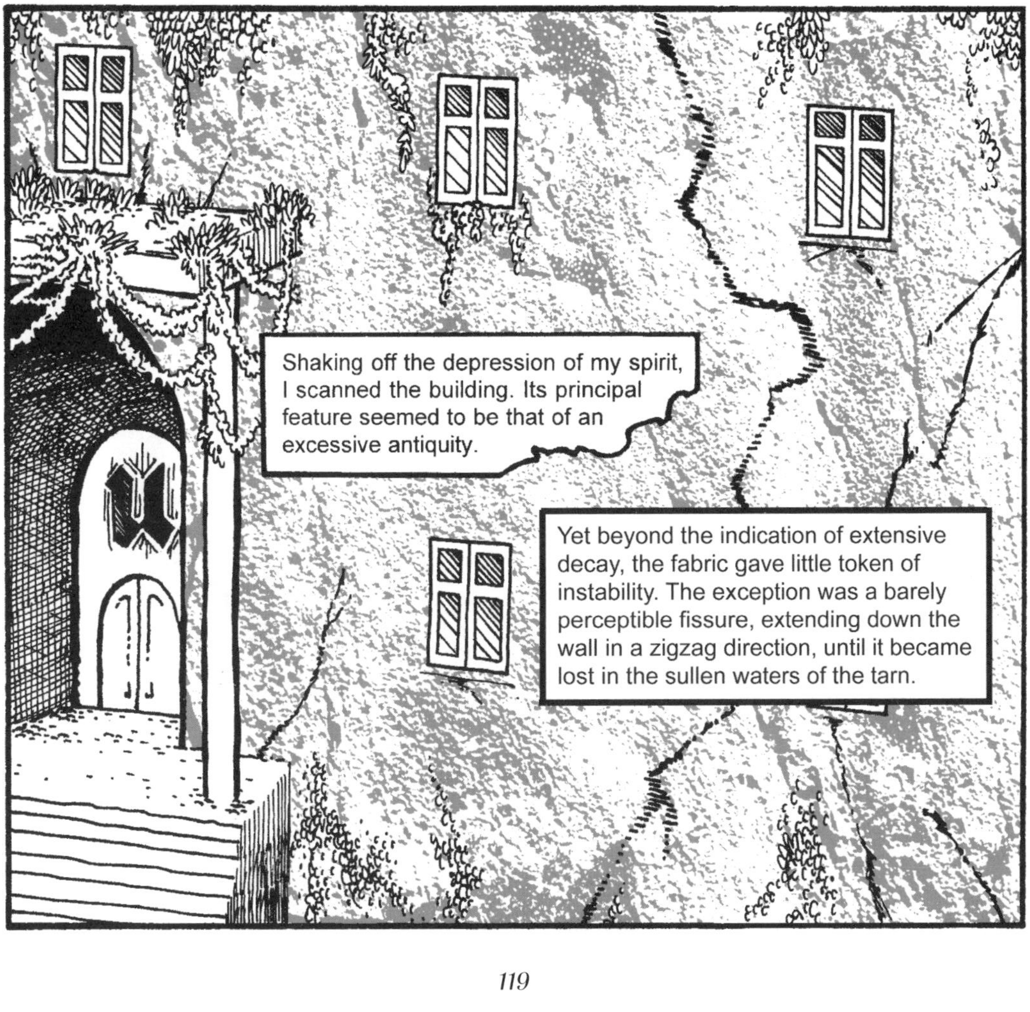
Shaking off the depression of my spirit, I scanned the building. Its principal feature seemed to be that of an excessive antiquity.
Yet beyond the indication of extensive decay, the fabric gave little token of instability. The exception was a barely perceptible fissure, extending down the wall in a zigzag direction, until it became lost in the sullen waters of the tarn.

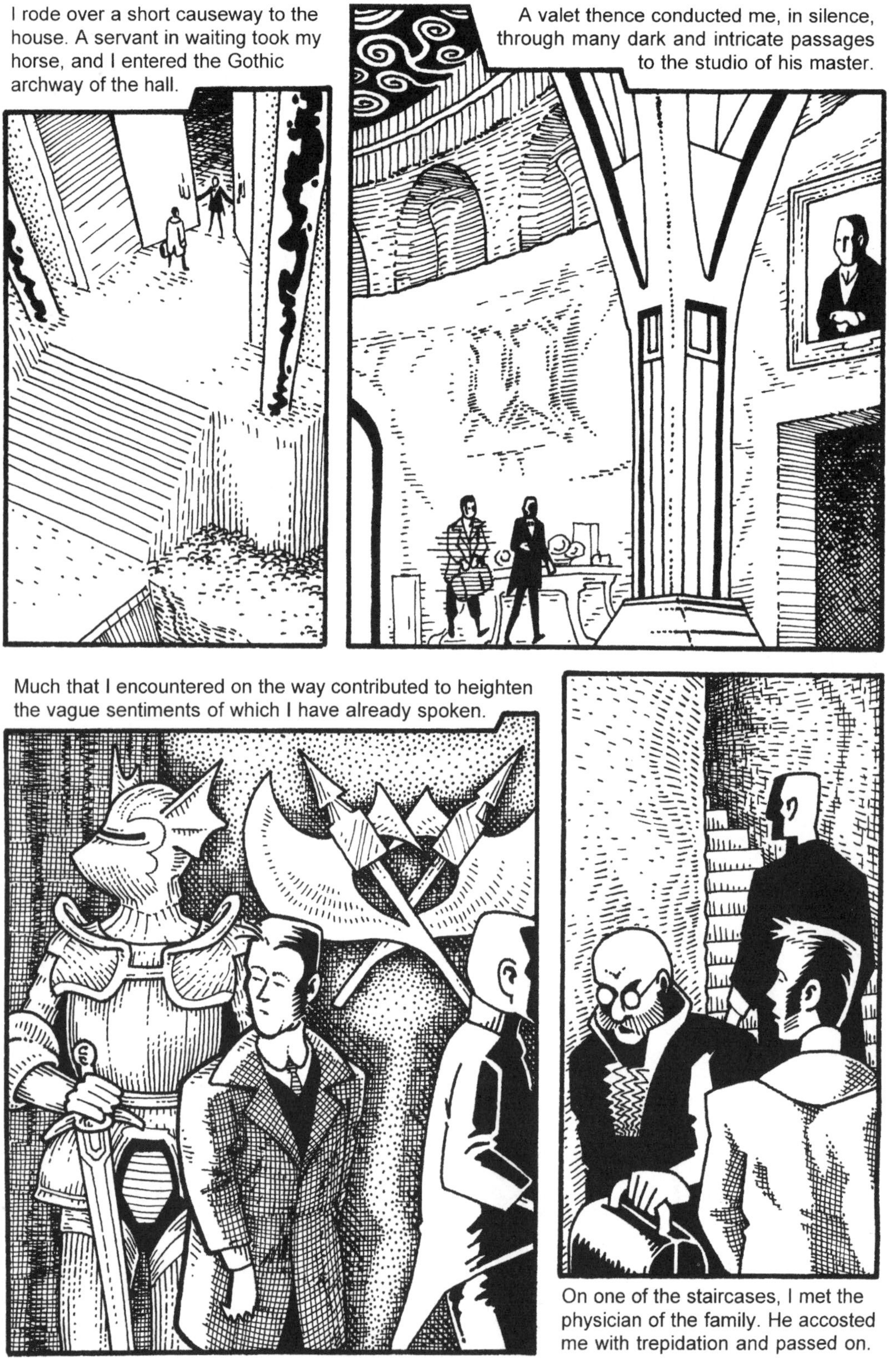
I rode over a short causeway to the house. A servant in waiting took my horse, and I entered the Gothic archway of the hall.
A valet thence conducted me, in silence, through many dark and intricate passages to the studio of his master.
Much that I encountered on the way contributed to heighten the vague sentiments of which I have already spoken.
On one of the staircases, I met the physician of the family. He accosted me with trepidation and passed on.

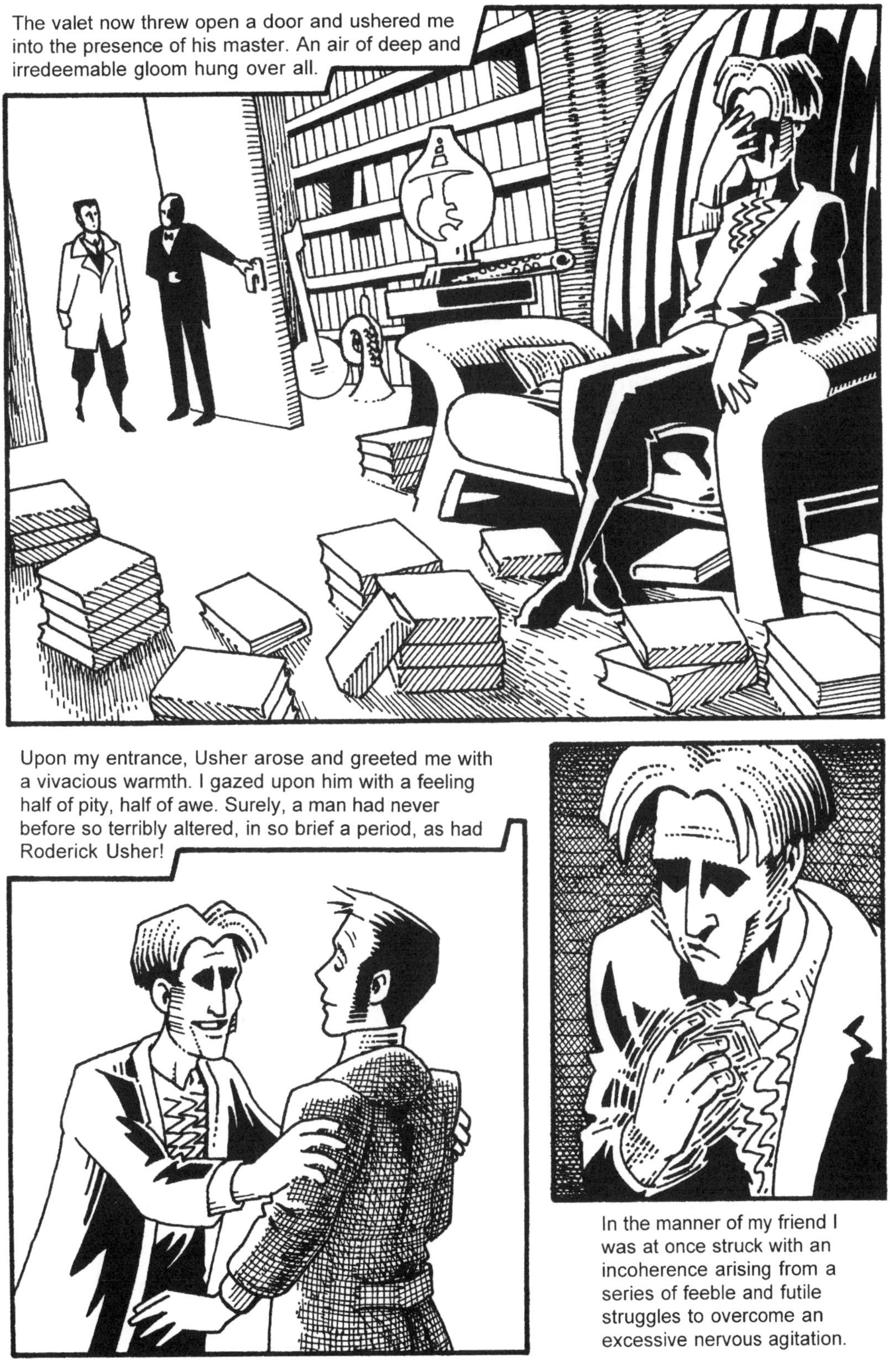
The valet now threw open a door and ushered me into the presence of his master. An air of deep and irredeemable gloom hung over all.
Upon my entrance, Usher arose and greeted me with a vivacious warmth. I gazed upon him with a feeling half of pity, half of awe. Surely, a man had never before so terribly altered, in so brief a period, as had Roderick Usher!
In the manner of my friend I was at once struck with an incoherence arising from a series of feeble and futile struggles to overcome an excessive nervous agitation.

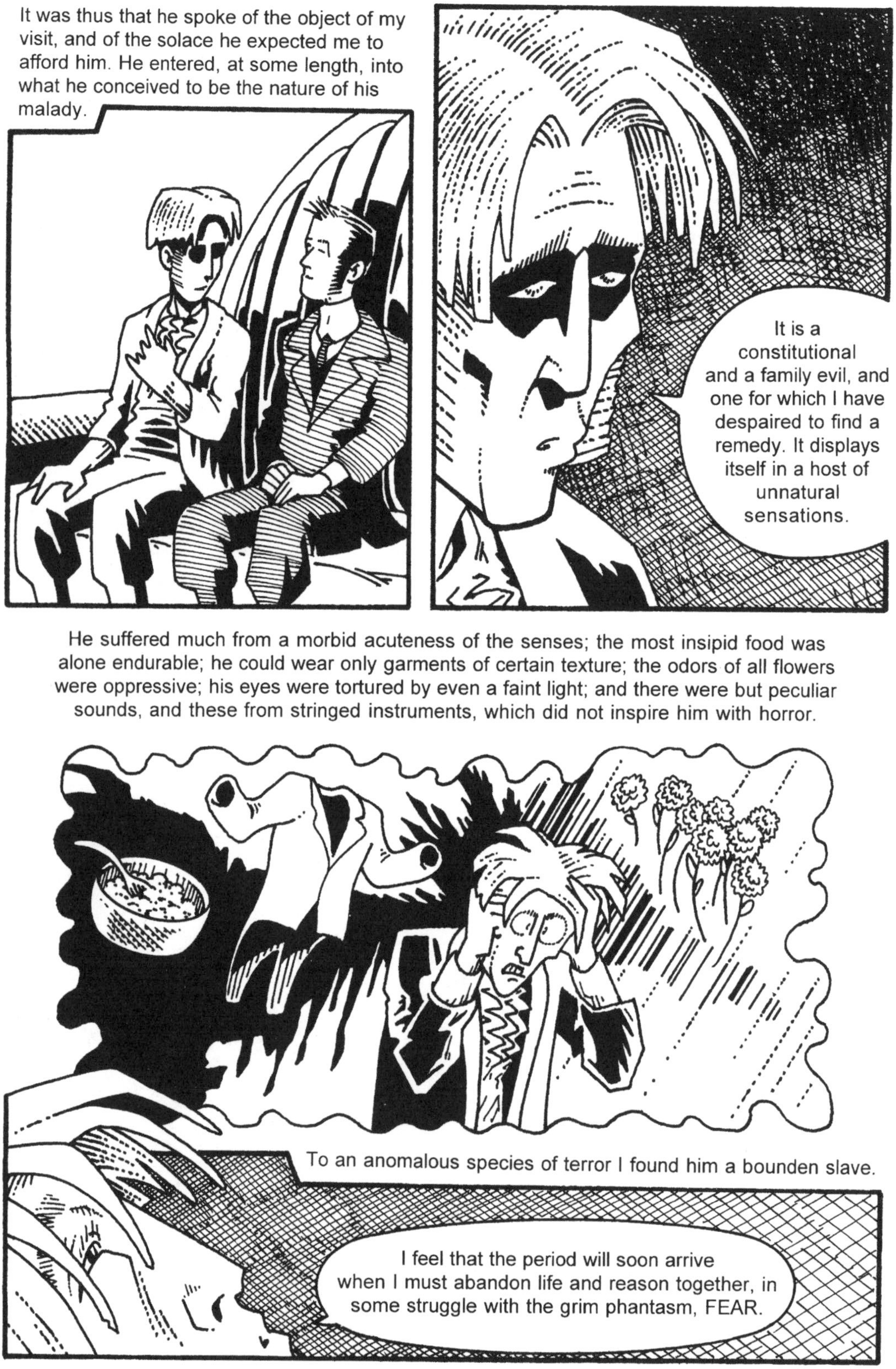
It was thus that he spoke of the object of my visit, and of the solace he expected me to afford him. He entered, at some length, into what he conceived to be the nature of his malady.
It is a constitutional and a family evil, and one for which I have despaired to find a remedy. It displays itself in a host of unnatural sensations.
He suffered much from a morbid acuteness of the senses; the most insipid food was alone endurable; he could wear only garments of certain texture; the odors of all flowers were oppressive; his eyes were tortured by even a faint light; and there were but peculiar sounds, and these from stringed instruments, which did not inspire him with horror.
To an anomalous species of terror I found him a bounden slave.
I feel that the period will soon arrive when I must abandon life and reason together, in some struggle with the grim phantasm, FEAR.

He admitted, although with hesitation, that much of the peculiar gloom which thus afflicted him could be traced to a far more palpable origin–to the severe and long-continued illness of a beloved sister–his sole companion for long years, and his last relative on earth.

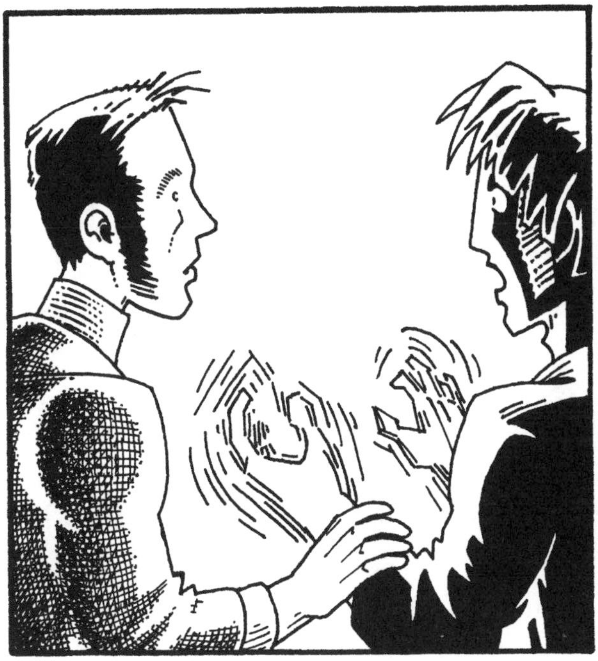

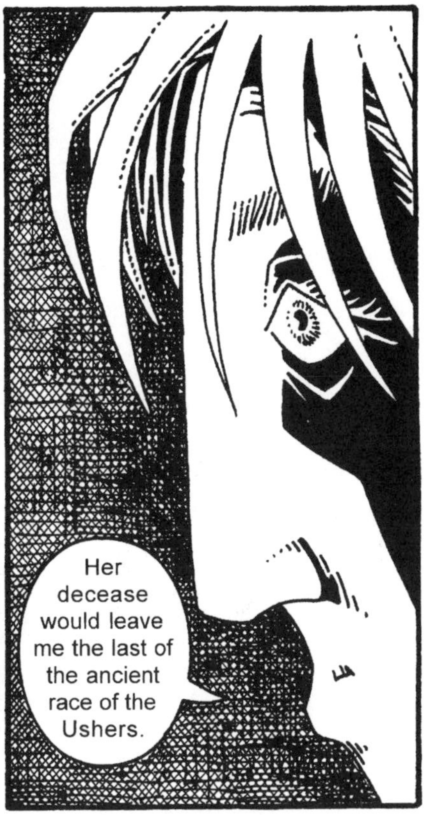
Her decease would leave me the last of the ancient race of the Ushers.

While he spoke, the lady Madeline passed slowly through the apartment. I regarded her with an astonishment not unmingled with dread.

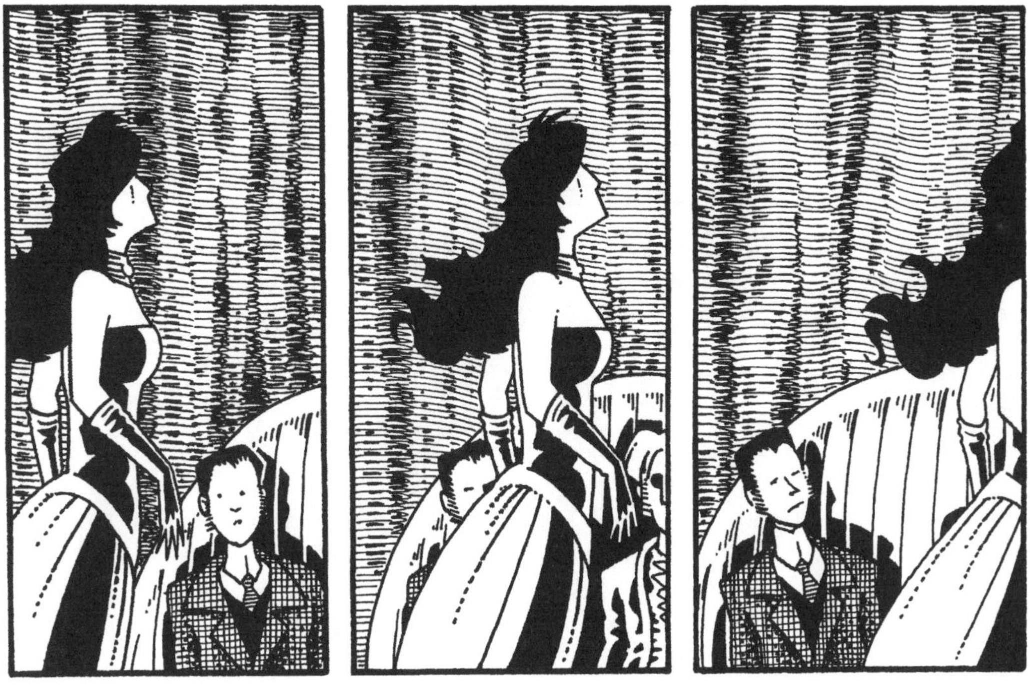

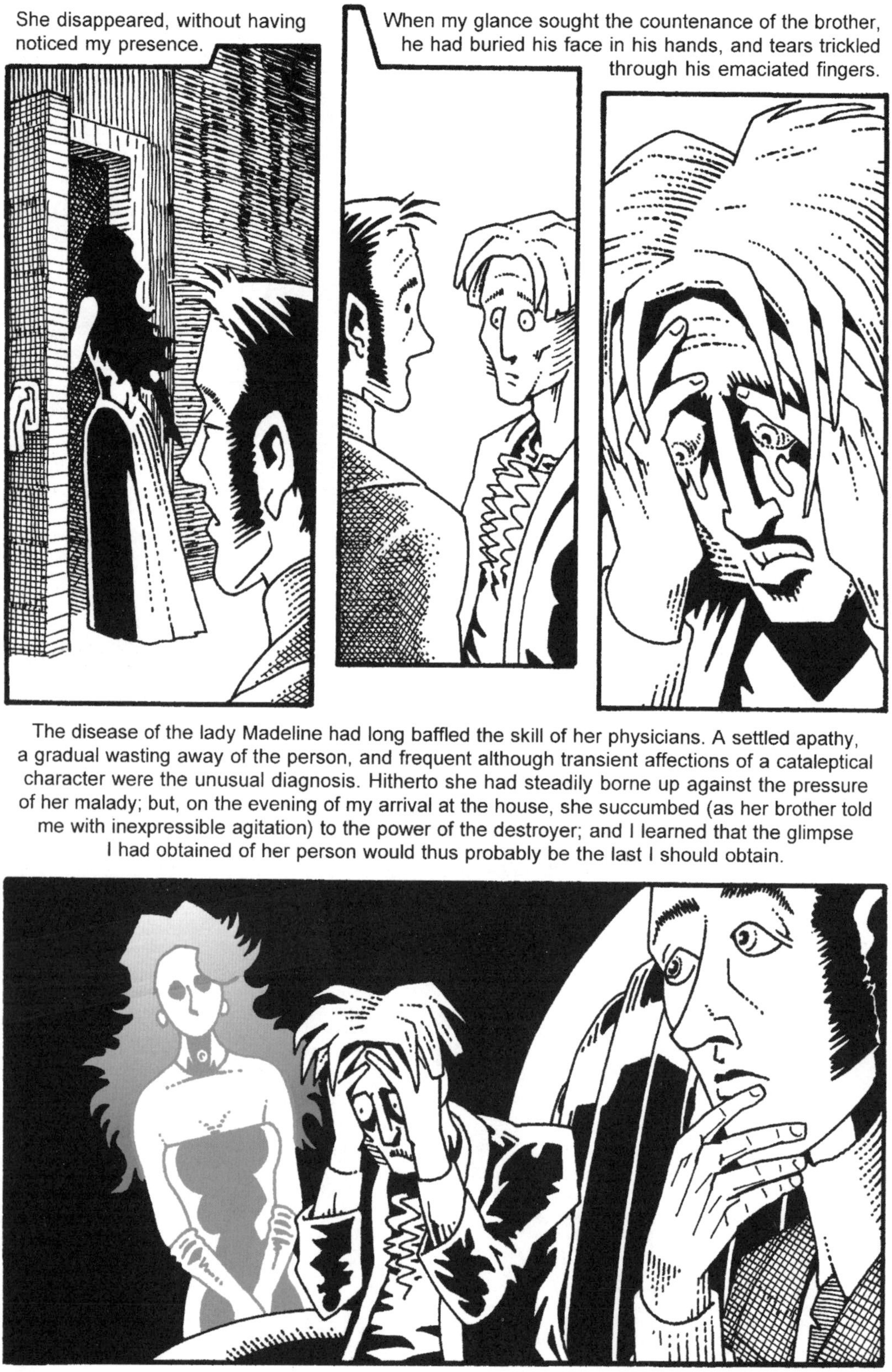
She disappeared, without having noticed my presence.
When my glance sought the countenance of the brother, he had buried his face in his hands, and tears trickled through his emaciated fingers.
The disease of the lady Madeline had long baffled the skill of her physicians. A settled apathy, a gradual wasting away of the person, and frequent although transient affections of a cataleptical character were the unusual diagnosis. Hitherto she had steadily borne up against the pressure of her malady; but, on the evening of my arrival at the house, she succumbed (as her brother told me with inexpressible agitation) to the power of the destroyer; and I learned that the glimpse I had obtained of her person would thus probably be the last I should obtain.

For several days ensuing, her name was unmentioned by either Usher or myself; and during this period I was busied in earnest endeavors to alleviate the melancholy of my friend.

We painted and read together; or I listened, as if in a dream, to the wild improvisations of his guitar. And thus, as a closer intimacy admitted me more unreservedly into the recesses of his spirit, the more bitterly did I perceive the futility of all attempt at cheering a mind from which darkness, as if an inherent positive quality, poured forth upon all objects of the moral and physical universe.

I shall ever bear a memory of the solemn hours I thus spent alone with the master of the House of Usher.

His long, improvised dirges will ring forever in my ears. Among other things, I hold painfully in mind a particular piece entitled "The Haunted Palace." I was, perhaps, the more forcibly impressed with it because, in the undercurrent of its meaning, I fancied that I perceived for the first time a full consciousness on the part of Usher of the tottering of his lofty reason upon her throne.

The paintings over which his elaborate fancy brooded grew, touch by touch, into vaguenesses at which I shuddered thrillingly.

There arose out of the abstractions which the hypochondriac contrived to throw upon his canvas, an intensity of intolerable awe.

The books which, for years, had formed no small portion of the mental existence of the invalid were, as might be supposed, in strict keeping with this character of phantasm. His chief delight was an exceedingly rare and curious book –the manual of a forgotten church–the "Vigiliae Mortuorum Secundum Chorum Ecclesiae Maguntinae."

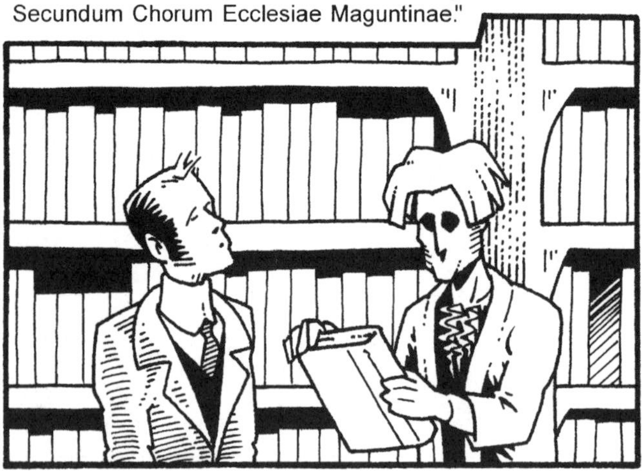

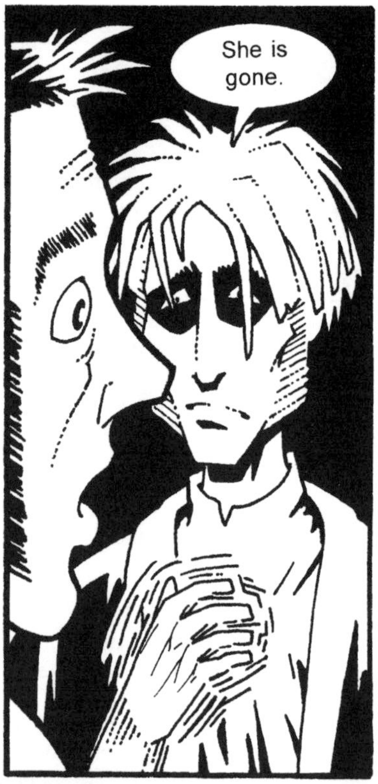
She is gone.

I could not help thinking of the wild ritual of this work, and of its probable influence upon the hypochondriac, when, one evening, having informed me abruptly that the lady Madeline was no more, he stated his intention of preserving her corpse for a fortnight (previous to its final interment), in one of the numerous vaults within the main walls of the building. The reason for this proceeding was a consideration of the unusual character of the malady of the deceased, of certain obtrusive inquiries on the part of her medical men, and of the remote and exposed situation of the burial-ground of the family. I had no desire to oppose what I regarded as at best but a harmless precaution.

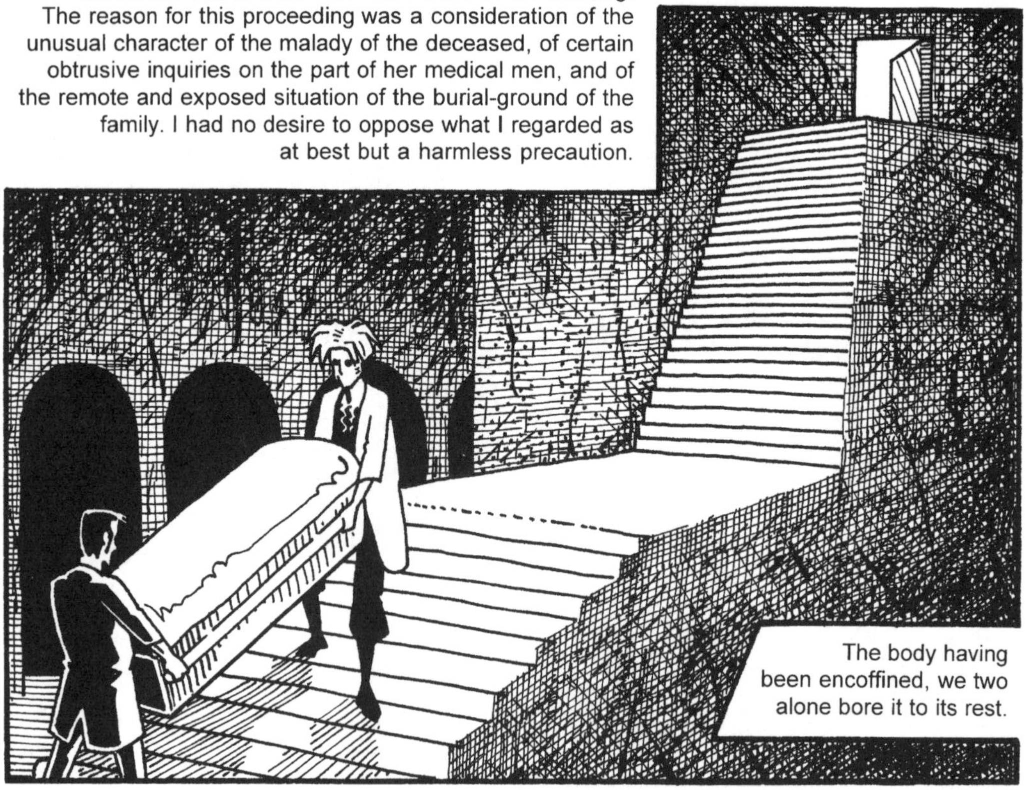
The body having been encoffined, we two alone bore it to its rest.

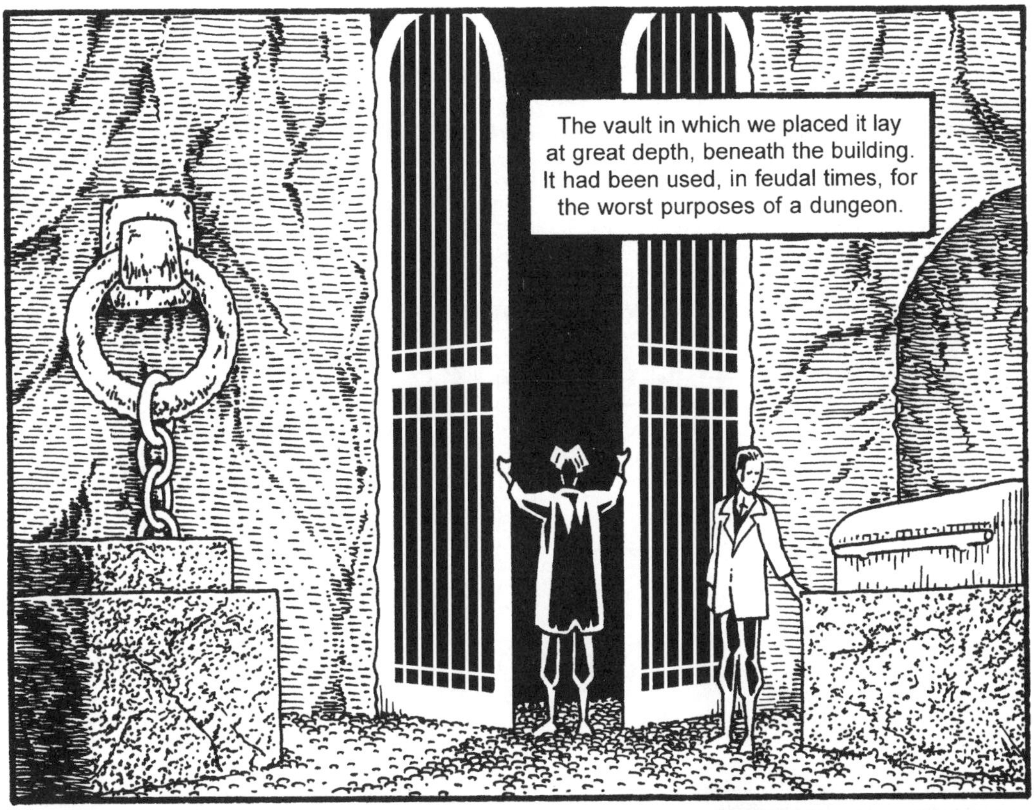
The vault in which we placed it lay at great depth, beneath the building. It had been used, in feudal times, for the worst purposes of a dungeon.

Having deposited our mournful burden within this region of horror, we partially turned aside the lid of the coffin, and looked upon the face of the tenant. A striking similitude between the brother and sister arrested my attention; and Usher, divining my thoughts, murmured that the deceased and himself had been twins, and that sympathies of a scarcely intelligible nature had always existed between them.

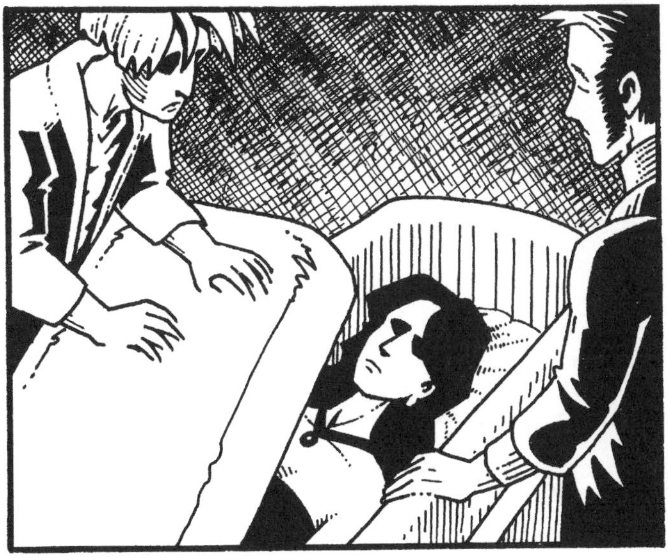

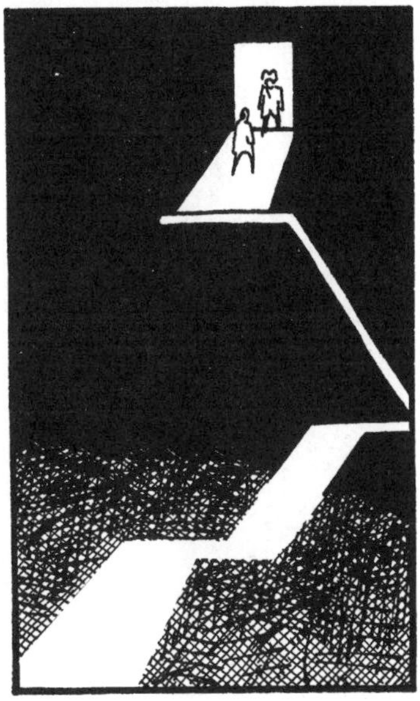

We replaced and screwed down the lid, and, having secured the door of iron, made our way into the scarcely less gloomy apartments of the upper portion of the house.

And now, some days of bitter grief having elapsed, my friend's ordinary manner had vanished. He roamed from chamber to chamber with hurried and objectless step. The pallor of his countenance had assumed, if possible, a more ghastly hue, and the luminousness of his eye had utterly gone out. There were times, indeed, when I thought his unceasingly agitated mind was laboring with some oppressive secret, to divulge which he struggled for the necessary courage.

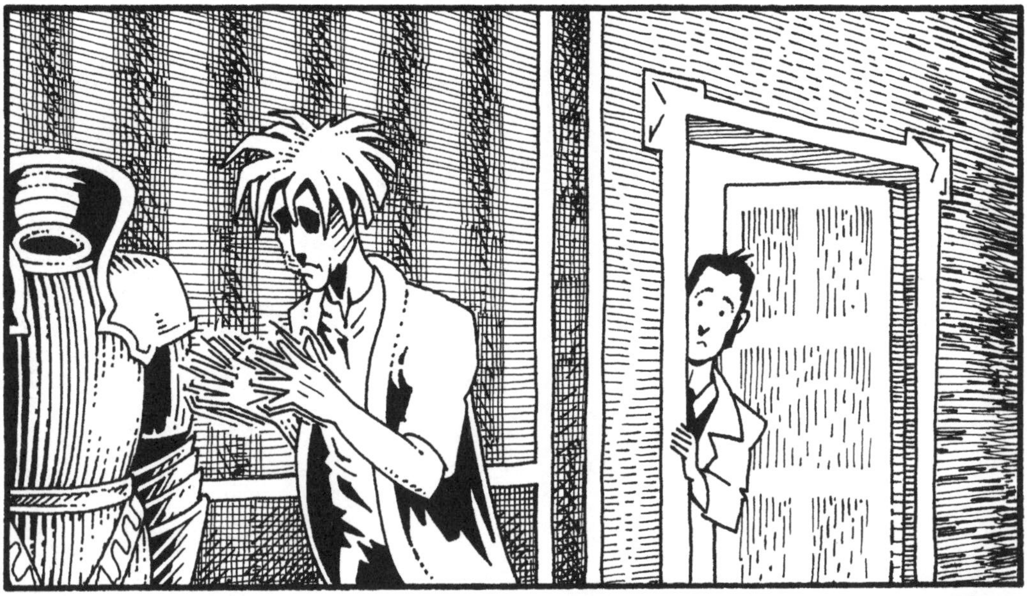

At times, I beheld him gazing upon vacancy for long hours, in an attitude of the profoundest attention, as if listening to some imaginary sound.

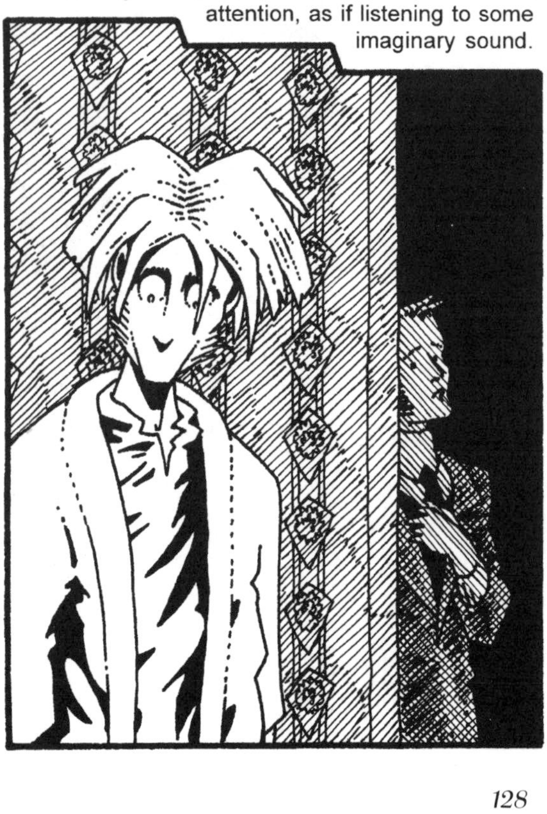

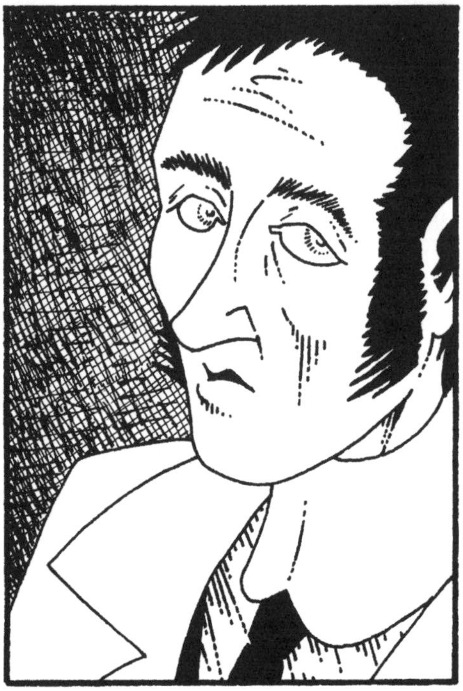

It was no wonder that his condition infected me. I felt creeping upon me, by slow yet certain degrees, the wild influences of his own fantastic superstitions.

It was upon retiring to bed late in the night of the seventh or eighth day after the placing of the lady Madeline within the dungeon, that sleep came not near my couch. I struggled to reason off the nervousness which had dominion over me. I endeavored to believe that much, if not all of what I felt, was due to the bewildering influence of the gloomy furniture of the room—of the dark and tattered draperies, which, tortured into motion by the breath of a rising tempest, swayed fitfully upon the walls. I listened earnestly, within the intense darkness of the chamber, to low and indefinite sounds which came, through the pauses of the storm, at long intervals, I knew not whence.

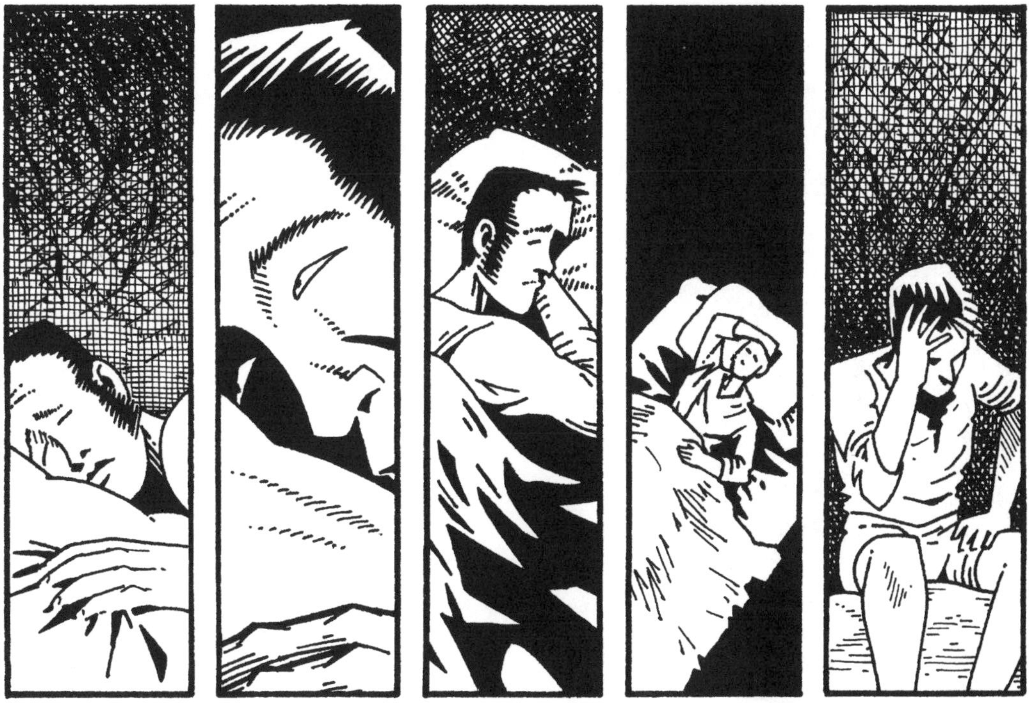

Overpowered by an intense sentiment of horror, I threw on my clothes and endeavored to arouse myself by pacing to and fro through the apartment.

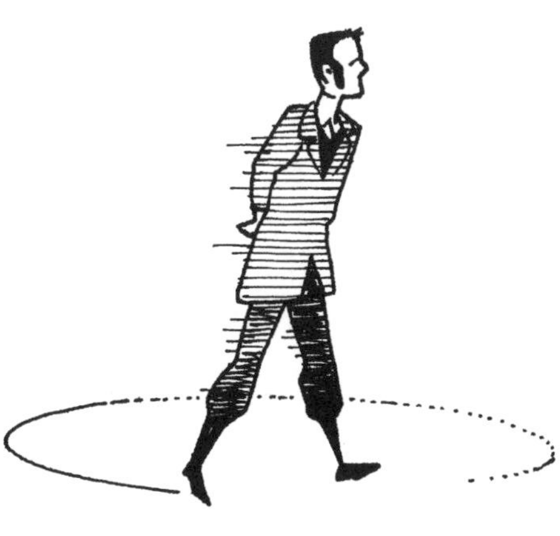

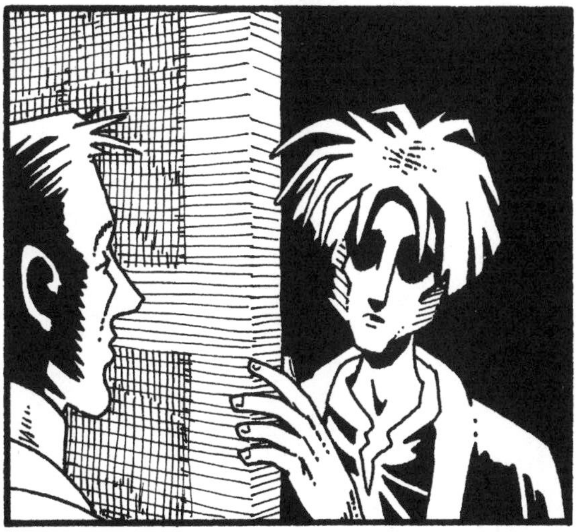

I had taken but few turns in this manner when Usher rapped at my door and entered, bearing a lamp. His countenance was, as usual, cadaverously wan—but, moreover, there was a restrained hysteria in his whole demeanor which appalled me.

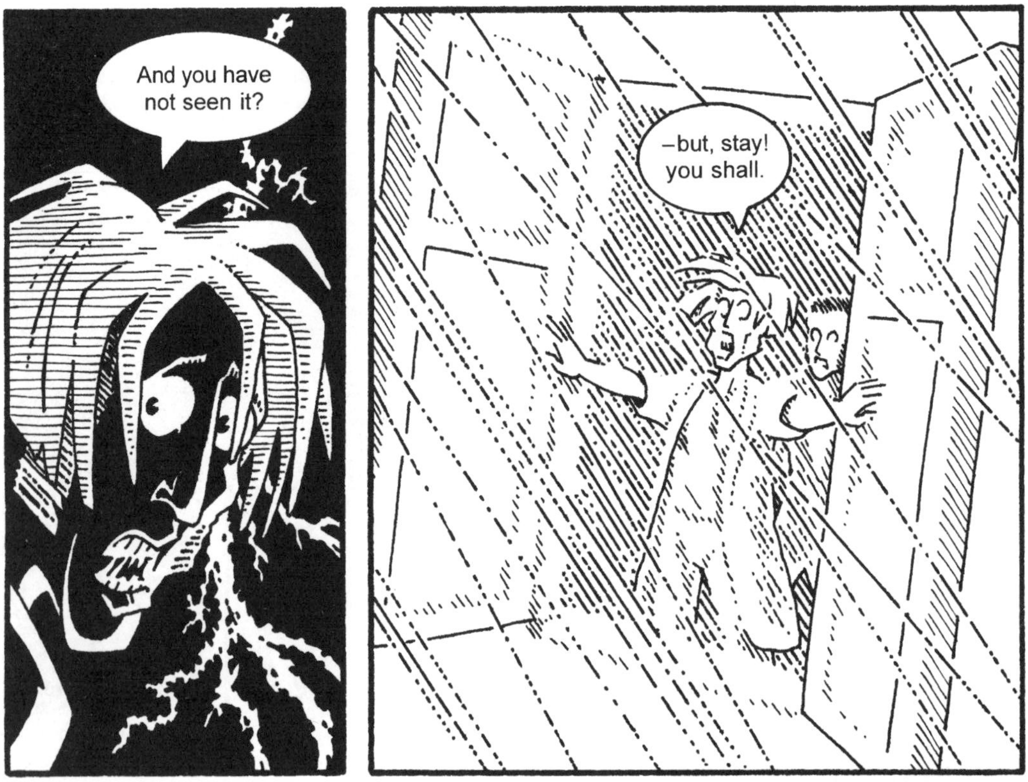
And you have not seen it?
–but, stay! you shall.

The impetuous fury of the entering gust nearly lifted us from our feet. It was, indeed, a tempestuous night, wildly singular in its terror and its beauty. There were frequent and violent alterations in the direction of the wind; and the clouds flew with life-like velocity.

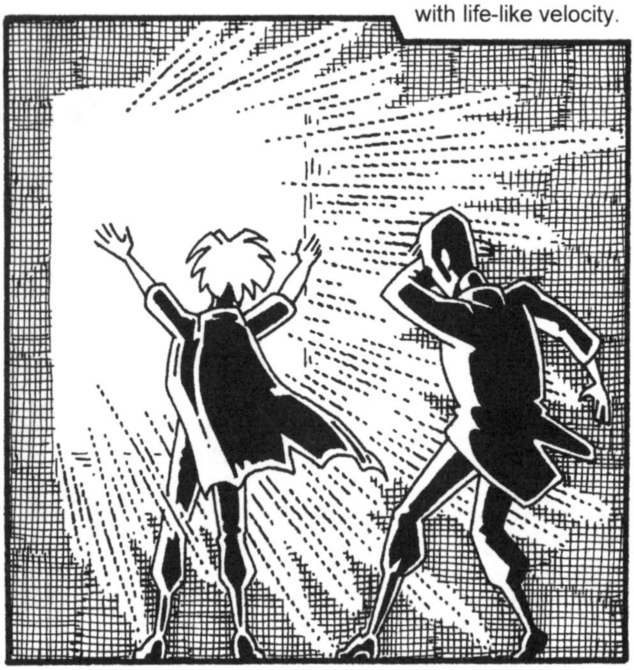

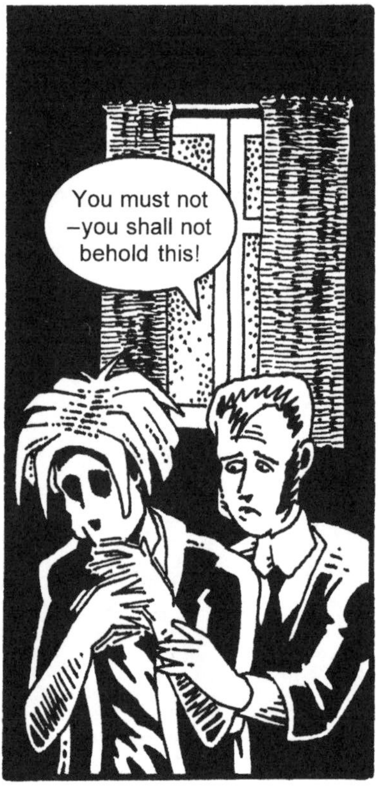
You must not –you shall not behold this!

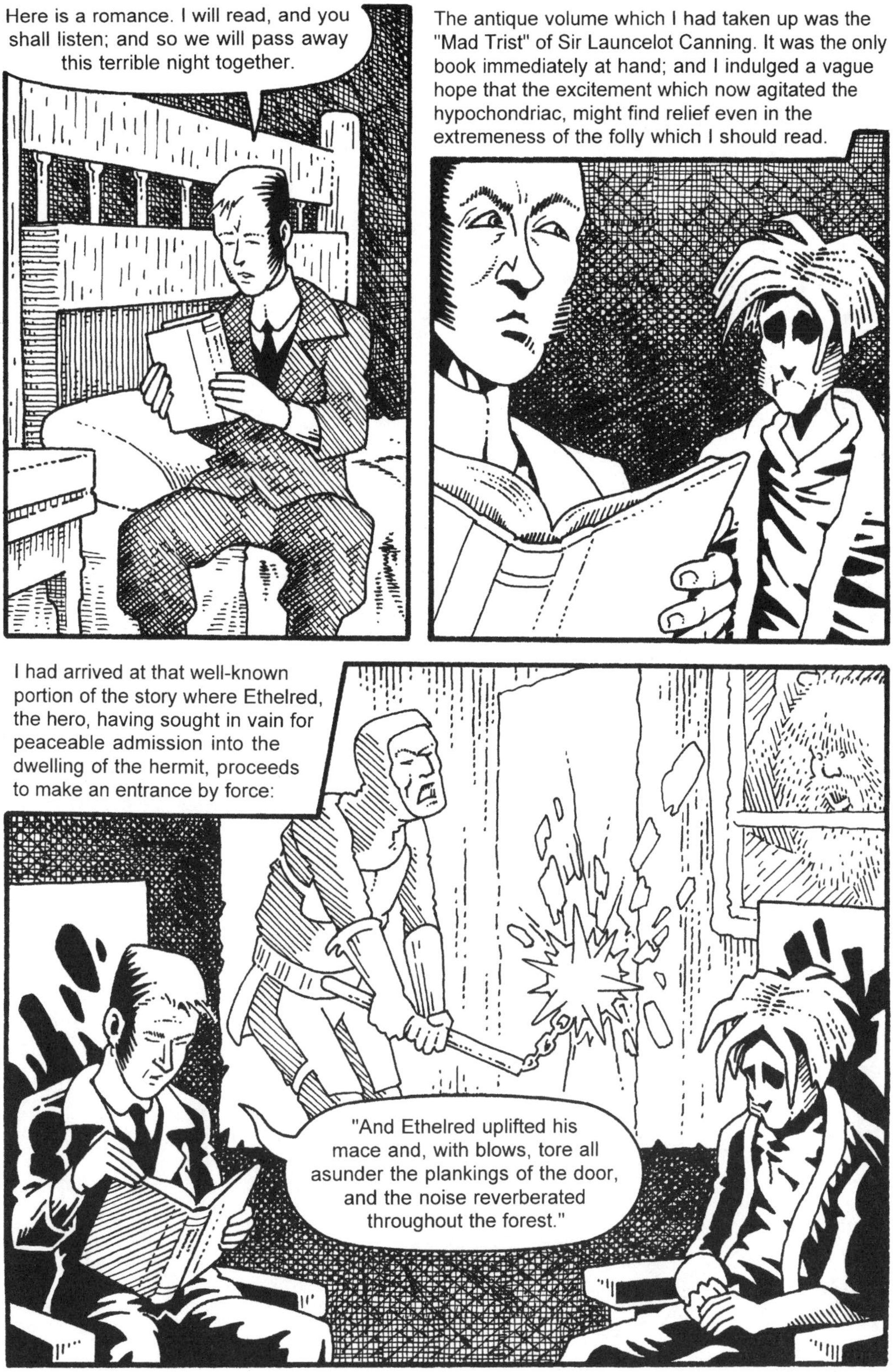
Here is a romance. I will read, and you shall listen; and so we will pass away this terrible night together.
The antique volume which I had taken up was the "Mad Trist" of Sir Launcelot Canning. It was the only book immediately at hand; and I indulged a vague hope that the excitement which now agitated the hypochondriac, might find relief even in the extremeness of the folly which I should read.
I had arrived at that well-known portion of the story where Ethelred, the hero, having sought in vain for peaceable admission into the dwelling of the hermit, proceeds to make an entrance by force:
"And Ethelred uplifted his mace and, with blows, tore all asunder the plankings of the door, and the noise reverberated throughout the forest."

At the termination of this sentence I started, and for a moment, paused; for it appeared to me (although I at once concluded that my excited fancy had deceived me)–that, from some very remote portion of the mansion, there came what might have been the echo of the sound which Sir Launcelot had described.

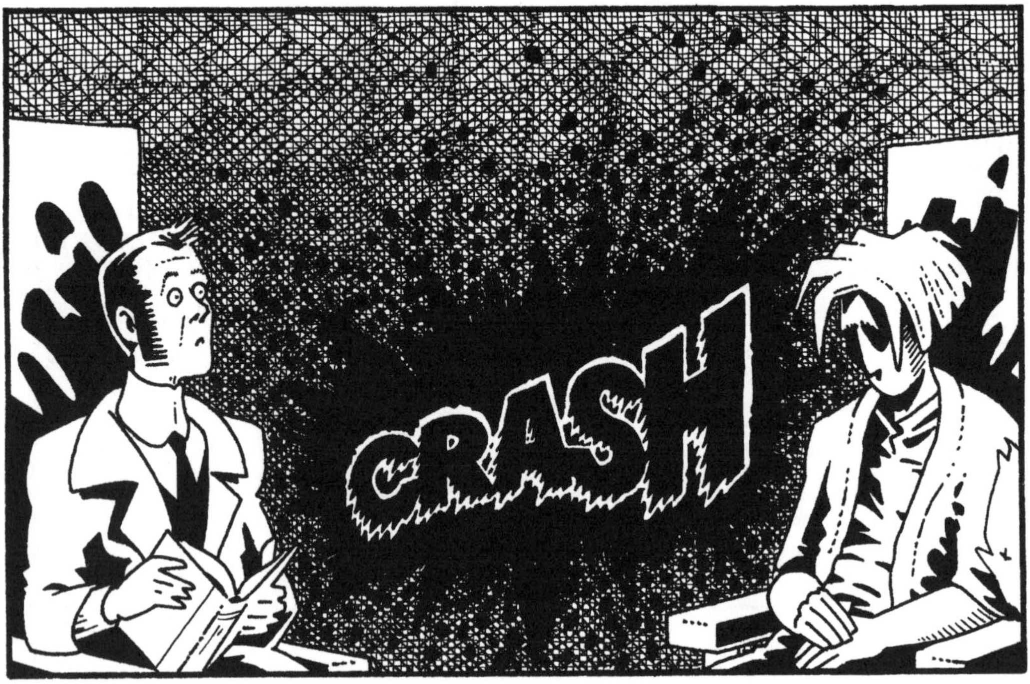
CRASH

It was, beyond doubt, the coincidence alone which had arrested my attention; for, amid the rattling of the sashes of the casements, and the ordinary noises of the still-increasing storm, the sound, in itself, had nothing which should have disturbed me.

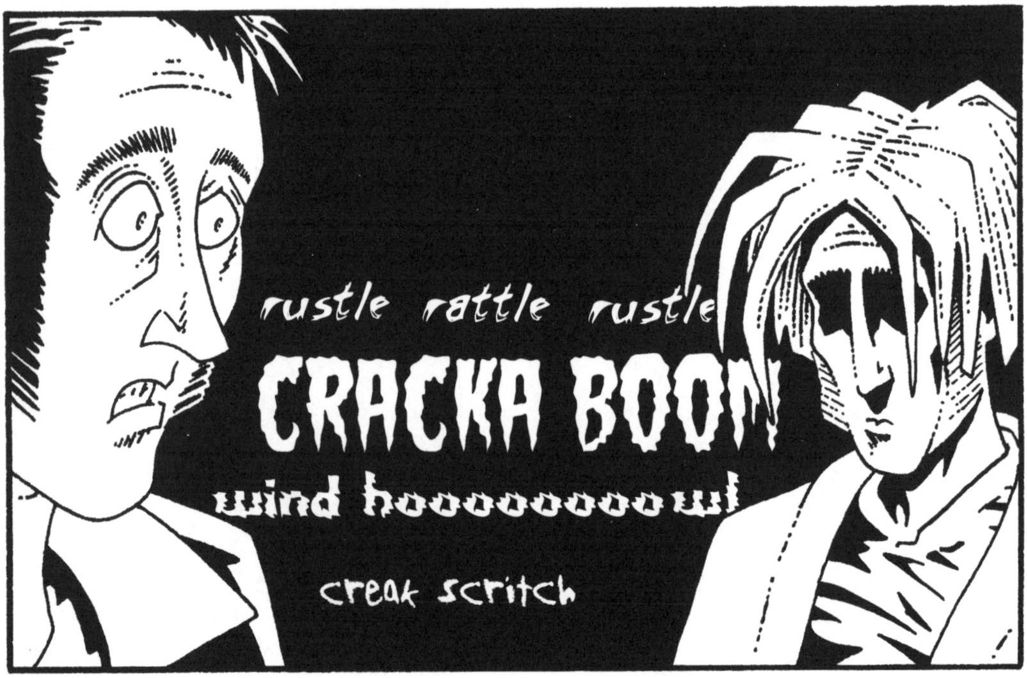
rustle rattle rustle
CRACKA BOOM
wind hoooooooooowl
creak scritch

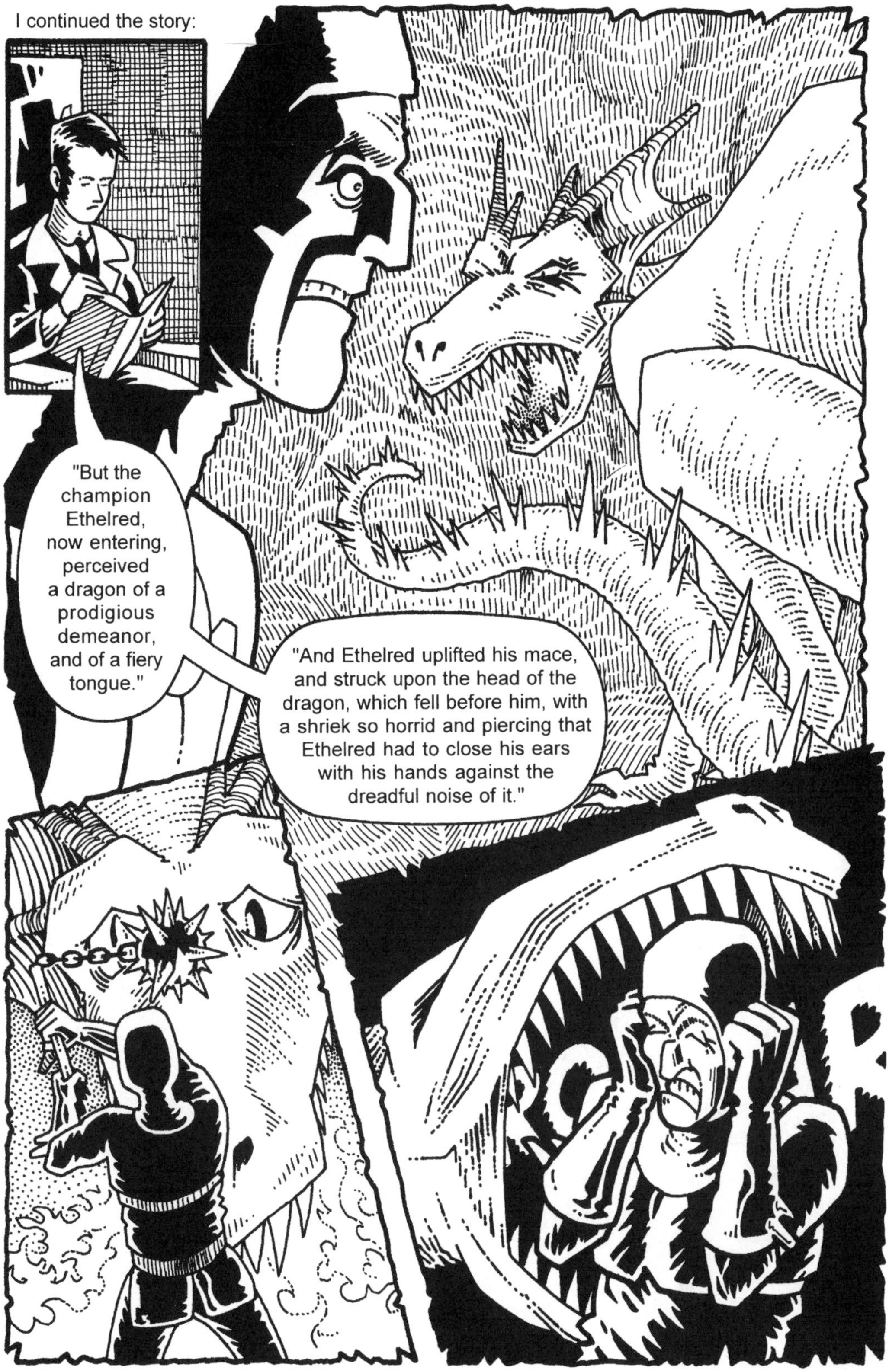
I continued the story:
"But the champion Ethelred, now entering, perceived a dragon of a prodigious demeanor, and of a fiery tongue."
"And Ethelred uplifted his mace, and struck upon the head of the dragon, which fell before him, with a shriek so horrid and piercing that Ethelred had to close his ears with his hands against the dreadful noise of it."

Here again I paused abruptly, and now with a feeling of amazement–for there could be no doubt whatever that I did actually hear a distant screaming sound–the exact counterpart of what my fancy had already conjured up for the dragon's unnatural shriek as described by the romancer.

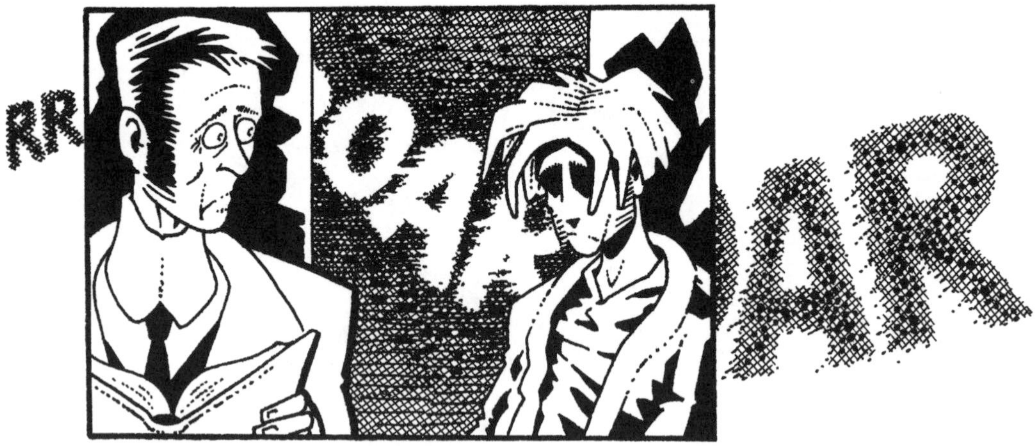

Oppressed with fear as I certainly was, upon the occurrence of this second and most extraordinary coincidence, I still retained sufficient presence of mind to avoid exciting the sensitive nervousness of my companion. I was by no means certain that he had noticed the sounds in question. He had gradually brought round his chair, so as to sit with his face to the door of the chamber.

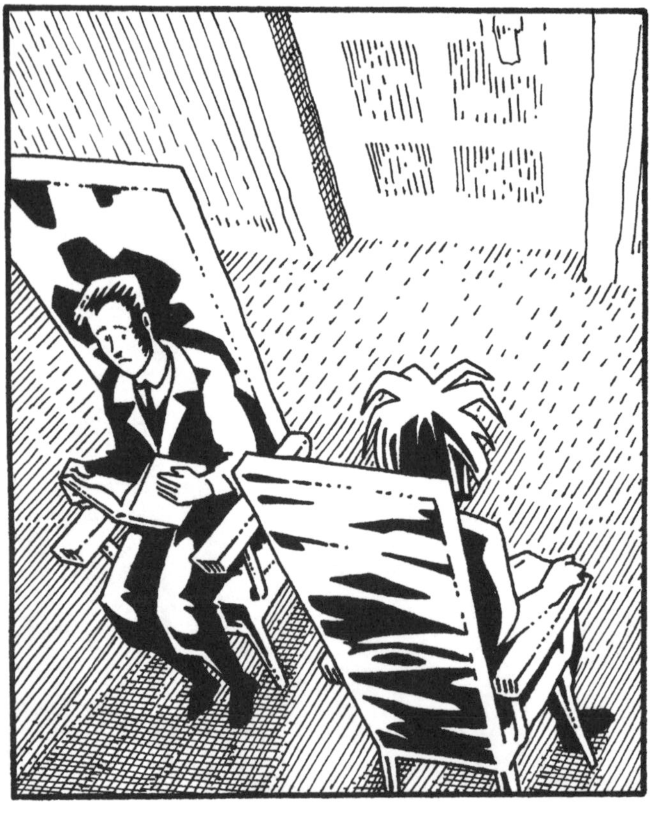

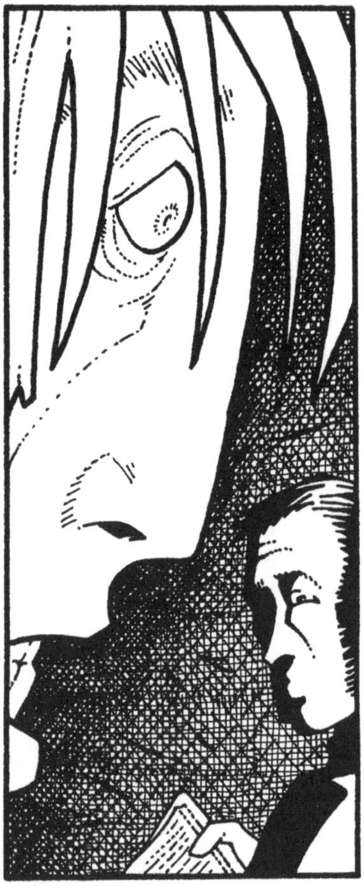

Thus I could but partially perceive his features, although I saw that his lips trembled as if he were murmuring inaudibly.

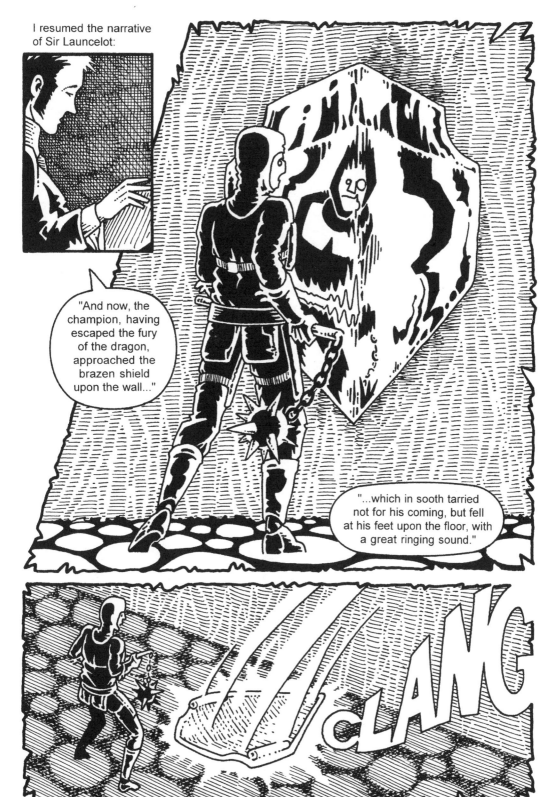

I resumed the narrative of Sir Launcelot:

"And now, the champion, having escaped the fury of the dragon, approached the brazen shield upon the wall..."

"...which in sooth tarried not for his coming, but fell at his feet upon the floor, with a great ringing sound."

CLANG

No sooner had these syllables passed my lips, than I became aware of a distinct, hollow, metallic, reverberation. Completely unnerved, I leaped to my feet.

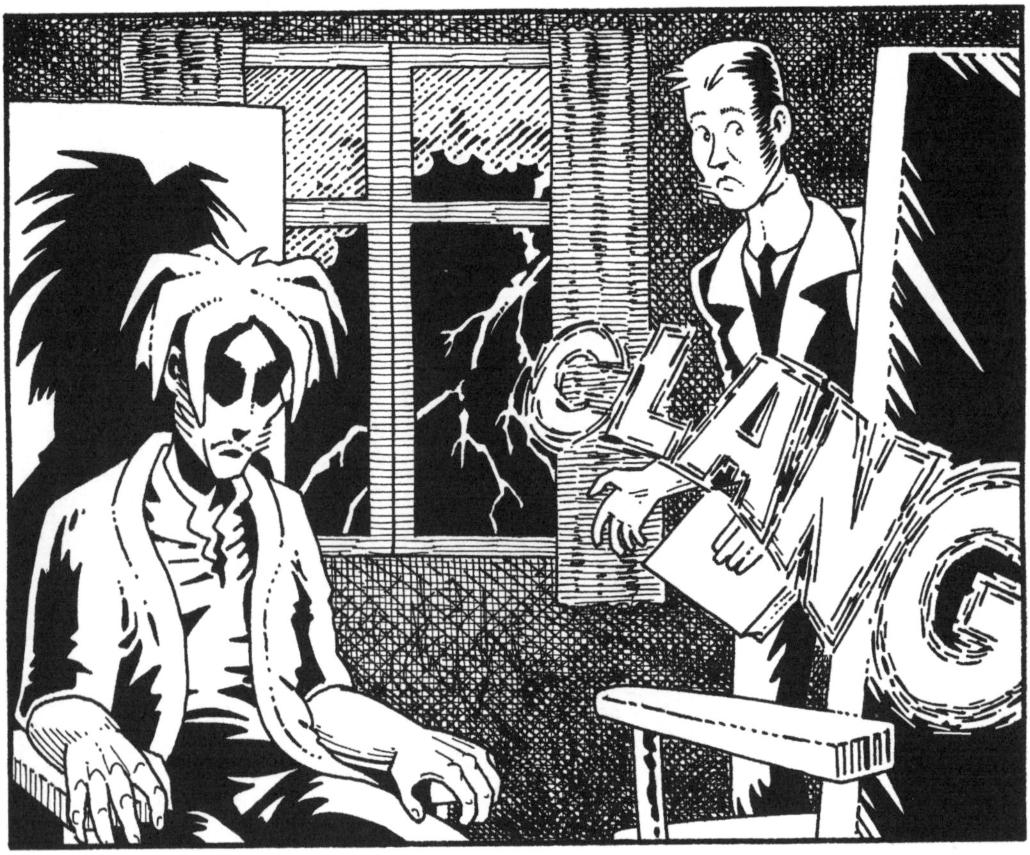
CLANG

As I placed my hand upon his shoulder, there came a strong shudder over his whole person; and he spoke in a gibbering murmur, as if unconscious of my presence.

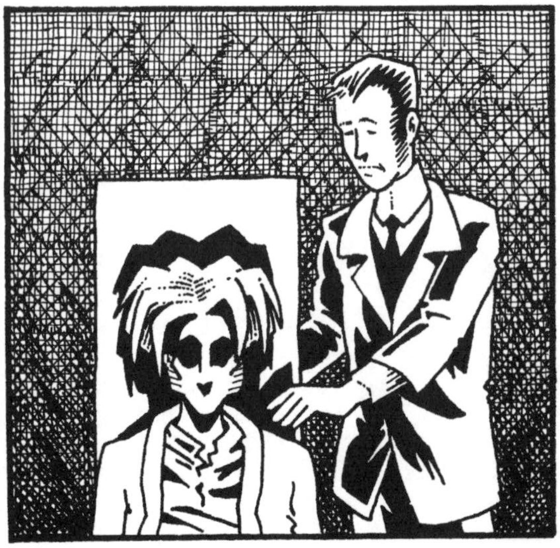

Bending closely over him, I drank in the hideous import of his words.

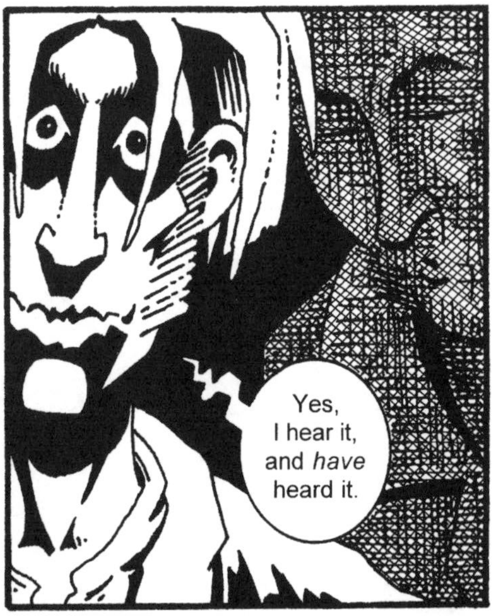
Yes, I hear it, and *have* heard it.

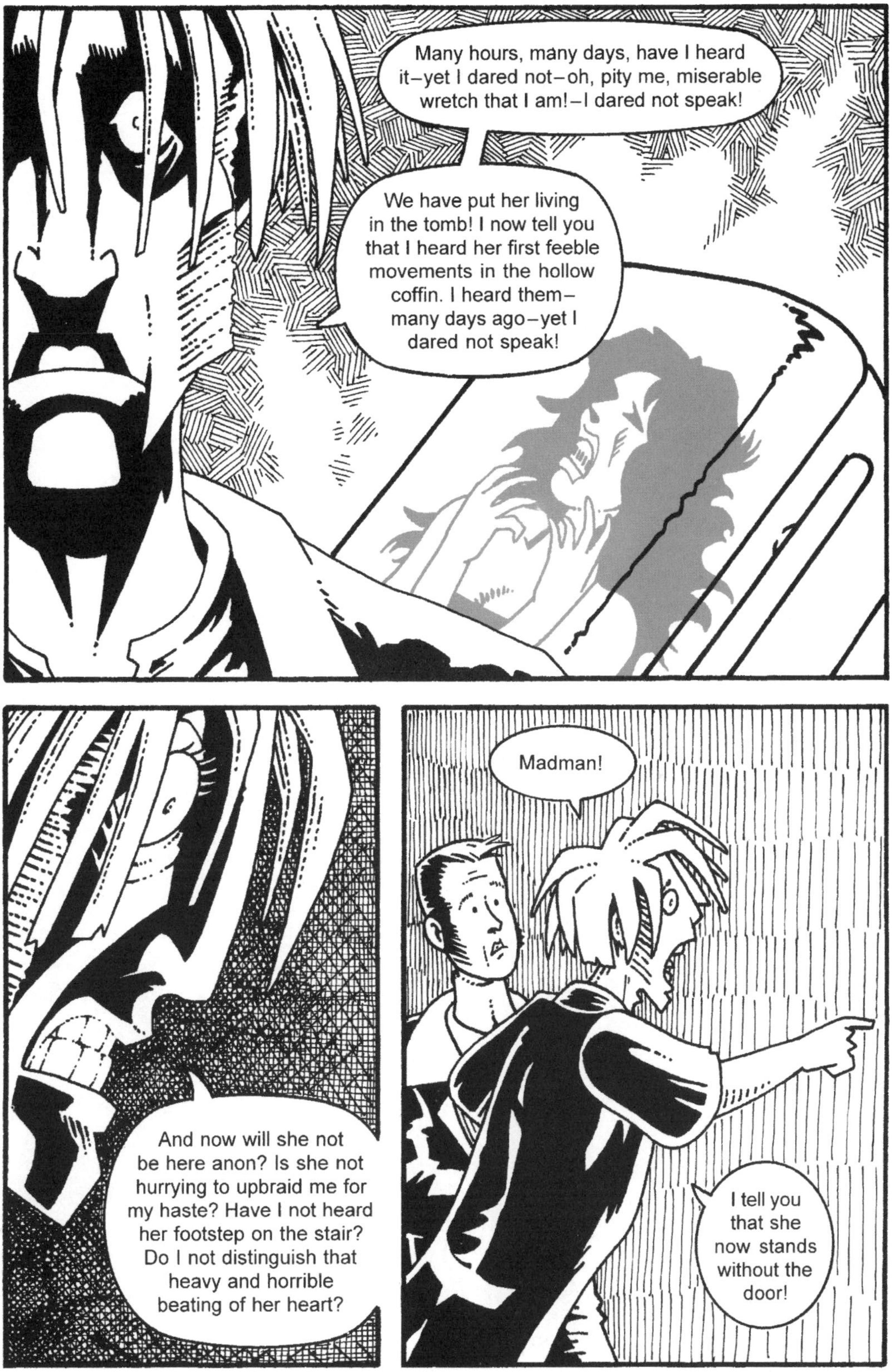
Many hours, many days, have I heard it—yet I dared not—oh, pity me, miserable wretch that I am!—I dared not speak!
We have put her living in the tomb! I now tell you that I heard her first feeble movements in the hollow coffin. I heard them—many days ago—yet I dared not speak!
And now will she not be here anon? Is she not hurrying to upbraid me for my haste? Have I not heard her footstep on the stair? Do I not distinguish that heavy and horrible beating of her heart?
Madman!
I tell you that she now stands without the door!

As if in the superhuman energy of his utterance there had been found the potency of a spell, the huge antique panels to which the speaker pointed threw back their ebony jaws.

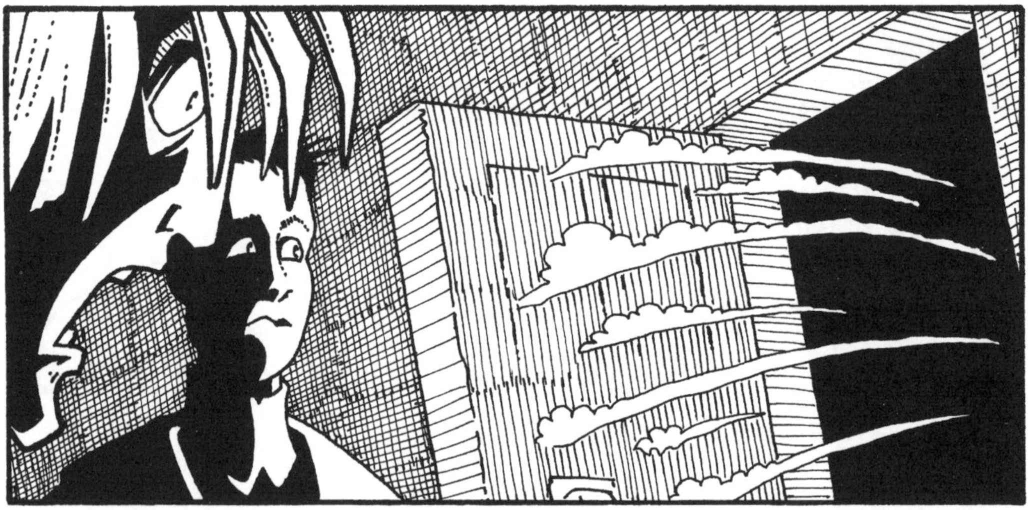

It was the work of the rushing gust–but then without those doors there did stand the lofty and enshrouded figure of the lady Madeline of Usher. There was blood upon her white robes, and the evidence of some bitter struggle upon every portion of her emaciated frame.

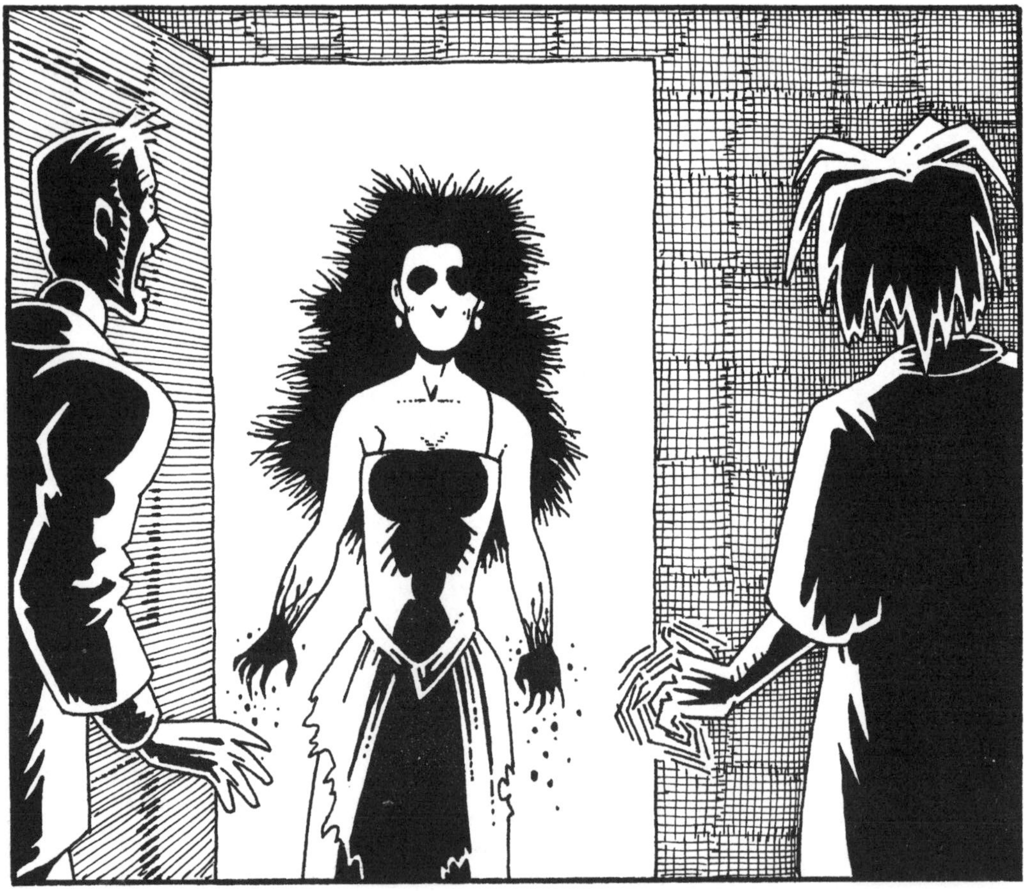

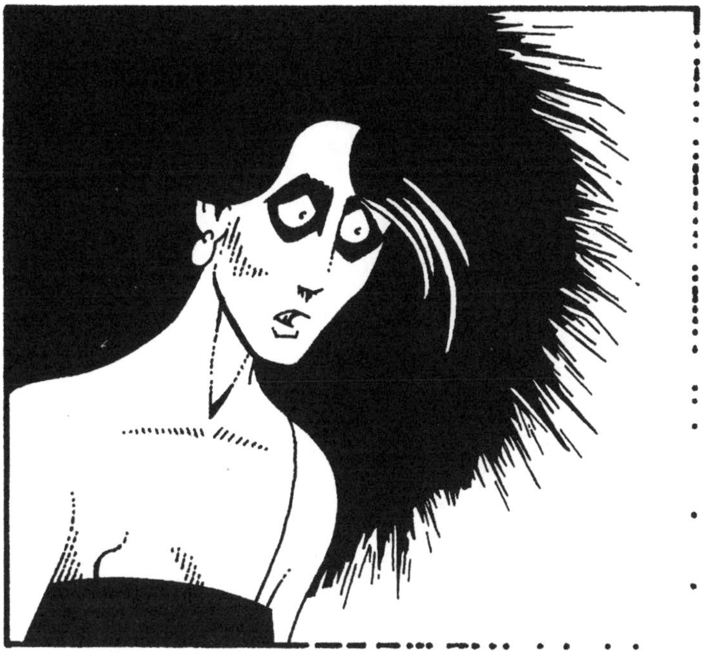

For a moment
she remained trembling
and reeling to and fro
upon the threshold.

Then, with a low moaning cry, fell heavily inward upon the person of her brother,
and in her violent and now final death-agonies, bore him to the floor a corpse!

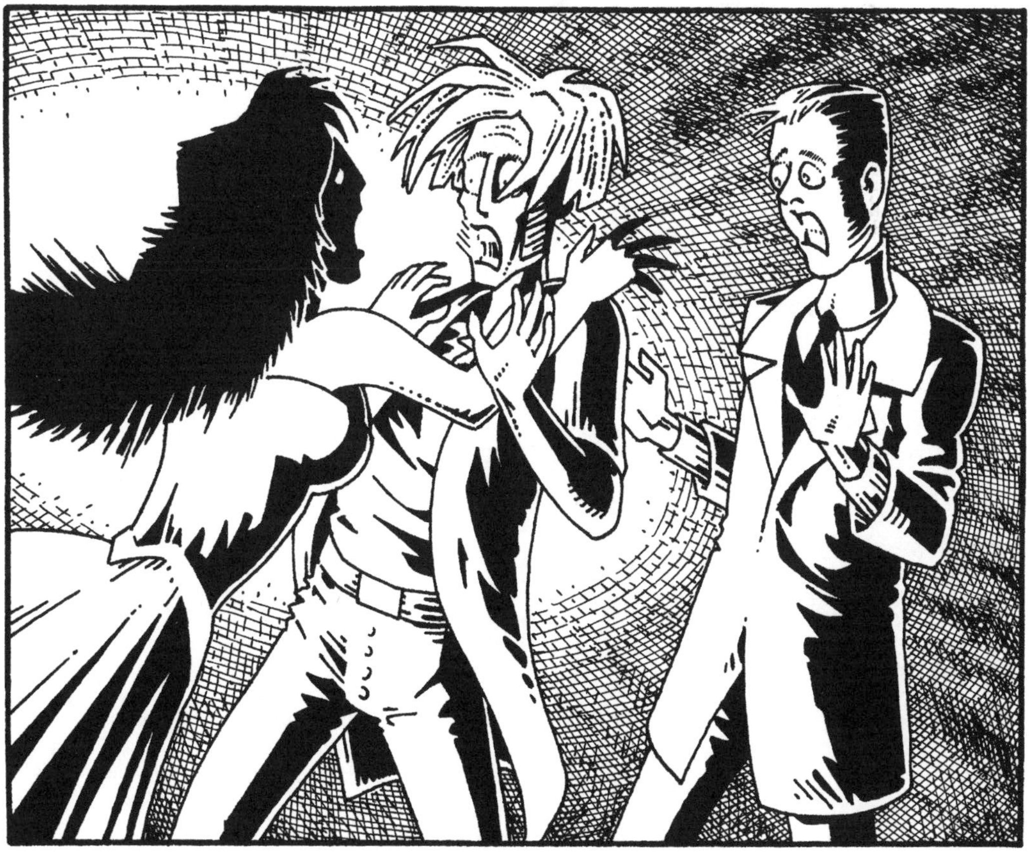

From that chamber, and from that mansion, I fled aghast. The storm was still abroad in all its wrath as I found myself crossing the old causeway.

Suddenly there shot along the path a wild light, and I turned to see whence a gleam so unusual could have issued. The radiance was that of the full, blood-red moon, which now shone vividly through that once barely-discernible fissure that extended from the roof of the building to the base.

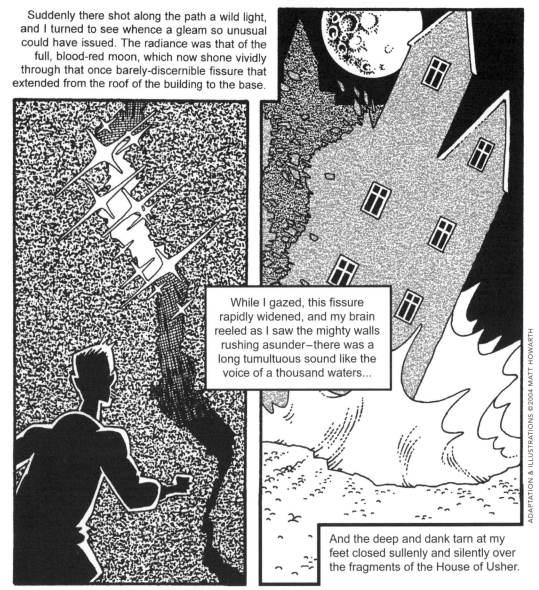

While I gazed, this fissure rapidly widened, and my brain reeled as I saw the mighty walls rushing asunder—there was a long tumultuous sound like the voice of a thousand waters...

And the deep and dank tarn at my feet closed sullenly and silently over the fragments of the House of Usher.

EDGAR ALLAN POE

Edgar Allan Poe, the orphaned son of itinerant actors, led a tumultuous adolescence of drink and gambling, which resulted in the failure of both his university and military careers. Throughout his life he was plagued by poverty, poor health, insecurity, and depression, much by his own doing and a result of his continuing problems with alcohol. He struggled unsuccessfully as a writer until winning a short story contest in 1833. Poe's subsequent writing ranged from his rigorously metrical poetry to short stories, from journalism and distinguished literary criticism to the pseudo-scientific essays of *Eureka*. Today he is generally acknowledged as the inventor of both the gothic short story and the detective story, a pioneer of early science fiction and the founding father of the horror genre. A comics adaptation of Poe's *Some Words with a Mummy* appears in *Horror Classics: Graphic Classics Volume Ten*, and *The Oval Portrait* will be included in the upcoming *Gothic Classics*.

MARCEL DE JONG *(cover)*

In the late 1990s Dutch artist Marcel de Jong formed AAARCH!!! Comics Amsterdam, a studio with Marco Kuipers. They published comics in the Netherlands, starting with *Kwaas Bloed* in 1999, and made their German comics debut with *Sadie*, "the ultimate gothic junky" in 2000. Marcel has also created comics for Eros/Fantagraphics in the U.S., including *Laque Noir*, but now concentrates on his painting, sculpture and music videos. You can see examples of all at www.marceldejong.com. For the cover image from *The Raven*, Marcel collaborated with another Dutch artist, Ramon Contini. You can view other examples of Ramon's work online at www.ramoncontini.com.

SKOT OLSEN *(pages 1, 59)*

While growing up in Connecticut, Skot and his parents spent their summers sailing up and down the coast of New England and all over the West Indies. It was on these long trips that he developed his love for the sea which forms the basis for much of his work. A graduate of the Joe Kubert School of Cartoon and Graphic Art, Skot now lives on the edge of the Florida Everglades, where he concentrates on paintings which have been featured in numerous publications and exhibited in galleries in Florida, New York and California. His illustrations are printed in *Graphic Classics: H.P. Lovecraft*, *Graphic Classics: Bram Stoker* and *Adventure Classics*, and a large collection of his work is online at www.skotolsen.com.

ANNIE OWENS *(page 2)*

Annie was born in Alabama, "parcel posted to the Philippines," and after three years was returned to the States and educated in the San Francisco Bay area where she earned her BFA in film and video. She is a fan of old horror films, the art of Charles Addams and Edward Gorey and the writings of Roald Dahl, Edgar Allan Poe and H.P. Lovecraft. Her adaptation of *Oil of Dog* appears in *Graphic Classics: Ambrose Bierce*, and she illustrated *Advice To Little Girls* in *Graphic Classics: Mark Twain*. Samples of Annie's comic strip *Ouchclub* can be seen at www.ouchclub.com, and she recently started publishing a magazine called *Hi-Fructose*.

MATT HOWARTH *(pages 3, 117)*

Matt Howarth has spent his career mixing the genres of science fiction, comic books, and alternative music. Probably best known for his *Those Annoying Post Bros.* comic book series, lately he has been doing a variety of graphic adaptations of stories by Greg Bear and Vernor Vinge. Other adaptations appear in *Graphic Classics: H.P. Lovecraft* and *Graphic Classics: Jack London*. Matt continues to explore the digital genre with a variety of online comics, plus his weekly music review column (at www.sonic-curiosity.com). Currently, he is working on a new *Bugtown* comic book series for MU Press, collaborating with New Zealander electronic musician Rudy Adrain, and has just finished his Lovecraftian SF novel, *The Eden Retrieval*. You are invited to visit www.matthowarth.com for more entertainment.

RICK GEARY *(page 4)*

Rick is best known for his thirteen years as a contributor to *The National Lampoon*. His work has also appeared in Marvel, DC, and Dark Horse comics, *Rolling Stone*, *Mad*, *Heavy Metal*, *Disney Adventures*, *The Los Angeles Times*, and *The New York Times Book Review*. He is a regular cartoonist in *Rosebud*. Rick has written and illustrated five children's books and published a collection of his comics, *Housebound with Rick Geary*. The seventh volume in his continuing book series *A Treasury of Victorian Murder* is *The Murder of Abraham Lincoln* (NBM Publishing, 2003). More of Rick's work has appeared in the *Graphic Classics* anthologies *Arthur Conan Doyle*, *H.G. Wells*, *H.P. Lovecraft*, *Jack London*, *Ambrose Bierce*, *Mark Twain* and *O. Henry*. You can also view his art at www.rickgeary.com.

ANTONELLA CAPUTO *(page 22)*

Antonella Caputo was born and educated in Rome, and is now living in England. She has been an architect, archaeologist, art restorer, photographer, calligrapher, interior designer, theater designer, actress and theater director. Antonella's first published work was *Casa Montesi*, a weekly comic strip that appeared in *Il Journalino*. She has since written comedies for children and scripts for comics in Europe and the U.S., before joining Nick Miller as a partner in Sputnik Studios. Antonella has collaborated with Nick, as well as with artists

Rick Geary, Mark A. Nelson and Francesca Ghermandi in the *Graphic Classics* volumes *Arthur Conan Doyle, H.G. Wells, Jack London, Ambrose Bierce, Mark Twain, O. Henry, Rafael Sabatini, Horror Classics* and *Adventure Classics.*

ANTON EMDIN (page 22)

"Sailing his drawing board in a sea of India Ink," Anton produces illustrations and comic art for a variety of books, magazines, websites and advertising agencies, both in Australia (where he resides) and internationally. Aside from the necessary commercial work, Anton contributes his weirdo comic art to underground comix anthologies, both in Australia and overseas, as well as self-publishing his own mini-comic, the now-sleeping ("soon, my pretties") *Cruel World.* You can find more of Anton's work on the cover of *Graphic Classics: Ambrose Bierce,* in *Graphic Classics: Bram Stoker, Graphic Classics: Mark Twain, Graphic Classics: Robert Louis Stevenson* and online at www.antongraphics.com. Between starting and finishing *King Pest,* Anton broke his drawing arm, and the story was finished with the able assistance of Sydney-based artist Glenn Smith. Glenn has published small press comics in Australia for fifteen years, including *Glenjamin, Entrailer Trash* and *Necrotardation.* Witness this obsession at www.glennoart.com.

JOE OLLMANN (page 39)

Joe Ollmann is a cartoonist and graphic designer who divides his time between Montreal, Quebec and Hamilton, Ontario. He has been publishing *Wag!,* a series of small-format books of his comics and fiction, for more than ten years. His comics and animations can be viewed at www.wagpress.net. Joe relates that his book of graphic short stories, *Chewing on Tinfoil,* was published by Insomniac Press in 2002, to "great acclaim and even greater lack of sales." He is now the art director at *ascent magazine,* Canada's only yoga magazine. Joe's first *Graphic Classics* appearance was as a co-illustrator of *Roads of Destiny* in *Graphic Classics: O. Henry.*

ROGER LANGRIDGE (page 48)

New Zealand-born artist Roger Langridge is the creator of Fred the Clown, whose online comics appear every Monday at www.hotelfred.com. Fred also shows up in print three times a year in *Fred the Clown* comics. With his brother Andrew, Roger's first comics series was *Zoot!* published in 1988 and recently reissued as *Zoot Suite.* Other titles followed, including *Knuckles, The Malevolent Nun* and *Art d'Ecco.* Roger's work has also appeared in numerous magazines in Britain, the U.S., France and Japan, including *Deadline, Judge Dredd, Heavy Metal, Comic Afternoon, Gross Point* and *Batman: Legends of the Dark Knight.* For *Graphic Classics* he has adapted a poem by Arthur Conan Doyle, a fable by Robert Louis Stevenson, a story

by Rafael Sabatini, and collaborated with Mort Castle on a comics bio of Jack London. Roger now lives in London, where he divides his time between comics, children's books and commercial illustration.

ANDY EWEN (page 50)

Andy Ewen's illustrations have appeared in *The Progessive, Isthmus,* and *The New York Times Book Review.* He was the featured artist in *Rosebud 10* and *Rosebud 22,* and his personal, dreamlike drawings also appear in *Graphic Classics: H.P. Lovecraft* and *Graphic Classics: Ambrose Bierce.* In addition to his ability as a graphic artist, Andy is also a talented musician. For over twenty years he has been the lead singer, guitarist and songwriter for Honor Among Thieves, one of the Madison, Wisconsin area's most respected bands, and the subject of the 2004 documentary *When the World Runs Fast.*

LANCE TOOKS (page 52)

As an animator for fifteen years, as well as a comics artist, Lance Tooks' work has appeared in more than a hundred television commercials, films and music videos. He has self-published the comics *Divided by Infinity Danger Funnies* and *Muthafucka.* His stories have appeared in *Zuzu, Shade, Vibe, Girltalk, World War 3 Illustrated, Floaters, Pure Friction,* the Italian magazine *Lupo Alberto, Graphic Classics: Ambrose Bierce, Graphic Classics: Mark Twain* and *Graphic Classics: Robert Louis Stevenson.* He also illustrated *The Black Panthers for Beginners,* written by Herb Boyd. Lance's first graphic novel, *Narcissa,* was named one of the best books of 2002 by *Publisher's Weekly,* and he has recently completed the third in his *Lucifer's Garden of Verses* series for NBM ComicsLit. Lance in 2004 moved from his native New York to Madrid, Spain, where he married and just finished a Spanish translation of *Narcissa.*

J.B. BONIVERT (page 57)

Jeffrey Bonivert is a Bay Area native who has contributed to independent comics as both artist and writer, in such books as *The Funboys, Turtle Soup* and *Mister Monster.* His art is also published in *Graphic Classics: Arthur Conan Doyle, Graphic Classics: Jack London, Graphic Classics: Ambrose Bierce, Graphic Classics: Bram Stoker* and *Adventure Classics,* and he was part of the unique four-artist team on *Reanimator* in *Graphic Classics: H.P. Lovecraft.* Jeff's biography of artist Murphy Anderson appears in *Spark Generators,* and *Muscle and Faith,* his Casey Jones / Teenage Mutant Ninja Turtles epic, can be seen online at www.flyingcolorscomics.com.

STEVEN CERIO (page 58)

"Artists try to create their surroundings to make the universe fit what they think it should be,"

Steven Cerio says. Cerio studied art in his hometown at Syracuse University, then moved to New York City in 1988. His first job was at Psychedelic Solution, a gallery at the center of Greenwich Village. There he encountered Robert Crumb, whose comment on Steven's work was "Hey Cerio, you think you're going to make a f— living drawing like this?" Steven responded by pursuing illustration work in *Village Voice*, *Guitar World* and *Entertainment Weekly*, as well as *Graphic Classics: H.P. Lovecraft*. His art is now shown in galleries nationwide. Steven's first full-length comic book, *PIE*, came out in 1996, *Steven Cerio's ABC Book – A Drug Primer* was published in 1998, and he continues to do commercial work for clients including Nickelodeon. Steven is also a drummer for his musical project, Lettuce Little, and he has long been involved artistically with legendary San Francisco group The Residents.

M.K. BROWN (page 60)

Mary K. Brown's 1972–1981 work in *National Lampoon* first brought her public notice. Her cartoons and illustrations have also appeared in *Playboy*, *Atlantic Monthly*, *Mother Jones* and *The New Yorker*. Her work has also been included in *The Big Book Of New American Humor* and numerous other anthologies. M.K.'s hilarious *Dr. Janice N!Godatu* animated shorts alternated with *The Simpsons* on *The Tracey Ullman Show* in 1987. She has written and illustrated several children's books. Her first, *Let's Go Swimming With Mr. Sillypants*, received the Junior Literary Guild Award. This was followed by *Sally's Room* and *Let's Go Camping With Mr. Sillypants*. Current projects include *Western Romance* and other cartoon collections and an illustrated novelette called *Wolf Boy*. In 2006, she will participate in the *She Draws Comics* show at the Museum of Comic and Cartoon Art, NYC, and have a one-person exhibition of paintings at Bonnafont Gallery, San Francisco. To see more cartoons, animation and posters by M.K., please visit www.benway.com/mkbrown.

MICHAEL MANNING (page 61)

Michael is the creator of the *Spider Garden* and *Tranceptor* erotic graphic novels series which are available from NBM/Amerotica. His latest release is *Inamorata*, a fine art collection published by Last Gasp. He studied at the School of the Museum of Fine Arts in Boston, and began publishing comics in 1987 while working as an animator and director of short films and music videos. A move to San Francisco's Mission District in 1991 coincided with Michael's decision to focus on erotic illustration and gallery shows full time. Michael's admiration for the Symbolist and Pre-Raphaelite movements as well as classical Japanese ukiyo-e and modern manga artists has contributed to the formulation of his distinct style. Michael's artwork can be seen online at

www.thespidergarden.net and in the pages of *Graphic Classics: Robert Louis Stevenson*, *Graphic Classics: Bram Stoker*, *Horror Classics* and *Adventure Classics*.

RYAN INZANA (page 62)

Ryan Inzana is an illustrator and cartoonist from Brooklyn, New York. His illustrations can be seen in publications including *The New York Times*, *The Wall Street Journal*, *The Nation* and *The Progressive*. Ryan's comics work has been published in *World War 3 Illustrated*, *New York Waste*, *Horror Classics* and online in *Slate Magazine*. His graphic novel, *Johnny Jihad*, was chosen as one of *Booklist's* top ten graphic novels of 2003. He is currently at work on a semi-autobiographical graphic novel series entitled *God-less America*, "a brutal memoir of the life and times of a foot-loose artist in the belly of the beast in Brooklyn, New York."

MARY FLEENER (page 63)

Besides doing comics, like her biweekly strip *Mary-Land*, autobiographical collection *Life of the Party*, and Eros title *Nipplez 'n' Tum Tum*, Los Angeles native Mary has also produced illustrations for magazines and books such as *Guitar Player*, *Musician*, *Spin*, *Hustler*, *The Book of Changes*, *Guitar Cookbook*, *RoadStrips*, and Poppy Z. Brite's *Plastic Jesus*. Her paintings have been shown at The American Visionary Art Museum, La Luz de Jesus Gallery, and the Laguna Beach Art Museum. She is currently painting on black velvet, and makes hand-thrown ceramics. Fleener also plays bass, and sings her own tunes in a band called The Wigbillies with her husband. She loves to surf, and walks a lot. Her art also appears in *Graphic Classics: Mark Twain* and *Adventure Classics*. Mary's website is at www.maryfleener.com.

EVERT GERADTS (page 64)

Evert Geradts is a Dutch comics artist now living in Toulouse, France. One of the founders of the Dutch underground comix scene, he started the influential magazine *Tante Leny Presents*, in which appeared his first *Sailears & Susie* stories. He is a disciple of Carl Barks, whom he names "the Aesop of the 20th century." Over the years Geradts has written about a thousand stories for Dutch comics of Donald Duck and other Disney characters. He also writes stories for the popular comic series *Sjors & Sjimmie* and *De Muziekbuurters*. Evert's work appears in *Graphic Classics: Ambrose Bierce*, *Graphic Classics: Bram Stoker* and *Graphic Classics: Robert Louis Stevenson*.

TONI PAWLOWSKY (page 65)

Toni Pawlowsky is both an exhibiting fine artist and a commercial illustrator. She shows her watercolors at the Fanny Garver Gallery in Madison, Wisconsin, and is represented by Langley and

Associates in Chicago. Her commercial work includes numerous CD covers for the series *Music for Little People*, including two covers for Taj Mahal. She has done work for the Wisconsin Dance Ensemble and Madison Ballet. Toni lives in Madison with her three sons, Jason, Justin, and Jared. She was the featured artist in *Rosebud 17* and appears in *Graphic Classics: Mark Twain*. Her greeting cards are available at www.redoakcards.com, prints can be purchased at www.guild.com, and more art can be viewed at www.kookykool.com.

TODD LOVERING *(page 66)*

Todd was born on the east coast, and "moved out to the Northwest at 21 years of age, took a few classes at the School of Visual Art and stuck my feet into illustration. Got out and into throwing pizza. A dear friend turned me on to the video game industry and I've been working in it to this day." Todd is also an editorial and commercial illustrator and has shown his paintings in several galleries in the Northwest. He says his strongest influences are Robert Williams, Rick Griffin, Jamie Burton, Jim Blanchard and "all the talented cats I work with." Todd's illustrations appear in *Graphic Classics: Ambrose Bierce* and *Graphic Classics: Bram Stoker*.

STANLEY SHAW *(page 67)*

Stan Shaw has been illustrating for more than twenty years. His clients include *The Village Voice*, *Esquire*, *Slate*, Starbucks, Nintendo, Rhino Records, Microsoft, DC Comics, Dark Horse, ABC-NEWS.com, Wizards of The Coast, *Vibe*, Hasbro, Washington Mutual, Lucas Film Licensing, *Mad*, *Premiere*, Penguin Books, Harcourt Brace, and *Washington Post Sunday Magazine*. His work has appeared in *How*, *CA*, *Print*, and *Covers and Jackets* by Steven Heller. Additional *Graphic Classics* stories are in the Ambrose Bierce, O. Henry and *Rafael Sabatini* volumes. In addition to practicing illustration Shaw also teaches it. He has taught at Cornish School of the Arts, School of Visual Concepts, Tacoma Art Museum, Charles Wright Academy, Seattle Public Library, AIGA Design Camp, local elementary schools and several LINKS workshops, sponsored by the Seattle AIGA. He currently teaches at Pacific Lutheran University, and was part of a group of artists advising "Exploring Illustration," an in-depth guide to the art and techniques of contemporary illustration. Stan hosts an illustration blog at drawstanley.blogspot.com.

MILTON KNIGHT *(page 81)*

Milton Knight claims he started drawing, painting and creating his own attempts at comic books and animation at age two. "I've never formed a barrier between fine art and cartooning," says Milt. "Growing up, I treasured Chinese watercolors, Breughel, Charlie Brown and Terrytoons equally." His work has appeared in magazines including *Heavy Metal*, *High Times*, *National Lampoon* and *Nickelodeon Magazine*, and he has illustrated record covers, posters, candy packaging and T-shirts, and occasionally exhibited his paintings. Labor on *Ninja Turtles* comics allowed him to get up a grubstake to move to the West Coast in 1991, where he became an animator and director on *Felix the Cat* cartoons. His comics titles include *Midnite the Rebel Skunk* and *Slug and Ginger*. His adaptation of *The Fool's Love Story* for *Graphic Classics: Rafael Sabatini* features characters from his long-running series *Hugo*. Milt has also contributed to the *Graphic Classics* volumes *H.G. Wells*, *Jack London*, *Ambrose Bierce*, *Mark Twain*, *O. Henry*, *Horror Classics* and *Adventure Classics*. Check the latest news at www.miltonknight.net.

LISA K. WEBER *(page 94, back cover)*

Lisa is a graduate of Parsons School of Design in New York City, where she is currently employed in the fashion industry, designing prints and characters for teenage girls' jammies, while freelancing work on children's books and character design for animation. Other projects include her "creaturized" opera posters and playing cards. Lisa has provided illustrations for *Graphic Classics: Ambrose Bierce*, *Graphic Classics: Bram Stoker* and *Graphic Classics: Mark Twain*, and adapted *The Gift of the Magi* in *Graphic Classics: O. Henry*. Art from her in-progress book *The Shakespearean ABCs* was printed in *Rosebud 25*. More of Lisa's work can be seen online at www.creatureco.com.

PEDRO LOPEZ *(page 106)*

Born in Denmark in 1974, Pedro is a comic artist inspired mostly by spaghetti westerns, Italian crime thrillers, and dark science fiction movies. His passion for these movies is obvious when you read his comics. He is also inspired by French comic artists such as Tardi, Hermann, and Mézières. He has published comics in Denmark and adapted *The Suicide Club* for *Graphic Classics: Robert Louis Stevenson*, *Roads of Destiny* for *Graphic Classics: O. Henry* and another O. Henry tale, *The Roads We Take*, for *Adventure Classics*. Pedro is now working on an online spaghetti western comic which you can see at www.pedrolopez.dk.

TOM POMPLUN

The designer, editor and publisher of the *Graphic Classics* series, Tom previously designed and produced *Rosebud*, a journal of poetry, fiction and illustration, from 1993 to 2003. He is now working on a revised edition of *Graphic Classics: Jack London*, scheduled for release in September 2006. You can find previews, sample art, and much more at www.graphicclassics.com.